Virtual Social Networks

Also edited by Niki Panteli

Exploring Virtuality within and beyond Organizations: Social, Global and Local Dimensions (with Mike Chiasson)

Virtual Social Networks

Mediated, Massive and Multiplayer Sites

Edited by

Niki Panteli

Selection and editorial content © Niki Panteli 2009
Individual chapters © contributors 2009

All rights reserved. No reproduction, copy or transmission of this publication may be made without written permission.

No portion of this publication may be reproduced, copied or transmitted save with written permission or in accordance with the provisions of the Copyright, Designs and Patents Act 1988, or under the terms of any licence permitting limited copying issued by the Copyright Licensing Agency, Saffron House, 6-10 Kirby Street, London EC1N 8TS.

Any person who does any unauthorised act in relation to this publication may be liable to criminal prosecution and civil claims for damages.

The author has asserted her right to be identified as the author of this work in accordance with the Copyright, Designs and Patents Act 1988.

First published 2009 by
PALGRAVE MACMILLAN

Palgrave Macmillan in the UK is an imprint of Macmillan Publishers Limited, registered in England, company number 785998, of Houndmills, Basingstoke, Hampshire RG21 6XS.

Palgrave Macmillan in the US is a division of St Martin's Press LLC, 175 Fifth Avenue, New York, NY 10010.

Palgrave Macmillan is the global academic imprint of the above companies and has companies and representatives throughout the world.

Palgrave® and Macmillan® are registered trademarks in the United States, the United Kingdom, Europe and other countries.

ISBN-13: 978-0-230-22928-0   hardback
ISBN-10: 0-230-22928-x   hardback

This book is printed on paper suitable for recycling and made from fully managed and sustained forest sources. Logging, pulping and manufacturing processes are expected to conform to the environmental regulations of the country of origin.

A catalogue record for this book is available from the British Library.

Library of Congress Cataloging-in-Publication Data

Virtual social networks : mediated, massive and multiplayer sites / edited by Niki Panteli.
    p. cm.
Includes bibliographical references and index.
ISBN 978-0-230-22928-0 (alk. paper)
1. Online social networks. 2. Virtual reality. I. Panteli, Niki.

HM742.V575 2009
303.48'33—dc22   2009013656

10 9 8 7 6 5 4 3 2 1
18 17 16 15 14 13 12 11 10 09

Printed and bound in Great Britain by
CPI Antony Rowe, Chippenham and Eastbourne

To James

Contents

List of Tables	viii
List of Figures	ix
Acknowledgements	x
Notes on Contributors	xi
1 Virtual Social Networks: A New Dimension for Virtuality Research *Niki Panteli*	1
2 Learning Virtually or Virtually Distracted? The Impact of Emerging Internet Technologies on Pedagogical Practice *Simran K. Grewal and Lisa Harris*	18
3 VU @ Second Life: A Report on Experiences with the Development of a (Virtual) Community of Learners *Frans Feldberg, Anton Eliëns, Sarah van der Land, Marleen Huysman, and Elly Konijn*	36
4 Patient Preferences for Online Person-Person Support *Ray Jones, Maged N. Kamel Boulos, Inocencio Maramba, Heather Skirton, and Jennifer Freeman*	52
5 The Social Impact of Online Games: The Case of Germany *Thorsten Quandt and Jeffrey Wimmer*	75
6 The Sexi(e)st of All: Avatars, Gender, and Online Games *Mia Consalvo and Todd Harper*	98
7 What Users of Virtual Social Networks Value about Social Interaction: The Case of GreyPath *Oliver K. Burmeister*	114
8 Labour's Second Life: From a Virtual Strike to Union Island *Bruce Robinson*	134
9 Community as Commodity: Social Networking and Transnational Capitalism *David Kreps and Erika Pearson*	155
10 Virtual Intimacy: Desire and Ideology in Virtual Social Networks *Rickard Grassman and Peter Case*	175
Index	194

Tables

2.1	Digital Natives versus Digital Immigrants	23
5.1	Distribution of online gamers/Quota matrix	81
5.2	Quota sample, arrangement before weighting, absolute numbers, and proportion	83
5.3	Played online genres	84
5.4	Top favourite games, main title per genre	85
5.5	Time spent playing per week on each online genre	86
5.6	Online gaming experience, differentiated by gender	90
5.7	Played online genres, differentiated by sex	90
5.8	Played online genres, differentiating adults vs adolescents	92
7.1	Value categories	124

Figures

1.1	Levels of virtuality research	2
2.1	A virtual office in Second Life	29
2.2	Online discussion forum	31
3.1	VU campus – outside view	39
3.2	VU campus – inside view	39
3.3	VU @ SL – visitors outside	40
3.4	Wheelchair race	40
3.5	Participants community of learners	42
4.1	Path of support at HealthInfo Island in Second Life	57
4.2	Avatars attending a seminar on 'Sex and Disability' in Second Life	58
4.3	Percentage of different age groups in Great Britain who have ever used the Internet	63
8.1	Protester excluded from IBM space	140
8.2	Pickets gatecrash an IBM meeting	141
8.3	The Union Island bar	144
8.4	The arena on Union Island	144

Acknowledgements

The book grew out of the interest of IFIP working group 9.5 in the subject of virtuality and society. My first acknowledgement therefore goes to those who actively took part in the workshops, conferences, and meetings organized to discuss issues on massive virtual communities and social networking sites as well as issues on virtuality in general. Furthermore, I wish to acknowledge Virginia Thorp and Paul Milner, who made this book possible, and their colleagues at Palgrave Macmillan. Special thanks also go to all the contributors to this book for their hard work and enthusiasm in pursuit of the study of virtual social networks.

Notes on Contributors

Oliver K. Burmeister (oburmeister@csu.edu.au) is an academic in the School of Computing and Mathematics at Charles Sturt University in Australia. He is a member of the Australian Computer Society (ACS), chairs its national committee on Computer Ethics, and is the current international ACS representative on International Federation for Information Processing – Technical Committee 9 (IFIP TC9) (computers and society). Oliver is a former director of the Australian Institute of Computer Ethics. His research interests cover predominantly the intersection between Human Computer Interaction (HCI) and computer ethics. Currently his research focus is on HCI design that takes the moral and social values of users into account.

Peter Case (Peter.case@uwe.ac.uk) is Professor of Organization Studies, Bristol Business School, University of the West of England and Director of the Bristol Centre for Leadership and Organizational Ethics. He served as Chairperson of the Standing Conference on Organizational Symbolism from 2002 to 2007 and is general co-editor of *Culture and Organization*. He is also a member of the editorial boards of *Leadership* and the *Leadership & Organizational Development Journal*. Peter has held visiting scholarships at the Helsinki School of Economics and the Royal Institute of Technology of Stockholm. His research interests encompass the ethics of leadership, organization theory and technologically mediated organization. Recent publications include *The Speed of Organization* (with S. Lilley and T. Owens, 2006: CBS & Liber) and *John Adair: the Fundamentals of Leadership* (with J. Gosling and M. Witzel, 2007: Palgrave Macmillan).

Mia Consalvo (consalvo@ohio.edu) is an associate professor in the School of Media Arts and Studies at Ohio University. She is the author of *Cheating: Gaining Advantage in Videogames* (MIT Press, 2007), and has edited *The Blackwell Handbook of Internet Studies* with Robert Burnett and Charles Ess. Her research focuses on women and games, the global videogame industry, and pedagogical uses of games. She has published related work in *The Video Game Theory Reader 1* and *The Video Game Theory Reader 2*, as well as the journals *Cinema Journal*; *Games and Culture*; *Television & New Media* and *Game Studies*. Mia has given more than 50 conference and invited presentations, is the vice president of the Association of Internet Researchers, and is on the steering committee of Women in Games International.

Anton Eliëns (eliens@cs.vu.nl) studied art, psychology, philosophy, and computer science. He is a lecturer at the Vrije Universiteit Amsterdam, where he teaches multimedia courses. He is also coordinator of the Master Multimedia for Computer Science. He has written books on distributed logic programming and object-oriented software engineering. Recently he has been appointed as Professor Creative Technology/New Media to set up a Bachelor's curriculum in Creative Technology at Twente University.

Frans Feldberg (jfeldberg@feweb.vu.nl) is Assistant Professor e-business at the Faculty of Economics and Business Administration of the Vrije Universiteit , Amsterdam and member of the Knowledge Information and Networks (KIN) research group. He holds a Ph.D. in online decision behaviour. His research is on the interface of business administration, cognitive psychology and information sciences. He specializes in decision-making behaviour and collaboration in computer-mediated environments. His research projects focus on online decision-making, decision support systems, computer-mediated communication, and relationship-building, collaboration and learning in virtual environments. He was the initiator and project manager of a multidisciplinary research team responsible for the Vrije Universiteit's Second Life research initiative. Feldberg has wide experience as business consultant for national and international companies, and actively participates in a network of researchers, managers and entrepreneurs that reflects on the economic, social and juridical relevance of online virtual worlds to society.

Jennifer Freeman (Jennifer.freeman@plymouth.ac.uk) is a reader in Physiotherapy and Rehabilitation in the School of Health Professions, Faculty of Health and Social Work, at the University of Plymouth; and also a lecturer within the Department of Clinical Neurology at the Institute of Neurology, Queen Square, London. Her research focuses mainly on the evaluation of rehabilitation interventions in people with long-term neurological conditions, such as multiple sclerosis. Jennifer is a member of the Chartered Society of Physiotherapy.

Rickard Grassman (Paul.Grassman@uwe.ac.uk) is a research and teaching associate within the field of Organization Studies at the Bristol Business School, University of the West of England. His current interests of research entail poststructuralist approaches towards the understanding of affect, in particular how commitment to certain belief systems is generated by different forms of organizing enjoyment, and the way in which this may bear extensive implications on sense making, power and politics. Recent projects within this area of interest include the publication of *The Masochistic Reflexive Turn* (with C. Cederström, 2008: Ephemera) and the paper 'Sustaining the Loss' (with A. Wozniak) presented at the conference 'Lacan at work', Copenhagen Business School, September 2008.

Simran K. Grewal (s.k.grewal@bath.ac.uk) is a lecturer in Organizational Behaviour at the School of Management, University of Bath. Simran's research takes an emerging critical stance in exploring the impact of virtual technologies on organizations and society. She has been invited to present her work at international conferences and is currently working on a number of research projects which examine learning, social identity, communication and leadership in virtual settings. Simran is open to the adoption of innovative pedagogical tools and has recently developed a teaching and learning approach which involves the use of Second Life.

Todd Harper (th298206@ohio.edu) is a doctoral student at Ohio University's School of Media Arts and Studies. His research interests include the meaning-making process of gameplay and the role of games in culture. His published work and presentation topics have ranged from the rhetoric of popular games to press framing of gay marriage.

Lisa Harris (l.j.harris@soton.ac.uk) is a senior lecturer in Marketing, School of Management, University of Southampton. Lisa is a chartered marketer and a director of the Chartered Institute of Marketing. Before joining the education sector, she worked for several years in marketing roles within the international banking industry. Lisa joined Southampton School of Management in September 2007 from Brunel University Business School, where she was Course Director of the Brunel MBA. She also developed and ran a cross-faculty undergraduate degree programme in e-commerce at Brunel. Lisa is a CIM Course Tutor and she has run marketing courses at the University of Weingarten in Germany and Zurich University in Switzerland. She is also a qualified e-tutor for the University of Liverpool online MBA. Lisa is currently working on a research project called 'Punch Above Your Weight', which is investigating how small firms are promoting themselves and growing their businesses using Web 2.0 technologies.

Marleen Huysman (mhuysman@feweb.vu.nl) is Professor of Knowledge & Organizations at the Department of Economics and Business

Administration, Vrije Universiteit, Amsterdam. She received her Master's degree in Sociology from the Erasmus University Rotterdam and her Doctoral degree in Information Systems from the Vrije Universiteit, Amsterdam. In 1994 she was a visiting researcher at Stanford University and from 2000 to 2001 she was affiliated to Harvard Business School. She is (co-)author of many international articles and books related to knowledge management, organizational learning and communities. Marleen heads the Knowledge, Information and Networks (KIN) research group, consisting of an enthusiastic community of scholars studying knowledge- and information-intensive processes in organizational (online) networks. Marleen is a frequent organizer of international workshops and conferences within the field.

Ray Jones (ray.jones@plymouth.ac.uk) is Professor of Health Informatics in the University of Plymouth. His research focuses mainly on the accessibility of health information to patients. This began in 1979 when he established the Nottingham Diabetes System, issuing paper copies of medical records to patients. He moved to Glasgow University in 1984, where he developed and evaluated the first public access health kiosks (Healthpoint) and researched patients' online access to their medical records. This included a series of randomized trials that included: patient-held records in primary care; a personalized touchscreen system for cancer patients, an education system for patients with schizophrenia, and a community based system for treatment of anxiety. He moved to Plymouth in 2002 and has been collaborating on the use of synchronous technologies and social networks. Ray is an elected Fellow of the Faculty of Public Health, a member of the British Computer Society, and a chartered engineer.

Maged N. Kamel Boulos (maged.kamelboulos@plymouth.ac.uk) is Senior Lecturer in Health Informatics at the University of Plymouth. He previously worked at the University of Bath where he was instrumental in developing the online MSc programme in Healthcare Informatics. He has a medical degree, an MSc in Dermatology, an MSc in Medical Informatics, and a Ph.D. in Measurement and Information in Medicine. He is well published on geographic information systems and Web X.0, including neogeography, the semantic web, the social web and the 3-D Internet. He is a Fellow of the Royal Geographical Society, a Fellow of the UK Higher Education Academy, a level-3 member of the UK Council for Health Informatics Professions, senior member of the Institute of Electrical and Electronics Engineers (IEEE) and of Engineering in Medicine and Biology Society (IEEE EMBS), and a member of the World Association of Medical Editors (WAME). He is also the founder editor-in-chief of *International Journal of Health Geographics*.

Elly Konijn (ea.konijn@fsw.vu.nl) is Associate Professor and Chair at the Department of Communication Science at the Vrije Universiteit, Amsterdam. She is an interdisciplinary scholar with backgrounds in psychology, social scientific information systems, and media studies, and was a visiting scholar at the City University of New York. Her research focuses on processing information via media, exploring the fuzzy borders between fiction and reality, and the role of emotions therein. She has published in major scientific journals – *Media Psychology, Pediatrics, Transactions on Computer-Human Interaction; CyberPsychology & Behavior*; and the *International Journal of Human-Computer Studies*. She serves on various editorial boards, has written several books, recently published the edited volume *Mediated Interpersonal Communication* (Routledge, 2008), and is currently a co-editor of *Handbook of Emotions and Mass Media* (Routledge, 2009). She is the elected vice-chair for the Information System's division of the International Communication Association.

David Kreps (d.g.kreps@salford.ac.uk) is an 'early adopter', pioneering thinker and commentator, with a fascination for technology and its impact upon society. A Web developer since 1995, following his career as a Local Authority Arts Centre director, he wrote his Ph.D. thesis on Cyborgism, and since completing it in 2003 has become an expert on Web Accessibility and an explorer of the philosophy of virtuality. David is Secretary of the IFIP working group 9.5 on virtuality and society, and has published widely in information systems journals and conferences on eAccessibility and virtuality. His background in cultural studies and sociology fosters a critical approach to his research in Information Systems. David lectures in Web Development, Emerging Technologies and Technoculture at the University of Salford.

Inocencio Maramba (Inocencio.maramba@plymouth.ac.uk) has a medical degree from the University of the Philippines, Manila. After graduation he worked as a researcher at the University of Philippines College of Public Health before becoming an assistant professor in 1996. In 1999 he transferred to the College of Medicine, as Assistant Professor in the Medical Informatics Unit. In 2000 he went on a scholarship to the University of Warwick where he completed his MSc in Health Information Science with distinction. He returned to the Medical Informatics Unit where he served in various capacities until his appointment as Director of the National TeleHealth Centre in 2004. In 2006 he moved to the University of Plymouth, where he now works as an e-Health e-Learning facilitator. His research interests are e-Health, e-Learning, and the use of open source software in health.

Niki Panteli (N.Panteli@bath.ac.uk) is a senior lecturer in Information Systems and Director for the Centre for Information Management at the University of Bath and the Chair of the IFIP working group. 9.5 on virtuality and society. Her main research interests lie in the area of IT-enabled transformation, virtual teams and computer-mediated communication. Within this field she has studied issues of trust, conflict and collaborations in virtual, geographically dispersed environments. She has published articles in numerous journals, including *Decision Support Systems*; *Information and Organization*; *Information and Management*; *IEEE Transactions on Professional Communication*; *Behaviour and Information Technology*; *European Journal of Information Systems*; *Futures*; *New Technology, Work and Employment* and the *Journal of Business Ethics*. Furthermore, her work has appeared in book chapters and conference proceedings. She is the co-editor of *Exploring Virtuality within and beyond Organizations* (2008: Palgrave Macmillan).

Erika Pearson (erika.pearson@otago.ac.nz) is a lecturer in the Department of Media, Film and Communication at the University of Otago, New Zealand and the founding convener of the Internet Research Group of Otago. She is also actively involved in a number of research projects focused on the Internet and mobile communication.

Thorsten Quandt (thorstenquandt@t-online.de) is a professor of Communication Studies (with a specialization in Interactive Media and Online Communication) in the University of Hohenheim. He has worked at the Free University Berlinthe Ludwig-Maximilians-University Munich and the Technical University Ilmenau. His research and teaching fields include online communication, media innovation research, communication theory and journalism. He (co)published more than 50 scientific articles and several books.

Bruce Robinson (bruce@brucerob.eu) is Honorary Research Fellow at the Research Centre on Information Systems, Organisations and Society, University of Salford. His research interests include: use of the Internet by social movements (particularly trade unions); the Internet and spatial relations; and foundational issues in Critical Information Systems Research. He is also a labour activist and involved in the 'No sweat, an anti-sweatshop' campaign that aims at linking United Kingdom unions and anti-capitalist movements with rank-and-file workers' organizations across the world.

Heather Skirton (heather.skirton@plymouth.ac.uk) is Professor of Applied Health Genetics in the University of Plymouth. Her research career stemmed from her clinical experience in midwifery and genetic counselling. Heather's main areas of interest are the impact of genetic conditions on families, ensuring informed consent for genetic testing and screening and professional and patient education in genetics. She has used asynchronous and synchronous methods in teaching in the health professions and to collect data for research. Currently she is involved in an innovative European project to develop a digital library of millions of learning objects to support teaching in genetics. She is a past president of the International Society of Nurses in Genetics and a current co-chair of the European Genetic Nurses and Counsellors Network.

Sarah van der Land (sland@feweb.vu.nl) graduated cum laude from the Radboud University in Nijmegen with a Master's degree in International Business Communication in 2006. After working in advertising for some time as a junior strategist, she joined the KIN research group in the Faculty of Economics and Business Administration of Vrije Universiteit, Amsterdam as a Ph.D. candidate. Her Ph.D. research focuses on group decision-making and co-creation in Second Life.

Jeffrey Wimmer (wimmer@uni-bremen.de) is currently a lecturer and postdoctoral research fellow at the Institute of Media, Communication and Information (IMKI), University of Bremen (Germany). Since 2005 he has been member of the network called 'integrative theories in communication science' promoted by the German research foundation (DFG). He has studied sociology, psychology, and political economy; in 1999 he gained a diploma in Social Sciences from University Erlangen-Nuernberg on the social change of Indian cities and its relationship with the computer industry in India. In 2006 he gained his Ph.D. on the topic of the modern public sphere. His primary research interests include sociology of media communication, in particular, digital games and public spheres. He has published in several English and German publications on public and counter-public spheres, digital games, and international communication.

1
Virtual Social Networks: A New Dimension for Virtuality Research

Niki Panteli

Introduction

Virtuality has been undergoing rapid and fundamental changes. As technology changes, so too have its applications and our uses of and experiences with them have changed as well. The emergence of new technologies such as Web 2.0 technologies offers individuals opportunities for new ways of interacting, playing, working, and learning, and companies new ways for promoting and advertising their products and services and interacting with their customers in general. The new possibilities are exciting, but there are uncertainties and anxieties too which affect individuals and organizations as well as societies in general. It is within this context, one of simultaneous excitement and anxiety, that we discuss virtual social networks in this edited collection.

The current public discourse refers to social networking sites and online games, showing the popularity and fascination that has developed with these emerging, multiplayer and interactive virtual networks. However, though there has been an exponential interest in virtual social networks within the media as well as in the business and academic communities, our understanding of these networks remains very limited. This book aims to embark on this journey of exploration with a collection of studies, both empirical and conceptual, on current academic thinking around virtual social networks.

In this introductory chapter, the primary aim is to position the current enthusiasm for and research interest in virtual social networks within the wider virtuality literature. There is currently overwhelming attention focused on virtuality and the dramatic effect it is having on an increasingly vast number of people, organizations, communities, and societies. For the first time, contemporary societies are seeing the large-scale attachment of individuals, regardless of location, language, education, gender, and age, to online social spaces and their involvement in them. These current trends have taken research in virtuality to a new level; needless to say, the speed of this change has taken many of us by surprise. We discuss these trends in virtuality research in the section that follows.

Levels of virtuality research

It has been posited that with virtuality individual choices are expanded to include numerous possibilities, unrestricted by local practices, with significant effects within and beyond organizations (Panteli and Chiasson, 2008). The literature guides us to the identification of different categories of research on virtuality. We position these in terms of a hierarchy and therefore call them 'levels of virtuality research'. These levels do not demonstrate stages of growth of virtuality, but rather they are distinct levels of virtuality research that have a presence and a sustainability of their own. Some researchers may choose to align themselves with one of these levels and develop expertise in one category of virtuality research (e.g. virtual teams), but others may prefer to follow the growth of virtuality and study certain topics at different virtuality levels. Figure 1.1 shows this representation of the four levels along with the two basic

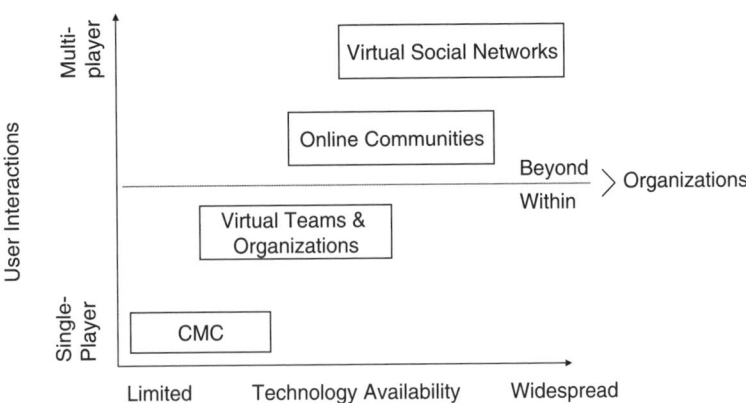

Figure 1.1 Levels of virtuality research.

dimensions: firstly, the degree of technology availability that the research takes account of. For example, a study may concentrate on exploring the interactions of a specific type of technology in a virtual environment (e.g. the use of email in conflict escalation) or it may study an environment where several technologies (e.g. email, instant messaging, videoconferencing, chat rooms) may be available to the users. Thus, the availability of technology may be either limited or widespread. Secondly, the nature of the interaction experienced among users in a specific virtual environment under consideration is shown. In this way, interaction with the technology could be either a single-player or a multiplayer one.

While Levels 1 and 2 include research that primarily takes place within an organizational context at both intra- and inter-organizational levels, Levels 3 and 4 go beyond the organization to explore wider virtual spaces, communities, and networks in the broader sense.

Level 1: Computer-mediated communication

Level 1 of virtuality research focuses on specific computer-mediated communication (CMC) technologies and their use by and/or impact on single-players. CMC is communication that takes place between human beings via the instrumentality of the computer (Herring, 2004). It has also been defined as any human symbolic text-based interaction conducted or facilitated through digitally based technologies (Spitzberg, 2006). This definition includes: the Internet; mobile phone text; instant messaging (IM); multi-user interaction (MUDS, multi-user dungeons; and MOOs, MUDS object oriented); email and listserv interactions; and text-supplemented videoconferencing (e.g. decision support systems). It requires people to be engaged in a process of message interchange in which the medium of exchange is computerised at some point.

Within Level 1, therefore, we can position research studies on the use of CMC in business or social interactions, and often their difference from other communication means such as face-to-face communication is discussed. Media choice theories play a dominant role in this category of research, with a vast number of studies discussing in different ways the levels of richness that diverse CMC media have. Indeed, historically, the theoretical research on CMC has fallen into two general types (Walther, 1994). The first examines the effects of CMC media on communication. The other seeks to explain media selection or media choice (e.g. Markus, 1994; Fulk and DeSanctis, 1995; Panteli, 2002; Rice et al., 1998; Rice and Shook, 1990), although there are some exceptions and hybrids. Recently, however, as CMC is gaining wide popularity, researchers are focusing more on the social aspects of CMC. Some researchers are focusing on the advantageous characteristics of CMC that have made it gain wide popularity. One important characteristic of CMC is that communicators can use it from different locations in the world, which makes it suitable for people who are geographically dispersed. It can enable people to communicate across boundaries. Different types of CMC have diverse characteristics and benefit users in a variety of ways.

Comparative studies of different CMCs have been published. For example, a vast number of studies in this category have examined the use of email as a business communication tool and contrasted its characteristics with other communication media, notably face to face. For example, Lee (1994) suggests that email messages are carriers of meaning; although email itself may not be a rich communication medium, it is the meaning given to email messages that contributes to its richness. He stresses that information richness is not just a function of the communication medium, but of the interaction between the communication medium and the organizational context in which it is used. Similarly, Markus (1994) has identified the role of organizational context on the choice of communication media. She found that email was used for communication tasks that involved high degrees of ambiguity and was used more intensively by senior managers. In fact, she also found that email was the preferred and promoted communication medium of senior managers across the organizational hierarchy. This is consistent with other findings on managerial email use (Rice and Shook, 1990; Soe and Markus, 1993).

The impact of these studies has been vital in developing an appreciation of the social construction of communication media. Over the years, this knowledge has been used, adapted, and enhanced in studies on other types of communication medium that include videoconferencing, instant messaging, and, more recently, blogging.

Level 2: Virtual teams and virtual organizations

Level 2 is concerned not just with the use of different technologies in enabling virtual interactions, but rather looks into how individuals, groups, and organizations could work collaboratively in a virtual environment where communication is primarily computer mediated. This level therefore focuses on group interactions and assumes that in a virtual environment there are various players/members who need to get together and work on a specific project.

From the wide variety of definitions of virtual teams, perhaps the most quoted is that of Lipnack and Stamps (1997): 'a group of people who interact through interdependent tasks, guided by a common purpose... with links strengthened by webs of communication technologies.' In a globally distributed environment collaboration between dispersed (virtual) teams/team members relies heavily on communication and groupware technology to achieve common outputs (Majchrzak et al., 2000; Kasper-Fuehrer and Ashkanasy, 2001; Panyasorn et al., 2008).

Whilst Lipnack and Stamps, in their definition of a virtual team, talk about links being 'strengthened by webs of communication technologies', a different perspective emerges when comparing these means to face-to-face communication, one that argues that links are being weakened: the leanness of the medium, in its inability to constantly transmit the subtleties of body language, eye movement etc. in the context of a group of collocated people. Even though these communication technologies are becoming richer with the increased use of web conferencing and videoconferencing, the use of email and conference calls still dominates today and is characterized by reduced or eliminated non-verbal cues and more asynchronous rather than synchronous activity. This limiting of the social cues that build context creates a sense of depersonalization (Montoya-Weiss, Massey et al., 2001) and has an impact on information exchange fundamental to establishing the normative, regulative, and cognitive structures that give meaning to social behaviour (Ahuja and Galvin, 2003). As a result, it raises the likelihood of misattribution. Equally it can encourage the positive expression of task-based conflict by reducing inhibitions, encouraging assertiveness, and reducing those emotionally rich communications associated with power, influence, and competitive behaviour.

The differences in information experienced as a result of lean communication media affect the inferences that dispersed members of virtual teams make with regard to the cause and effect of events as they take place (Cramton, 2001). Misattribution occurs in collocated teams, but it is aspects of virtual teams such as temporal delays in information exchange, a lack of shared context, etc. that can exacerbate this issue, particularly where one or more team members lack previous experience of these characteristics (Walther et al., 2002).

Studies at this level increase our understanding of the challenge in building and sustaining effective virtual collaborations at both the group and the organizational level. Further, such studies warrant the further exploration of how soft human factors can be integrated into our better understanding behaviour in virtual work arrangements and ultimately developing strategies for managing individuals, teams and organizations virtually.

Level 3: Online communities

Level 3 is online communities, concerned with the formation, development, and sustainability of communities within the virtual environment. Fernback and Thompson (1995: p. 8) provide the definition of online community as 'social relationships forged in cyberspace through repeated contact within a specified boundary or place that is symbolically delineated by topic of interest'. The words 'online' and 'virtual' have a similar meaning and are used interchangeably in the literature.

Although not communities in the traditional sense, virtual communities are similar to traditional ones as they are formed through a common interest rather than due to a shared physical space (White and Dorman, 2001). These communities exist in an Internet environment, and enable their members to carry out interactive activities through CMC. They therefore offer opportunities to people, despite their geographical dispersion, to develop relationships, to exchange information, to trade with one another. Rheingold (1993) suggests that a virtual community is a social aggregation; it has sufficient population and discussion and adequate interactive intercourse in cyberspace for the purpose of developing long-term relationships through the Internet. Indeed, research has shown that relationships developed in such environments are healthy and complement face-to-face relationships (Peris et al., 2002). A question, however, has arisen in the recent literature on the sustainability of these communities, and several studies on this topic have been pursued as a result, as discussed by Koh et al. (2007).

Studies exist at this level in an attempt to understand how members of virtual communities manage to develop common values and interests using electronic media and communicate within a shared semantic space on a regular basis (Guru and Keng, 2008). Similarly, studies have also shown that a sense of identification with like-minded individuals may drive participation in virtual communities (Blanchard and Markus, 2002). Within this area of research, identity, trust, and deception have played a key role (Donath, 1998; Joinson and Paine, 2007; Merchant, 2006; Pluempavarn and Panteli, 2008). Donath refers to new ways of establishing and hiding identity that evolve in virtual communities. Though these encourage freedom and self-expression, they also raise concerns about privacy and security. Mechanisms for dealing with these concerns have included the use of anonymity and the restriction of content and personal information when communicating online (Goldie, 2006).

Studies at this level take our understanding of virtuality further and into the wider 'space' and give insights into the development of communities beyond organizations. Nevertheless, organizations can benefit from these insights as these show the factors that draw individuals into unknown virtual spaces and how they manage to develop social as well as professional relationships using CMC (Guru and Keng, 2008). Moreover, by exploring the opportunities and challenges that virtual communities provide for self-presentation and impression formation in human communication, we are able to develop richer views of the different contexts and audiences for identity performance (Merchant, 2006).

Level 4: Virtual social networks

Finally, Level 4 is virtual social networks, concerned with the sudden but rapid emergence of massively multiplayer virtual sites. Virtual social networks – networks used for creating and maintaining social interactions among geographically dispersed individuals around the globe – have become an important way for interacting in today's world. The emergence of Web 2.0, user-orientated technologies allow massive, mediated networking opportunities to develop online. Miller (2005), for example, refers to the enhanced opportunities for user participation as opposed to the one-sidedness of Web 1.0, where content simply flowed from provider to viewer. Accordingly, at this level of virtuality research, a massive number of users interact using the widespread availability of different technological tools and capabilities.

It is not therefore surprising that in the current age of global and digital economy and virtuality there has been an overwhelming interest in online social networks. Bringing people together in this way calls for a change in traditional social interactions, particularly where multiple players are involved. These types of network show that having a presence and being present online matter.

When online, people want to be in the same space as other individuals; they like interacting on issues they have a personal interest in and thus enjoy spending time on. There is a sense of fascination with the unknown but also a fascination with being able to extend one's reach beyond the traditional boundaries of their physical world. Being present also indicates a sense of adventure which emerges from the opportunities to create and enact roles that are different from one's own identity. However, as Robinson (Chapter 8) explains, virtual social networks such as Second Life can replicate established social practices and forms of collectivity and solidarity that are evident in traditional collocated networks and organizations.

It follows that virtual social networks share three key characteristics: they are multimediated, massive and multiplayer.

Multimediated

Following Jenkins (2006), we consider virtual social networks as spaces where multiple media (e.g. audio, video, text, blogging software, and taggable photos) intersect, collide, and interact in multiple and even unpredictable ways (pp. 259–60). Jenkins refers to this as the phenomenon of media convergence, which characterizes Web 2.0 sites. Access to such dynamic Web 2.0 sites enables network development and promotes a participatory culture (Jenkins, 2006) despite the lack of familiarity with other participating individuals. When individuals do not have access to or lack an understanding of how these types of technology function, they may be excluded from virtual networks and subsequently from the digital society. But when they do have access to such media, the opportunities for networking, at both a personal and a professional levels are countless.

Massive

This characteristic is related to the membership size of a network. Virtual networks, social or otherwise, depend on members' involvement and commitment. Networks may have several thousands or even several millions of members. For example, Facebook, which was founded only in 2004, is reported to have 80 million active users (Facebook site, as at July 10, 2008). The mass of users generates the effect of a cluster. When they form a strong group, naturally more people are drawn into the network too. Research has shown that the longer users spend in such communities, the more likely it is that they develop personal and emotional connections with this community (Alon et al., 2004) and therefore their visit frequency increases (de Valck et al., 2006).

Multiplayer

Emerging social networks are able to support synchronous interactions among several (at times hundreds or even thousands) user-players. For example, the so-called massively multiplayer online games (MMOGs) may have up to thousands of players competing against one another. The real identity of the gamers in these sites does not matter. People geographically distributed in different places create roles through networks in real time. For example, World of Warcraft has been the most successful MMOG ever created, with over 9 million players worldwide to date (Henein, 2007). In such environments, MMOGs players have been found not only to play, but also to interact, share experiences, and socialize with one another (Papargyris and Poulymenakou, 2008).

It is important to note that social networking sites do share the above characteristics and we make sure that sufficient attention is given to them in this collection. However, we also allow for other contributions and for this we adopt the more generic title: virtual social networks. This also agrees with Boyd and Ellison (2007) who posit that often the primary function of the so-called social networking sites is not necessarily to promote relationship initiation and therefore the most appropriate term to adopt is 'social networks' rather than 'networking sites'. This view also agrees with a recent report (King, 2008) on the use of virtual worlds such as Second Life, where it is stated that companies have begun to use these spaces less publicly and for internal organizational use only (e.g. intra-organizational collaboration, recruitment, and mentoring).

Significance of the four-level model

The four-level model is based on the nature and characteristics of virtuality research that have evolved in the literature over the recent years. It should not be seen as limiting the scope of virtuality. The model allows us to pay sufficient attention to the different levels of virtuality research and provides coherence and synergy in our treatment of the topic. It is therefore important to emphasize that though there has recently been an overwhelming number of studies on Level 4, the other levels still remain important and continue to require the attention of researchers. Each level is being informed by and informs the others. Accordingly, all the levels collectively are vital to our understanding of virtuality. With new technologies emerging all the time, research is required to explore their uses, challenges, and the opportunities they bring to our lives.

It follows that even though at the outset Level 1 may seem the most basic type of virtuality research, it is perhaps the most critical of all in terms of guiding research in this field. We need to understand how different CMC media are used and that the interactions which take place when using these means of communication not only affect the individuals involved but also have implications at the team, community, and network levels. Ultimately, therefore, though there has been overwhelming attention focused on virtual social networks, the argument being made is that research on social networks can be informed by previous strands of research on virtuality. Accordingly, all levels of research continue to deserve further exploration and discussion.

Structure of the book and contributions

Having positioned the study of virtual social networks within the arena of virtuality research, we now move on to present what this book aims to achieve. The aim of the book is to advance theoretical and empirical understanding of virtual social networks. In doing so, it addresses the latest thinking on the growth, relevance, and sustainability of such networks across different sectors of society. The book has relevance to researchers, managers, educators, and policymakers in beginning to recognize the importance of addressing the technological, organizational, and social impacts that relate to the exponential growth of virtual social networks.

Collectively, the chapters illustrate the wide variety of applications and opportunities afforded by virtual social networks, not just at the social level but at the organizational and pedagogical levels too. The authors present their most recent and emerging research in this field. They raise their own questions and concerns about the subject and discuss the implications of their research for theory and practice.

Chapters 2 and 3 examine the potential of virtual social networks to enhance teaching and learning practices. Grewal and Harris (Chapter 2) begin by taking an emerging critical stance in exploring the impact of Internet-based technologies on pedagogical practice. They argue that virtual technologies, spurred on recently by the popularity of social networking sites such as Second Life, Facebook and Ning, offer new opportunities for the ways in which we interact socially with one another, conduct our business practices, communicate, gather information, and learn. Taking advantage of these opportunities will inevitability affect the processes through which we carry out these activities, raising serious questions about the wider implications of such technological advancements. Their chapter seeks to address some of these issues by exploring the impact of emerging internet development on teaching and learning practices, drawing upon two practical case studies to illustrate the ways in which these technologies are indeed contributing towards the teaching and learning process.

In Chapter 3, Feldberg, Eliëns, Van der Land, Huysman, and Konijn present their experiences in creating a presence for their university in the Second Life environment as well as their experiences with educational and research projects executed in Second Life. In doing so, they discuss the merits of Second Life as an educational platform, and as a platform that supports the development of an online community of learners.

Continuing along the same line of enquiry on the pedagogical significance of virtual social networks, in Chapter 4 Jones, Kamel-Boulos, Maramba, Skirton, and Freeman posit that both information and emotional support can be gained by participation in online networks. Taking the case of patients with chronic illnesses and disabilities, they identify a wide range of factors which may affect one's preferences for online support, including, but not limited to, age, gender, ease of use, and type of condition.

What these chapters have in common, in addition to their pedagogical perspective, is that they show excitement about the learning potential in these emerging new virtual worlds and the opportunities they provide to different categories of learners (e.g. students and patients).

The second section of the book examines how different groups make use of virtual social networks.

Quandt and Wimmer (Chapter 5) pursue a German-based study on the user composition of MMOGs. Regardless of popular beliefs that online gamers are primarily young and male, they show that a significant number of users are females, though their use patterns tend to differ from those of male users. Further, older players are found to make up an increasing part of the online gaming community. This study shows that online games are good exemplars of virtual social worlds as on average, players, regardless of gender and age, are found to spend twenty hours a week on online gaming, which exceeds many other forms of media use. In addition, users were found not only to participate but also to feel socially engaged with their fellow gamers, an engagement which, according to the researchers, may clash with engagements in the 'real social world'.

Within the same context of MMOGs, Consalvo and Harper (Chapter 6) examine representations of female avatars and players' reactions to them. They use two of the most popular MMOGs currently released—World of Warcraft and Age of Conan—and study each game's set of avatars, including the visual presentations of their bodies, armour and clothes, and how those choices differ (or not) based on gender, as well as players' responses to those design choices. From these sources, they sketch a portrait of how MMOGs are constructing gender and sex, and how players are responding to very different conceptions of those avatars. They conclude by arguing that the sexist or gendered nature of avatars is of less importance to the players taking part than the ability to control characters which they often see as extensions of themselves.

The use of virtual social networks by different age groups is further explored in Chapter 7. Here, Burmeister explores the values embedded in a virtual social network developed and maintained by senior members of society, notably the elderly. He found seven value categories that could be incorporated into the design of online networks and suggests that these need to be considered as they are important in making the use of these networks sustainable among similar online groups.

In Chapter 8 Robinson examines how real-life events are replicated in cyberspace. Using the case of a 'virtual strike' and demonstration which took place in the virtual world of Second Life in support of Italian workers for IBM, this chapter describes the action, its background, and subsequent developments in trade union use of Second Life. The initial action is used to discuss the nature of the real and the virtual, the concept of the 'production of space' as a social process, the possibility of labour remaking the spaces defined by capital, and the connection between the social relationships created in Second Life and pre-existing forms of collectivity.

The final section consists of studies concerned with the commodification and commercialization of virtual social networks. Chapters 9 and 10 both adopt a critical stance on virtual social networks and identify the power games as well as the commercial and political interests that surround the development and use of these sites.

Using the cases of Facebook and OpenSocial, Kreps and Pearson argue that there is growing evidence that such social networking sites are part of a hegemonic transnational agenda of conservative venture capital which reinforces hierarchies of consumption. By appropriating these various virtual social networks, either as part of the development of the infrastructure or during their use, the emergence of social networking sites demonstrates the continued and thriving hegemony of capitalism in today's virtual world.

Grassman and Case discuss commodification (as what is, or is perceived to be, the desire of the other) within the context of virtual social networks. In such spaces, they argue, subjects endow their identity and lifestyle with the mark of particular brands and products, which may help them to represent what they consider to be the other's desire. More radically, the subjects embody appearance itself by enacting images of their lives framed by brands like Facebook and MySpace and presented for the other's gaze. Through this framing, the authors encourage reflection on and observation of the current social realities evident in emerging virtual worlds.

Virtual social networks: Emerging themes

Within only a short period of time, virtuality has rapidly become more prevalent, unveiling modern Internet-based societies. This is now leading to a significant change in the manner in which everyday life is conducted and how our personal and organizational lives are shaped. Tapscott and William (2006), for example, argue that the emergence of Web 2.0 technologies, along with a new generation of Internet users born in the 1980s who are likely to play an active role in creating and editing online content, has created a 'perfect storm' that is revolutionizing the Internet and changing the way business is done. The implications are that mass collaboration changes the rules of the game, enabling cheaper and easier communication for individuals and organizations alike. These changes will have a definite and long-standing effect on the individuals and other entities involved. We therefore do not consider that virtual social networks will be a passing fad; technologies may change but our dependence on them will remain.

The chapters in this collection, as well as prior research on virtual social networks, provide some clues about the role that these online networks play and will increasingly play in our lives. But many questions still remain. What are the motivations, expectations, and preferences of users and players and how do these change over time? If users spend a significant amount of their time online as reported in different chapters here (i.e., Chapters 5, 6 and 7), then conflicts may arise between the real and the virtual. How do we resolve these conflicts and, perhaps more appropriately, how can we go beyond a mere differentiation between 'real' and 'virtual' phenomena to a phenomenon that is both real and virtual?

Rheingold (1993) has posited that although CMC technology offers a new capability of 'many to many' communication, the way in which and the extent to which this capability would be used would depend 'on the way we, the first people who are using it, succeed or fail in applying it to our lives'. Based on the increasing number of reports on the uptake of these sites, there is little doubt that indeed we have succeeded in applying such massively mediated and multiplayer capabilities to our lives. We can therefore assume that this many-to-many communication is here to stay as its adoption and use have been overwhelming. Despite this, the speed of change has made it difficult for academics to follow the pace of growth with sufficient empirical and conceptual studies that would give us insights into these emerging virtual networks and explanations of their growth, operations, and impact. These issues are still largely under-researched.

Understanding virtual social networks, especially with the increasing commercialization and commodification that we see evident in the studies presented here, reveals issues of privacy and data protection. These issues are in need of further debate and discussion. The language we use to talk about different phenomena matters as it affects the way we think about them and our engagement with them. The same sites we refer to as 'social networking' sites (e.g. Facebook) also have other roles; they are companies, too, as Kreps and Pearson discuss in this book, with their adopted revenue model being that of 'advertising' (Enders et al., 2008). They have directors and employees and, like all the other companies, they are profit-making entities. It is not surprising, therefore, that it has been predicted that by 2010 marketers will spend £1860 billion on online advertising and venture capitalists have been quizzing Web entrepreneurs about their 'Facebook strategy' (Reuters, 2007). Promoting them as 'networking' sites but using them for advertising and profit-making raises many ethical issues that require the attention of researchers and policymakers alike.

The existing literature on social networking sites places an overemphasis on the active agency of individual users; several studies, for example, discuss the demographic characteristics of users and their behaviour in these online spaces. However, contextual factors also need to be considered. The significance of virtual networks, as Castells (2001) has very thoughtfully acknowledged, goes beyond the number of users:

> Core economic, social, political, and cultural activities throughout the planet are being structured by and around the Internet, and other computer networks. In fact, exclusion from these networks is one of the most damaging forms of exclusion in our economy and in our culture.
>
> (p. 3)

It follows that social inclusion and social exclusion from virtual social networks is a matter that needs exploration. What are the short-term and long-term implications if members of society passively or actively exclude themselves from these networks? Are they winners or losers, and in what ways?

Last but not least, there are different types of virtual social networks. They should not therefore be treated as homogeneous. Some networks may be more collaborative than others, creating a strong sense of identity and belongingness. Others may be bypassed or just used to 'kill time'. Their heterogeneity should therefore be used to explain participants' diverse experiences and different degrees of exposure to the virtual world. Overall, however, each of them deserves particular attention by researchers as a means of examining issues of trust, collaboration, identity, power, and other relationship dynamics. Collectively, the studies presented here support the need for more research into this topic in order to lead us to deeper insights into these new and dynamic, but highly unknown, networks.

References

Ahuja, M.K. and Galvin, J.E. (2003). 'Socialization in Virtual Groups', *Journal of Management*, 29, 2, 161–85.

Alon, A., Brunel, F. and Siegal, W.S. (2004). 'Ritual Behavior and Community Life-Cycle: Exploring the Social Psychological Role of Net Rituals in the Development of Online Consumption Communities'. In: C. Haugvedt, K. Machleit and R. Yalch (eds) *Online Consumer Psychology: Understanding How to Interact With Consumers in the Virtual World*. Hillsdale, NJ: Erlbaum.

Blanchard, A.L. and Marklus, M.L. (2002). 'Sense of Virtual Community: Maintaining the Experience of Belonging', Proceedings of the 35th Hawaii International Conference on Systems Sciences, HICSS-35.

Boyd, D.M. and Ellison, N.B. (2007). 'Social Network Sites: Definition, History and Scholarship', *Journal of Computer-Mediated Communication*, 13, 1, article 11. http://jcmjc.indiana.edu/vol13/issue1/boyd.ellison.html

Castells, M. (2001). *The Internet Galaxy: Reflections on the Internet, Business, and Society*. Oxford: Oxford University Press.

Cramton, C.D. (2001). 'The Mutual Knowledge Problem and Its Consequences for Dispersed Collaboration', *Organization Science*, 12, 3, 346–71.

de Valck, K., Langerak, F., Verhoef, P.C. and Verlegh, P.W.J. (2006). 'Satisfaction with Virtual Communities of Interest: Effect on Members' Visit Frequency', *British Journal of Management*, 18, 241–56.

Donath, S.J. (1998). 'Identity and Deception in the Virtual Community'. In: P. Kollck and M. Smith (eds) *Communities in Cyberspace*. Routledge, London.

Ellison, N.B., Steinfiled, C. and Lampe, C. (2007). 'The Benefits of Facebook 'Friends': Social Capital and College Students' Use of Online Social Network Sites', *Journal of Computer-Mediated Communication*, 1143–68.

Enders, A., Hungenberg, H., Denker, H-P. and Mauch, S. (2008). 'The Long Tail of Social Networking: Revenue Models of Social Networking Sites', *European Management Journal*, 26, 199–211.

Fernback, J.E. and Thompson, B. (1995). *Virtual Communities: Abort, Retry, Failure?* http://www.rheingold.com/texts/techpolitix/VCcivil.html

Fulk, J. and DeSanctis, G. (1995). 'Electronic Communication and Changing Organizational Forms', *Organization Science*, 6, 4, 337–49.

Goldie, J.L. (2006). 'Virtual Communities and the Social Dimension of Privacy', *University of Ottawa Law and Technology Journal*, 3, 1, 133–67.

Guru, A. and Keng, S. (2008). 'Developing the IBM iVirtuality Community: iSociety', *Journal of Database Management*, Oct–Dec, 19, 4, i–xiii.

Henein, M. (2007). 'The WoW Factor', *Mix*, 31, 12, 54–9.

Herring, S.C. (2004). 'Slouching Toward the Ordinary: Current Trends in Computer-Mediated Communication', *New Media and Society*, 6, 1, 26–36.

Jarvenpaa, S.L. and Leidner, D.E. (1999). 'Communication and Trust in Global Virtual Teams', *Organization Science*, 10, 5, 791–815.

Jenkins, H. (2006). *Convergence Culture: Where Old and New Media Collide*. New York: New York University Press.

Joinson, A.N. and Paine, C.B. (2007). 'Self-Disclosure, Privacy and the Internet'. In: A.N. Joinson, K.Y.A. McKenna, T. Postmes and U-D. Reips (eds) *Oxford Handbook of Internet Psychology*, 237–52. Oxford: Oxford University Press.

Kasper-Fuehrer, E.C. and Ashkanasy, N.M. (2001). 'Communicating Trustworthiness and Building Trust in Interorganizational Virtual Organizations', *Journal of Management*, 27, 235–54.

King, R. (2008). 'The (Virtual) Global Office', Business Week, May 2, Special Report, p. 3–3.

Koh, J., Kim, Y-G., Butler, B., Bock, G-W. (2007). 'Encouraging Participation in Virtual Communities', *Communications of the ACM*, 50, 2, 69–73.

Lee, A. (1994). 'Electronic Mail as a Medium for Rich Communication: An Empirical Investigation Using Hermeneutic Interpretation', *MIS Quarterly*, 18, 2, 143–57.

Lipnack, J. and Stamps, J. (1997). *Virtual Teams: Reaching across Space, Time and Organizations with Technology*. New York: Wiley.

Majchrzak, A., Rice, R.E., King, N., Malhotra, A. and Ba, S. (2000). 'Technology Adaptation: The Case of a Computer-Supported Inter-Organizational Virtual Team', *MIS Quarterly*, 24, 4, 569–600.

Markus, M.L. (1994). 'Electronic Mail as the Medium of Managerial Choice', *Organizational Science*, 5, 4, 502–27.

Merchant, G. (2006). 'Identity, Social Networks and Online Communication', *E-Learning*, 3, 2, 235–44.

Miller, P. (2005). 'Web 2.0: Building the New Library', *Ariadne*, 45, October. http://www.ariadne.ac.uk/miller

Montoya-Weiss, M.M., Massey, A.P. and Song, M. (2001). 'Getting it Together: Temporal Coordination and Conflict Management in Global Virtual Teams'. *Academy of Management Journal*, 44, 6, 1231–62.

Panteli, N. (2002). 'Richness, Power Cues and Email Text', *Information and Management*, 40, 75–86.

Panteli, N. and Chiasson, M. (2008). 'Rethinking Virtuality'. In: N. Panteli and M. Chiasson (eds) *Exploring Virtuality Within and Beyond Organizations: Social, Global and Local Dimensions*. Basingstoke: Palgrave Macmillan.

Panyasorn, J., Panteli, N. and Powell, P. (2008). 'An Interaction Model in Groupware Use for Knowledge Management', *Encyclopedia for E-Collaboration*, 398–404. London: IGI Global.

Papargyris, A. and Poulymenakou, A. (2008). 'Playing Together in Cyberspace: Collective Action and shared meaning constitution in virtual worlds'. In: N. Panteli and M. Chiasson (eds) *Exploring Virtuality Within and Beyond Organizations: Social, Global and Local Dimensions*. Basingstoke: Palgrave Macmillan.

Peris, R., Gimeno, M.A., Pinazo, D., Ortett, G., Carrero, V., Sanchiz, M., Ibaniez, I. (2002). 'Online Chat Rooms: Virtual Spaces of Interaction for Socially Oriented People', *CyberPsychology and Behavior*, 5, 1, 43–51.

Pluempavarn, P. and Panteli, N. (2008). 'Building Social Identity through Blogging'. In: N. Panteli and M. Chiasson (eds) *Exploring Virtuality within and beyond Organizations: Social, Global and Local Dimensions*. Basingstoke: Palgrave Macmillan.

Reuters 2007, July 6, VCs Factor in Facebook, Red herring the business on technology.

Rheingold, H. (1993). *The Virtual Community. Homesteading on the Electronic Frontier.* New York: Harper Collins.

Rice, R.E., D'Ambra, J.E. and More, E. (1998). 'Cross-Cultural Comparison of Organizational Media Evaluation and Choice', *Journal of Communication*, 48, 3, 3–26.

Rice, R.E. and Shook, D.E. (1990). 'Relationships of Job Categories and Organizational Levels to Use of Communication Channels, Including Electronic Mail: A Meta-Analysis and Extension', *Journal of Management*, 27, 2, 195–229.

Soe, L.L. and Markus, M.L. (1993). 'Technological or Social Utility? Unraveling Explanations of Email, Vmail, and Fax Use', *The Information Society*, 9, 213–36.

Spitzberg, B.H. (2006). 'Preliminary Development of a Model and Measure of Computer-Mediated Communication (CMC) Competence', *Journal of Computer-Mediated Communication*, 11, 2, article 12. http://jcmc.indiana.edu/vol11/issue2/spitzberg.html

Tapscott, D. and Williams, A. (2006). *Wikinomics: How Mass Collaboration Changes Everything.* New York: Portfolio.

Walther, J. (1994). 'Anticipated Ongoing Interaction Versus Channel Effects on Relational Communication in Computer-Mediated Interaction' *Human Communication Research*, 20, 473–501.

Walther, J.B., Boos, M. and Joas, K.J. (2002). 'Misattribution and Attributional Redirection in Distributed Virtual Groups', Proceedings of the 35th Annual Hawaii International Conference on Systems Science HICSS-35, 7–10 January.

2
Learning Virtually or Virtually Distracted? The Impact of Emerging Internet Technologies on Pedagogical Practice

Simran K. Grewal and Lisa Harris

Introduction

Incremental and radical innovation

Technological innovation is a very normal and anticipated part of social and organizational life and a critical ingredient in safeguarding societal and organizational progression. Certain types of 'sustained' innovation go relatively undetected; they are gradual and incremental in nature, as small extensions or developments are made to an existing product or service, building on and reinforcing existing technologies. These small changes strengthen the value of technology either by making the product easier to use or by reducing the cost. For instance, if an innovation has reached the maturity stage of the product life cycle, then perhaps its functionality will be developed to provide a 'bolt-on', with the core of the innovation remaining essentially the same. A classic example of a sustained innovation is the mobile phone, where functionality is increased by adding on extra capabilities, such as video, Internet access, GPS tracking systems, music, and email. In contrast, a radical innovation has a more profound effect on existing industries, business practices, and society as it often renders existing products, industries, or practices obsolete. Radical innovations destroy the value of an existing technology by providing an alternative that is markedly different and to which existing technologies cannot be adapted to. In recent years, the most radical technological innovation that we have seen is undoubtedly the Internet. Quite clearly, through its communication capabilities the Internet has paved the way for providing more efficient ways of conducting social, organizational, and pedagogical practices.

A useful way to analyse the impact of emerging Internet technologies on traditional social, organizational, and pedagogical practices is through the notion of 'creative destruction'. This term was coined by Schumpeter (1942) to describe the process of transformation that accompanies radical innovation. Creative destruction occurs when a radical innovation renders existing practices or products obsolete. For example, the cassette tape replaced the eight track, only to be replaced by the compact disc, and then more recently it was replaced by the iPod or mp3 players. We only have to look at the computer industry to illustrate further the concept of creative destruction. For instance, personal computer (PC) companies have destroyed many mainframe computer companies, but in doing so have created one of the most important inventions of this century: the PC. Nevertheless, while it is an important concept, creative destruction became one of the most overused terms during the dotcom era through suggestions that creative destruction would replace the old economy with the new. In reality, many traditional business practices continue to exist alongside innovative practices brought about by the Internet.

Although the notion of creative destruction was originally used to explain the economic cycles of industrial innovation, this theory has indeed been put forward as a useful model to explain the disruptive potential of emerging technologies (Smith, 2007). It therefore serves as a useful framework to help us to better understand how the creation of the Internet is affecting other social, organizational and pedagogical practices. Christensen et al. (2004) alert us to the tacit power of disruptive technologies over time. They argue that disruptive technologies provide unique capabilities which a small niche market values. Because these capabilities serves the needs of only an insignificant niche market in comparison to the primary target market, industry leaders view the capability as insignificant. This lack of significance stems either from the small market size or from the relatively small profit margin which such innovations generate. Therefore, rather than rapidly destroying the value of existing technologies, disruptive innovations gradually cannibalize the value of such technologies through a systematic process of eroding away customers from the bottom of the value chain. Over time disruptive innovations gradually improve their processes, products, and services to customers, moving up the value chain. As they move up, they become a genuine threat to existing market leaders. In similar vein, over the last 15 to 20 years the gradual way in which emerging Internet technologies (in particular Web 2.0 technologies) have been permeating through society can be viewed as disruptive. Initially the capabilities afforded by the Internet appealed to a relatively niche market, but over time and through developments to the innovation as well as increased exposure and accessibility,

Internet technologies have disrupted existing products and services and our traditional modes of social interaction.

While the literature is bursting with various interpretations of Internet opportunities and developments, relatively little is known about the pervasive impact of such radical innovation on existing organizational, social, and pedagogical practice. For this reason the opportunities offered by the Internet can be viewed as a double-edged sword: there is undoubtedly a darker side to such technological advances and it is this issue that serves as the focal point of this chapter. In the next section we introduce the Web as a teaching and learning environment, before exploring the tension between the opportunities and threats created by recent technological developments and concurrent changes in the learning styles and expectations of students. We then consider the implications of emerging Internet technologies on pedagogical practice by drawing upon two practical case studies.

The use of Web 2.0 environments for teaching and learning

The use of the Web as an effective teaching and learning medium has been widely researched (Gee, 2003; Arbaugh, 2000; Bigelow, 1999; Farmer, 2004; Bradshaw and Hinton, 2004; McLoughlin and Luca, 2000; Bunker and Ellis, 2001; Oliver, 2000; Grewal, 2002, 2003, 2004a, 2004b, 2007, 2008). Recent developments in modes of social interaction facilitated by Web 2.0 technologies have the potential to shift the boundaries of teaching and learning again. To this end, the use of social software, such as wikis, blogs, podcasts, instant messaging, VoIP, 3D computer simulation, and online gaming, prescribes to our dynamic society our evolving modes of social interaction and offers tremendous scope for teaching and learning by providing a stimulating, interactive, and engaging learning environment.

Erosion of traditional learning styles

All around us we are beginning to see evidence of the way in which emerging Internet technologies are beginning to erode more traditional ways of teaching and learning. For instance, many university classrooms are now equipped with network facilities that provide course instructors with live access to Internet-based resources. Live network access offers an opportunity to access a wider range of resources in a more efficient way. One such tool which is being increasingly used in management education is YouTube. This website provides links to video clips which serve as a useful aid in illustrating contemporary case study examples of work-based issues and scenarios, and help students to make sense of abstract theoretical constructs. Consequently, less reference is being made to traditional textbook resources, which date very quickly.

Another example of how emerging Internet technologies are eroding traditional teaching and learning practices is the use of virtual learning environments such as Moodle, WebCT, and Blackboard. Many courses across the higher education sector are now supported by e-learning resources. These provide students with additional support material, including lecture slides, links to readings, communication forums, and assessment tools, which include quizzes and assignment submission functions. University libraries are providing wider access to electronic journals, which reduces the need to stock hard copies of journals while allowing more efficient remote access to academic resources. Increasingly, students are turning to the Internet as a resource for information. Google and Wikipedia have now become powerful first points of reference for students seeking information about concepts and issues related to course topics.

However, these technological developments have not occurred in a vacuum. If we go back to Christensen's notion of disruptive technologies, and in particular think about how certain innovations gradually permeate through existing systems and processes interlinked with the technology, it helps us to contextualize the impact that emerging Internet technologies are having on teaching and learning. Prensky (2001) alerts us to the disruptive potential of emerging Internet technologies vis-à-vis the current generation of students. He argues that this group constitutes the first generation of students to grow up with the Internet, and they will have spent their entire lives exposed to computers, videogames, digital music players, video cams, and mobile phones. For instance, he notes that the current generation of university students in the United States have spent less than 5000 hours of their lives reading, yet in excess of 10,000 hours playing video games. Of course, there may now be an even greater divide in these statistics, given that the research was conducted seven years ago.

The way in which the Internet is eroding traditional learning methods is not country specific. In the last few years, research conducted by the European Interactive Advertising Agency (EIAA, 2005) has highlighted the phenomenon that the current generation of European students is dedicating a greater percentage of its time to Internet-related activities, including information-gathering, online gaming, and online chats as opposed to watching TV, talking on the phone, or reading newspapers and books. The data show that 46 per cent of 15- to 24-year-olds are watching less TV, preferring instead to browse the Internet. It is also increasingly common for people to 'watch' TV while simultaneously using their laptops to carry out multiple Instant Messaging (IM) conversations and surf the Internet. A number of terms have been used to describe this current generation of students:

- V Gen = Virtual Generation (Proserpio and Gioia, 2007)
- Net Gen = Net Generation (Oblinger and Oblinger, 2005)
- D Gen = Digital Generation (Papert, 1996)
- Digital Natives (Prensky, 2001)
- Google Generation (O'Brien, 2008).

A literal interpretation of these statistics shows that this generation of students is becoming increasingly reliant on Internet technologies as a learning resource, which raises some important questions: If students are relying increasingly on the Internet, how will these technologies affect the processes through which students learn? And, as instructors, how will we affect the methods we use to teach them?

Different generational attitudes to new technologies

Prensky (2001) begins to address the first part of this question by making a useful distinction between the current generation of students, whom he describes as 'the digital natives', and their predecessors, 'the digital immigrants'. He suggests that like natives the current generation of students has grown up and been exposed to all things digital and can therefore speak the 'digital language'; the digital immigrants, on the other hand were not born into the digital world but were exposed to it at a later stage of their lives. Therefore the way in which they think and process information will be significantly different. For instance, digital immigrants will probably have spent many hours locked away in a bedroom revising for exams from textbooks and classroom notes with minimal distraction, whereas in stark contrast the digital natives will probably supplement the textbook and class notes with a laptop screen displaying a number of tabbed pages that provide multiple sources of information. This is often carried out in tandem with checking emails and updates of friends' profiles on Facebook while downloading the latest iTunes onto an iPod, the epitome of multitasking. The outcome is that the current generation of students is able to absorb information quickly and from multiple sources, adapt more easily to change, and have amazingly flexible minds. This means that they assume a 'process' rather than a 'content' view to problem-solving and searching for information. Accordingly, there is a greater focus on the development of skills that promote problem-solving

Table 2.1 Digital Natives versus Digital Immigrants

Digital natives like...	Digital immigrants like...
receiving information quickly from multiple sources	slow and controlled release of information from multiple media sources
parallel processing and multitasking	singular processing and single or limited tasking
processing pictures, sounds, and video before text	processing text before pictures, sounds, and video
random access to hyperlinked multimedia information	to receive information linearly, logically, and sequentially
to network with others	to work independently
to learn 'just in time'	to learn 'just in case'

Source: Adapted from Times Online (2008).

in a world where information is abundant, rather than on memorizing a contained amount of tutor-directed content (Tapscott, 1998).

The following table (Table 2.1) outlines the key distinctions between the digital natives and the digital immigrants.

There has been a large amount of media coverage of the supposed divide between digital natives and digital immigrants, but in practice the distinction is less clear. Recent research by the British Library (Manchester, 2008) found that the skills and enthusiasm for Web 2.0 tools among the 'Google generation' have been highly overrated, because while the students surveyed used social networks for personal activities, they were sceptical about their wider relevance, and they actually expected more traditional means of interaction to take place in the office or classroom. Also, a recent study of technology usage among first-year students in Australia (Kennedy et al., 2007) of indicated that there is greater diversity in the use of technology by students than many commentators have so far suggested. In particular, they found that usage of Web 2.0 technologies was quite low among their sample of digital natives.

It may therefore be too simplistic to assume that digital natives have fundamentally different learning styles which require new methods of teaching. In the next section we delve a little deeper into the changes taking place in order to shed more light on these issues.

Multiple processing of information

What is the impact of the type of multiple processing of information, identified above, on the learning process? Mounting evidence suggests that although these virtual technologies are making the information-gathering process more efficient by making it simpler to collate information, there is a real danger that processing information in this way can lead to 'skimming' or a surface approach to learning. A five-year study into the 'Google Generation' conducted by researchers at University College London (2008) examined the behaviour of students logging on to websites of journals and e-books. They found widespread evidence of skimming activity involving 'bouncing out' and 'flicking' behaviour. For instance, users viewed no more than three pages before 'bouncing out'. This suggests that users are searching for information horizontally rather than vertically. Quite clearly, the gathering of multiple sources of information allows knowledge to be broadened but it doesn't act as a substitute for analysing and developing the critical skills to assess the information.

Bauerlein (2007) and Jackson (2008) alert us to a hidden danger of multitasking that is facilitated by emerging Internet technologies. They argue that these technologies are creating a 'culture of distraction' in which users are finding it increasingly difficult to sustain concentration levels as they have the capacity to assimilate information much faster and from multiple sources of information. They therefore expect a wider variety of information from more dynamic sources, which include visual, sound, and textual data. Some would argue that this could be regarded as evidence of a short attention span.

Nevertheless, it can also be argued that the dynamic processing of multiple sources of information, harnessed by more efficient accessibility to this information, enables the current generation of students to evaluate critically and form judgements more quickly than their predecessors who would have processed information from singular sources in a more sequential fashion. So perhaps the question should be more about whether speed and multiple processing of information affects one's ability to provide in-depth critical evaluation. Further research is necessary in this area.

Moving from institutional to social learning

According to Brown and Sadler (2008) the most profound impact of the Internet is its ability to support and extend the various aspects of social learning. This means that our understanding of content is influenced not just by *what* we are learning but by *how* we are learning. The authors cite Light's (2001) discovery that one of the strongest determinants of students' success in higher education was their ability to form or participate in small study groups. These students were more engaged in their studies than their peers who worked alone, better prepared for class, and learned significantly more. By working in groups students can clarify areas of uncertainty or confusion and in turn help their colleagues who may be struggling.

A second aspect of social learning involves acquiring the practices and behavioural norms of established practitioners within a community of practice, a skill which has historically been acquired through an apprenticeship or a mentor–mentee relationship. The authors also note how traditional education systems encourage students to spend years learning about a subject before acquiring the tacit skills associated with being an active practitioner in a field. This approach worked well in a relatively stable world in which careers were based within one organization. But nowadays the wheels turn much faster and one person may move between many different jobs as their skills become outdated, and without the luxury of a lengthy re-training period each time. Viewing learning as a process that involves joining a community of practice reverses the traditional pattern of knowledge acquisition, and encourages the practice of 'productive inquiry' in which knowledge is acquired as it is needed in order to carry out a specific task.

Tools such as blogs, wikis, social networks, tagging systems, mashups, and content-sharing sites are examples of a new infrastructure that focuses on conversation, participation, and action-based learning. These Web 2.0 technologies provide many opportunities for social learning to occur, together with the additional advantage of overcoming geographical boundaries to group work and community development. Brown and Sadler (2008) sum up their argument by calling for a new approach to learning that is characterized by *'demand-pull'* (meaning driven by the particular interests of the learner) rather than the traditional *'supply-push'* mode of knowledge acquisition (where specific content is dictated by the tutor or institution).

Siemens (2008) takes this argument further by suggesting that Web 2.0 technologies could be instrumental in moving away from traditional hierarchical models of education that are structured around a defined body of knowledge and broadcast to learners in a controlled manner, towards a networked approach which is more adaptive to the needs of learners. Communication could be facilitated through the use of wikis, blogs, and global communities of expertise, while the relative value of diverse sources of information is assessed through social bookmarking tools such as Digg or Del.icio.us. This means that learners can get a sense of the importance of an article or video in terms of the number of viewers who have bookmarked it or commented favourably on it, although admittedly such ranking is subjective and hardly an exact science. In this environment, the role of the tutor changes or can even disappear altogether. Students move from a learning environment controlled by the tutor and the institution to one where they direct their own learning according to personal interests, find their own information and create knowledge by engaging in relevant networks of expertise that could be physically located anywhere in the world.

We have so far discussed the ways in which emerging Internet technologies are eroding the traditional learning process and highlighted some of the advantages and disadvantages associated with these changes. We need to be aware that because emerging Internet technologies are becoming closely intertwined with our social and organizational lives, we are gradually being locked into a system in which we are becoming increasingly dependent upon these technologies to support the ways in which we facilitate the learning process. Consequently, there is a real need to revisit our current teaching styles and make sure that they are aligned with changes in the ways that students are processing information, otherwise we are in danger of creating a significant division between teaching methods and learning styles.

Aligning teaching methods with changing learning styles

In particular, we need to think about ways of developing more specific methods of encouraging a deeper approach towards learning. Proserpio and Gioia (2007) have identified the danger of this mismatch between the ways in which information is processed across generations in the context of the teaching and learning processes. What they highlight is the evident risk of creating a division between learning styles and teaching practices. They suggest that technological developments based on 'out of classroom' media have meant that 15- to 24-year-olds are (typically) more familiar with Internet-based technologies than previous generations. They term this demographic group the Virtual Generation (or VGen) as their increased exposure to 'out of class' virtual media is likely to influence their learning style.

As noted earlier, Prensky (2001) also alerts us to the widening gap between today's university students and their teachers, the so-called digital immigrants. He argues that lecturers need to tailor their teaching to match the skills, experiences, and expectations of their 'digital native' students. All too often teaching styles tend to lag a generation behind as lecturers tend to adopt styles that are consistent with their own learning styles, based on their familiarity with the media they have been exposed to in their formative years. Therefore, when teaching the current generation of students, we need to be sensitive to changing learning styles, while at the same time remembering that such changes are not distributed uniformly across all members of this generation: we also need to be aware that students will exhibit a range of aptitudes for new technologies. Similarly, educators display a range of attitudes towards technological developments. As Martin (2006) notes, some lecturers will be reluctant to engage with the new technologies and may even see such trends as undermining the traditions of adult education. Others will be more receptive of the need to change but still be slow to change their own behaviour until they have assimilated new skills. Some lecturers will be keen to experiment with new teaching methods – and we outline two such approaches below.

The pedagogical potential of virtual social networks

Second Life

A good example of Web 2.0 technology is Second Life. It has the potential to encourage a richer approach to learning, supports the development of process-based skills, and facilitates productive enquiry. Media hype suggests that this virtual parallel universe is capable of transforming social, organizational, and pedagogical practice as they exist in real life. While the notion of participating in a virtual existence may appear far-fetched for some, the increase in the number of virtual communities of avatars appearing in Second Life indicates that this is a phenomenon which simply cannot be taken lightly. At the beginning of April 2008 Second Life reported a global membership of 13 million registered users. Businesses such as Accenture and IBM have adopted this platform for graduate recruitment. Adidas, BMW, Coca Cola, Cisco, Sky News, Sony Ericsson, Penguin Publishing, Sony BMG, IKEA, and Reuters have established a brand presence within this platform. And it is not only businesses that recognize the potential that such a platform holds: entire real-life cities such as Tokyo have been re-created in a virtual sense. At a political level, in the recent 2008 United States democratic elections, Hillary Clinton and Barack Obama were reported to have been conducting election campaigns in Second Life. The Swedish and Mauritian embassies have also been quick to stake their territory within this virtual jungle. Then there are the ever-increasing social islands that are emerging, like the Isle of Ballymore originating in Holland in which a community of avatars gathers in a conservatory to be entertained by virtual rock stars.

However, Second Life is not without controversy. In recent months a number of unsavoury incidents have raised the question of the appropriateness of adopting Second Life as an educational platform. For instance, media coverage recently reported Second Life as a breeding ground for terrorist activity, with militants using this virtual world to hunt for recruits and mimic real-life terrorist activity (griefing), against avatars and buildings. These virtual atrocities in Second Life are being used to facilitate the formation of a community of extremists (Guest, 2007). Moreover, the ability of avatars to engage in promiscuous activity raises further questions about the appropriateness of using this virtual platform for educational purposes. Yet the existence of Ivy League academic institutions in Second Life such as Stanford, Harvard, and Princeton universities implies a degree of educational merit.

According to Fink (2003), using a diverse range of teaching and learning activities stimulates the student learning experience, which in effect can lead to a richer learning outcome. He suggests that engaging in active learning activities increases the likelihood that learners will experience significant and meaningful learning as 'all learning activities involve some kind of "experience" or some kind of "dialogue"'. In line with Fink's (2003) concept of active learning, participating in a learning activity in Second Life should enhance a student's learning experience as the technology offers a platform for interaction with a community of learners by simulating a real-life dynamic learning environment.

Quite clearly, if we want to engage with the current generation of students, we need to design teaching activities through media that these students are familiar with. Second Life offers the potential to develop problem-solving skills and provides an environment in which students can engage with other learners through interaction with other students in a 3D environment. This environment offers the potential to create simulation activities based on key subject areas.

If an activity is designed carefully, this can provide a rich learning experience for the student. In management education one of the key topic areas often studied is group decision-making (Kolb, 1999). Second Life offers an ideal simulation environment from which students can experience the group decision-making process through dynamic media they are familiar with. For instance, a pilot group decision-making activity was recently designed and implemented in Second Life for 196 undergraduate students on an organizational behaviour course at the University of Bath to assess the pedagogical suitability of this platform for management education. The rationale behind designing this activity was for students to experience conflict and negotiation in the context of group decision-making.

The pedagogical activity was structured around a role-play scenario in a hypothetical organization in which students were required to participate in a virtual group meeting. Students were allocated predefined conflicting roles on an executive board consisting of five to six members and were expected to negotiate a change proposal. To enhance the experience of conflict, the use of non-verbal communication channels was restricted to allowing the use of chat tools only to obstruct the flow of conversation and the meeting time was limited to 20 minutes. Forty virtual meetings were conducted over a two-week period. Prior to the virtual meeting, students were provided with instructions for creating an avatar and installing Second Life on laptops.

Six virtual offices were built in a meeting space on the Eduserv Island in Second Life. The offices were connected via a central pathway, which provided a link to each office, and a central meeting point, which allowed the students to socialize with one another in between meetings. The virtual offices were designed to simulate 'real-life' meeting rooms. Each office was equipped with a round table and six chairs, a whiteboard outlining meeting protocol, and a reception desk with a computer. (Please see Figure 2.1.)

Although accessibility and technical issues were minimal, upon reflection a number of other issues emerged in the pilot project. One of the key issues for the lecturer was the organization of such a large cohort of students and as a result the design and set-up of the activity proved extremely time-consuming. More efficient ways of organizing large groups of

Figure 2.1 A virtual office in Second Life.

students need to be considered. However, it is important to bear in mind that although the initial set-up was time-intensive, the same meeting space can be recycled and used again.

Another issue that emerged was language barriers; these affected the participation levels of certain cohorts. The international student cohort constituted 25 per cent of the course out of this percentage approximately 13 per cent were students whose first language was not English. Given that the primary language of communication was English, this resulted in this cohort being slightly slower to respond and contribute to the discussion. Subsequently, this led to lower levels of chat contribution during the virtual meetings. Maintaining an even flow of conversation was difficult, which resulted in students having to type extremely fast or simultaneously with each speaker to keep up. Often the flow of conversation was difficult to follow due to the pace at which a meeting progressed, and this often led to instances of miscommunication. Nevertheless, this experience brought to the surface a very useful example in inner-group dynamics and highlighted contemporary issues in working with diverse groups. At the time of writing this chapter, student reaction to the Second Life activity is still being analysed, but initial indications would suggest that the overall experience was positive.

Ning

Another experiment that we are carrying out to enhance the learning experience is the development of an online community for MSc students using Ning. This is a free resource (or, rather, it is paid for by advertising) which allows a 'social network in a box' to be created – meaning that such features as discussion boards, video, photos, and RSS feeds from relevant blogs can be incorporated into one place for the benefit of invited community members only. Students can create a profile which can be customized to their individual tastes.

At the University of Southampton we have created a community using Ning for those studying towards our Marketing MSc. The majority of students on this course study in a second language and many of them were also new to the whole social networking experience at the start of their course. We have created a number of discussion topics, as shown in Figure 2.2 below.

The objectives were to create a central resource for information relating to studying and living in Southampton, with opportunities to interact with tutors or past students out in the workplace, to encourage small groups of students to work together and support one another, and organize and publicize social or networking events. Given that many of the

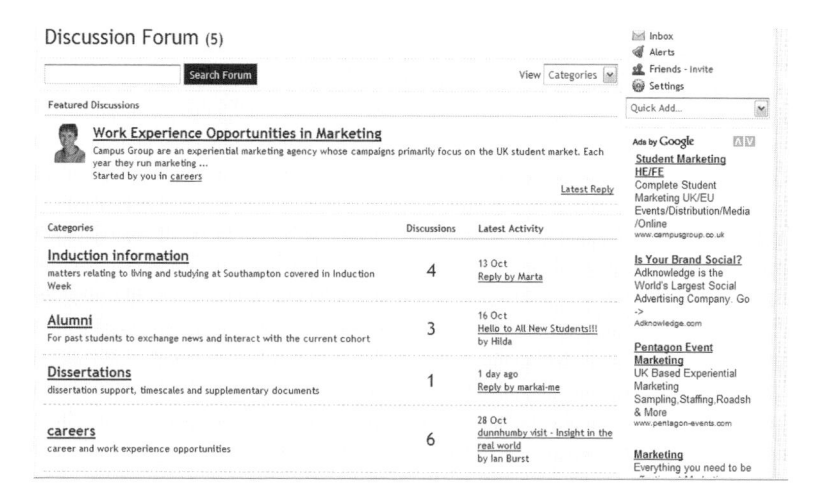

Figure 2.2 Online discussion forum.

students are resident in the United Kingdom for the first time, and in fact are studying abroad for the first time, there is a lot to be gained from encouraging them to interact with other ethnic groups, support one another and share their experiences. A lot of the information provided on the site would have been discussed with the students during Induction Week, a time when they are bombarded with vast amounts of new information which can all be too much to take in, particularly in a second language. The Ning community allows relevant links and contact details to be displayed throughout the year and read by the students on a 'need-to-know' basis.

It is still too early to judge how successful this experiment has been. It is already evident that simply signing up to the community does not guarantee active participation, but this is an issue for all online communities, where typically just 5 to 10 per cent of members are regular contributors. The content can still be useful for those who prefer not to engage directly themselves, and we have encouraged alumni to contribute their advice about surviving the course, writing dissertations, and applying for jobs for the benefit of the current group of students. It was pleasing to note that, after playing a video for the group in class, one of the students went online and found another video made by the same presenter and posted a link to it on the Ning community for the benefit of the group as a whole. This is exactly the type of response that we hope to encourage. One of last year's students who now has a graduate job has used the site to publicize a visit he is undertaking to the university with his boss to deliver a presentation about careers in his industry and to encourage other students to apply to the company for a job.

Conclusion

Emerging Internet technologies are permeating our social and organizational lives and a consequence of these technological developments is the way in which they are eroding traditional learning styles, as evidenced by changes in the ways that the current generation of students learns. Our experience shows that labels such as 'digital native' are oversimplistic and do not reflect the wide variety of attitudes towards new technologies and their role in learning that a number of researchers have observed among their students.

We have noted that Web 2.0 technologies, though they seem disruptive to traditional learning approaches, can facilitate social learning and the development of process-based skills due to their focus on information-gathering through interaction with a community of learners and the creation and sharing of user-generated content. However, at the same time virtual social networks such as Ning and Second Life also offer the potential for students to develop process-based skills through media they are familiar with. This allows them to engage with the technology and can lead to a richer learning experience. Nevertheless, the level of integration and the degree to which the use of the technology is aligned with the learning objectives of a course will be critical to its success.

Implications for further research and practice

Our discussion on the impact of virtual social networks on pedagogical practice suggests that there is a need to reassess our teaching methods in order to engage more meaningfully with the current generation of students, and in practice to design our teaching to match students' learning styles so that there is closer alignment between the two. At the same time we should bear in mind that any group of students may well encompass individuals with a broad range of learning styles, and so some form of 'hybrid' approach may be necessary which can easily be adapted to suit the needs of the majority, or offer a degree of choice to the group, once the learning profile of the group has been identified.

While we have identified a need to redefine pedagogical practice, at the same time we also need to go one step further and think about the implications of our findings on practice and further research, as we cannot view these developments in a vacuum. For example, the practical implications of introducing innovative teaching methods into the classroom will of course require, in the first instance, an adequate infrastructure, access to resources and senior management support and will force lecturers to acquire the necessary knowledge and skills to use the technology. The suitability of the technological environment to the topic of study will also have to be assessed.

At a more intrinsic level our findings outline how emerging Internet technologies are permeating social and organizational lives. The technology facilitates the multiple and dynamic processing of information and, consequently, this may be causing a reduction in learners' attention spans, resulting in a surface approach to learning, particularly as exposure to the technology increases. Clearly, further scientific research is required to ascertain whether these technologies do indeed contribute towards a surface approach to learning and, if so, how this problem may be mitigated. However, using the same traditional measures to assess depth of learning appears rather limited. What has changed is the rate at which we are processing information and therefore we should also be exploring whether the rate at which a learner processes information influences the depth of their learning.

References

Appleyard, B. (2008) 'Stooopid...why the Google Generation isn't as smart as it thinks', *Times Online*, 20 July 2008. http://www.timesonline.co.uk (accessed on 30 July 2008).

Arbaugh, J.B. (2000) 'Virtual classrooms versus physical classroom: An exploratory study of class discussion patterns and student learning in an asynchronous Internet MBA course'. *Journal of Management Education*, 24(2): 213–34.

Bauerlein, M. (2007) *The dumbest generation. How the digital age stupefies young Americans and jeopardises our future.* New York: Tarcher.

Bigelow, J.D. (1999) 'The web as an organizational behaviour learning medium'. *Journal of Management Education*, 23: 635–50.

Bradshaw, J. and Hinton, L. (2004) 'Benefits of an online discussion list in a traditional distance education course'. *Turkish Online Journal of Distance Education (TOJDE)*, 5(3). http://tojde.anadolu.edu.tr/tojde15/articles/hinton.htm (accessed on 14 October 1996).

Brown, J.S. and Adler, R.P. (2008) 'Minds on fire, open education, the long tail and learning 2.0', *Educause Review*, January–February.

Bunker, A. and Ellis, R. (2001) 'Using bulleting boards for learning: What do staff and students need to know in order to use boards effectively?' In A. Hermann and M.M. Kulski (eds), *Expanded horizons in teaching and learning, Proceedings of the 10th Annual Teaching Learning Forum*, 7–9 February 2001, Curtin University of Technology, Perth. http://lsn.curtin.edu.au/tlf2001/bunker.html (accessed on 14 October 2006).

Christensen, C.M., Antony, S.D. and Roth, E.A. (2004) *Seeing What's Next: Using Theories of Innovation to Predict Industry Change*. Boston: Harvard Business School Press.

CIBER (2008) 'Information behaviour of the researcher of the future', University College London, 11 January 2008. http://www.bl.uk/news/pdf.googlegen.pdf (accessed on 12 July 2008).

European Interactive Advertising Association (2005) http://www.eiaa.net/news/eiaa-articles-details.asp?lang=1&id=66 (accessed on 27 March 2008).

Farmer, J. (2004) 'Communication dynamics: Discussion boards, weblogs and the development of communities of inquiry in online learning environments'. In R. Atkinson, C. McBeath, D. Jonas-Dwyer and R. Phillips (eds), *Beyond the comfort zone: Proceedings of the 21st ASCILITE Conference*. Perth, 5–8 December 2004, 274–83. http://www.ascilite.org.au/conferences/perth04/procs/farmer.html (acessed on 21 February 2005).

Fink, L.D. (2003) *Creating Significant Learning Experiences: An Integrated Approach to Designing College Courses*. San Francisco: Jossey Bass.

Gee, J.P. (2003) *What videogames have to teach us about learning and literacy*. Basingstoke: Palgrave Macmillan.

Grewal, S.K. (2003) 'The Social Dynamics of Integrating E Mediated Learning into Traditional UK Universities', *Conference Proceedings E-LEARN-World Conference on E Learning in Corporate, Government, Health and Higher Education 2003*, 1: 503–6.

Grewal, S.K. (2004a) 'Coerced evolution: Integrating e learning into traditional UK universities'. In Budd, L. and Harris, L., *E-Economy: Rhetoric or Business Reality*. London: Routledge, 106–22.

Grewal, S.K. (2004b) 'E mediated learning in traditional UK universities: A panacea for change?' *Conference Proceedings ED MEDIA – World Conference on Educational Multimedia, Hypermedia and Telecommunications 2004*, 1: 2883–9.

Grewal, S.K. (2007) 'Active learning: A reflection on the pedagogic use of social software in a campus-based UK university'. In C. Crawford, D. A. Willis, R. Carlsen, I. Gibson, K. McFerrin, J. Price & R. Weber, *Proceedings of Society for Information Technology and Teacher Education International Conference 2007* (pp. 1500–05). Chesapeake, VA: AACE. San Antonio, Texas, USA, March 26, 2007.

Grewal, S.K. (2008) 'Second Life: Black hole or Baby universe', *IFIP WG 9.5 International Working Conference on Virtuality and Society: Massive Virtual Communities*. Leuphana University, Luneburg, Germany, 1–2 July 2008.

Guest, T. (2007) *Second Lives: A Journey through Virtual Worlds*. London: Hutchinson.

Jackson, M. (2008) *Distracted: The Erosion of Attention and the Coming of the Dark Age*. New York: Prometheus Books.

Kennedy, G., Dalgarno, B., Gray, K., Judd, T., Waycott, J., Bennett, S., Maton, K., Krause, K.L., Bishop, A., Chang, R. and Churchward, A. (2007). 'The net generation are not big users of Web 2.0 technologies: Preliminary findings'. In *ICT: Providing choices for learners and learning. Proceedings ascilite Singapore 2007*. http://www.ascilite.org.au/conferences/singapore07/procs/kennedy.pdf

Kolb, J. (1999) 'A project in small group decision making', *Journal of Management Education*, 23(1): 71–9.

Light, R.J. (2001) *Making the most of college: Students speak their minds*. Cambridge, Mass.: Harvard University Press.

Martin, I. (2006) 'In whose interests? Interrogating the metamorphosis of adult education'. In A. Antikainen, P. Harinen & C.A. Torres (eds), *In from the

Margins: Adult Education, Work and Civil Society. Rotterdam, The Netherlands: Sense Publishers.

McLoughlin, C. and Luca, J. (2000) 'Cognitive engagement and higher order thinking through computer conferencing: We know why but do we know how?' In A. Hermann and M.M. Kulski (eds) *Flexible Futures in Tertiary Teaching, proceedings of the 9th Annual Teaching Learning Forum*, 2–4 February 2000, Curtin University of Technology. http://lsn.curtin.edu.au/tlf/tlf2000/mcloughlin.html (accessed on 16 October 2006).

Oblinger, D.G. and Oblinger, J.L. (2005) *Educating the Net generation*, Educause.

O'Brien, C. (2008) 'How the Google generation thinks differently', *Times Online*, 8 July 2008. http://www.timesonline.co.uk (accessed on 8 November 2008).

Oliver, R. (2000) 'When teaching meets learning: design principles and strategies for web-based learning environments that support knowledge construction'. In R. Sims, M. O'Reilly and S. Sawkins (eds), *Learning to choose: Choosing to learn*. Proceedings of the 17th Annual ASCILITE Conference. Lismore, NSW: Southern Cross University Press, 17–28.

Papert, S. (1996) *The Connected Family: Bridging the Digital Generation Gap*. Atlanta: Longstreet Press Inc.

Prensky, M. (2001) 'Digital natives, digital immigrants', *On the Horizon*, MCB University Press, 9, 5, October.

Prensky, M. (2001) 'Digital natives, digital immigrants, do they really think differently?' *On the Horizon*, MCB University Press, 9, 6, October.

Proserpio, L. and Gioia, D.A. (2007) 'Teaching the virtual generation', *Academy of Management Learning and Education*, 6(1): 69–80.

Schumpeter, J.A. (1942) *Capitalism, Socialism and Democracy*. New York: Harper Row.

Second Life. Available at http://secondlife.com/whatis/economy_stats.php (accessed on 21 August 2008).

Smith, R. (2007) 'The disruptive potential of game technologies', *Research Technology Management*, 50(2): 57–64. (Accessed 5 August 2008 from Business Source Premier Database).

Tapscott, D. (1998) *Growing up digitally: The rise of the net generation*. New York: McGraw-Hill.

3
VU @ Second Life: A Report on Experiences with the Development of a (Virtual) Community of Learners

Frans Feldberg, Anton Eliëns, Sarah van der Land, Marleen Huysman, and Elly Konijn

Introduction

Online virtual worlds have been present for more than ten years and the recent substantial media attention on Second Life can be considered an indication that virtual worlds are no longer the domain of a selective group of fanatical online gamers. For example, the number of registered residents in Second Life increased from two million at the beginning of 2007 to more than 12 million in February 2008, at times even reaching a growth of 1 million new registrations a month.[1] Big companies such as Reebok, IBM, Philips, Randstad, and ABN AMRO organize press meetings to announce their presence in virtual worlds. Even governments, municipalities, and NGOs have entered Second Life with an eagerness comparable to the 'don't miss the boat' feeling experienced during the early days of the Internet.

On 28 February 2007, the VU University Amsterdam announced its presence as the first Dutch university in Second Life. Why does a respectable university want to be present in Second Life? And what are the prospects for or benefits to an educational institute with a strong research reputation to be present in Second Life? Is it publicity we are after, the momentary attention of the press, taking profit from the (current) hype around Second Life? Or are there more sustainable reasons that make such a presence worthwhile, from both educational and research perspectives? In this chapter we address these questions and give an account of the process that led to our establishing a presence in Second Life.

The structure of this chapter is as follows: first, we explain our motivation(s) for entering Second Life and explore its potential as a pedagogical platform. Then we outline the actual building of our virtual campus and briefly report on our experiences when going live. After presenting some insights with the development of a community of learners in Second Life, we discuss the implications for practice and policymaking and suggest directions for further research. Finally, we present our conclusions.

Creating a presence in a virtual world

In less than a decade since the publication of William Gibson's novel *Neuromancer*, the *metaverse* was realized, albeit in a primitive way, through the introduction of virtual reality modelling language (VRML),[2] and introduced at the International Web Conference of 1992 (Anders, 1999). The German company *blaxxun*,[3] named after the virtual environment in Neil Stephenson's *Snowcrash*, was one of the first to offer a 3D community platform. It was soon followed by *AlphaWorld*, which offered a richer repertoire of avatar gestures as well as limited in-game building facilities. However, somehow 3D virtual communities never seemed to fulfil their initial promises. Furthermore, the adoption of VRML as a 3D interface to the Web never really took off.

The history of Second Life is extensively described in the official *Second Life* guide (Rymaszweski et al., 2007). Beginning in 2004, almost out of the blue, Second Life[4] appeared with a high adoption and a low churn rate, and in the autumn of 2008 it had over 16 million inhabitants.[5] Considering the cost of ownership of virtual estate, which easily amounts to €200 per month rent after an initial investment of €1500 for a single piece of virtual land measuring 65,536 square metres, the adoption of Second Life by individuals as well as companies such as ABN AMRO and Philips and institutions such as Harvard is surprising.

From a technical point of view, it seems that in comparison to other platforms for immersive worlds, including massively multiplayer online roleplaying games (MMORPGs)[6] such as *World of Warcraft* (*WoW*)[7] and *Everquest*,[8] Second Life offers an optimal combination of avatar modification options, gesture animations, in-game construction tools, and facilities for communication and social networking such as chatting and instant messaging (Utz, 2003). Incorporating elements of community formation, commonly denoted as Web 2.0, and exemplified by MySpace, YouTube, and Flickr, the immersive appearance, perhaps also the built-in physics and the inclusion of elementary economic principles, seem to be important ingredients in the success of Second Life. In addition, the possibility of recording collaborative enacted stories (Davenport, 2000) using built-in *machinima*[9] certainly also contributes to its appeal. Next to these technical opportunities that Second Life has to offer, one of the decisive reasons for our university's creating a presence in

Second Life is the opportunity to build a virtual platform that may embody our so-called *community of learners* vision, where both staff and students collaborate in contributing content in the context of knowledge development.

Building a virtual campus

To explore the opportunities virtual worlds can offer in support of the development of a community of learners we decided to build a virtual campus. In December 2006 we first discussed the idea of creating a presence in Second Life. Our initial aim was to explore the opportunities of Second Life by building a prototype of our university campus, by developing tutorials for further content creation, and by analyzing the functional and technical requirements and opportunities for use in education and research.

Two-and-a-half months later we were online, with a virtual campus that contains a lecture room, a telehub from which teleports[10] are possible to other places in the building, billboards containing snapshots of our university's website from which the visitors can access the actual website, as well as a botanical garden mimicking the VU's Hortus and a white-walled experimentation room suggestive of a 'real' scientific laboratory. A group of four students from all the faculties involved did all the building and scripting. A weekly walkthrough took place in our 'builders' meeting' to reassess our goals and solve technical and design issues.

Our virtual campus (see Figures 3.1, 3.2 and 3.3) is meant to serve as an *information portal* and as a *meeting ground* where students, staff, and visitors can meet and communicate. It should also be a place where teachers and researchers can conduct experiments aimed at discovering new ways of teaching and doing research. The overall style is realistic, although not in all its detail. It was considered most important to create a visual resemblance and to offer visitors the opportunity to be presented with relevant information in easily accessible, yet immersive, ways (e.g. Bolter and Grusin, 2000; Hoorn et al., 2003).

On 1 March 2007 we opened the doors of our virtual campus to the public. A university creating a presence in Second Life appeared to be an issue for the media. In the evening a news item on national television featured students showing the virtual campus and our project leader explaining the reasoning behind our presence in Second Life, and how to present a course in the virtual classroom. A similar item appeared on the local Amsterdam television channel, and various national newspapers published a multiple-column article reporting on our efforts. Not surprisingly,

Figure 3.1 VU campus – outside view.

Figure 3.2 VU campus – inside view.

Figure 3.3 VU @ SL – visitors outside.

Figure 3.4 Wheelchair race.

all the items focused on what we have characterized as the naive interpretation of our efforts, exemplifying the old credo 'the medium is the message'.

The initial feedback on our virtual efforts exceeded our expectations. The students were praised for the results of their building efforts but, more importantly, we were approached by many organizations, both corporate and non-profit, and asked to share our experiences of Second Life. We were also invited to participate in their educational, business and research projects.

From project to process: Development of a community of learners

After the successful introduction of our university in Second Life the next challenge was the implementation of an important driver behind the 'raison d'être' for creating a presence in this virtual world: to use Second Life to develop a *community of learners*. Although the initial project, which aimed at creating a presence, showed that Second Life offers useful community support features (e.g. multimodal communication, group (membership) management, access management, etc.), our ultimate aim was to transfer the initial project findings to our daily educational and research practices. In order to do so many initiatives were launched, ranging from student thesis projects to courses which used Second Life as enabling technology. For example, a teacher from the Faculty of Law used Second Life to explore the opportunities of virtual worlds for online dispute resolution. They also organized two tutorials in Second Life in which students and lecturers from the VU University Amsterdam collaborated with a group of international students and lecturers, who were geographically dispersed, on the solution of a relevant law case. To explore fully the opportunities of virtual worlds as enabling technology for the development of a community of learners we setup a dedicated 'master's course' that, among other educational objectives, specifically aimed at meeting the following 'community' requirements:

- multidisciplinary approach: participation of students and researchers from more than one faculty, and
- broad participation: participation of external parties (going beyond the boundaries of the university).

For the purposes of this course, called Capita Selecta Virtual Worlds, students and researchers from the Faculty of Economics and Business Administration and the Faculty of Sciences, as well as three external parties (ABN AMRO,[11] an international bank, and two NGOs, the Dutch Red

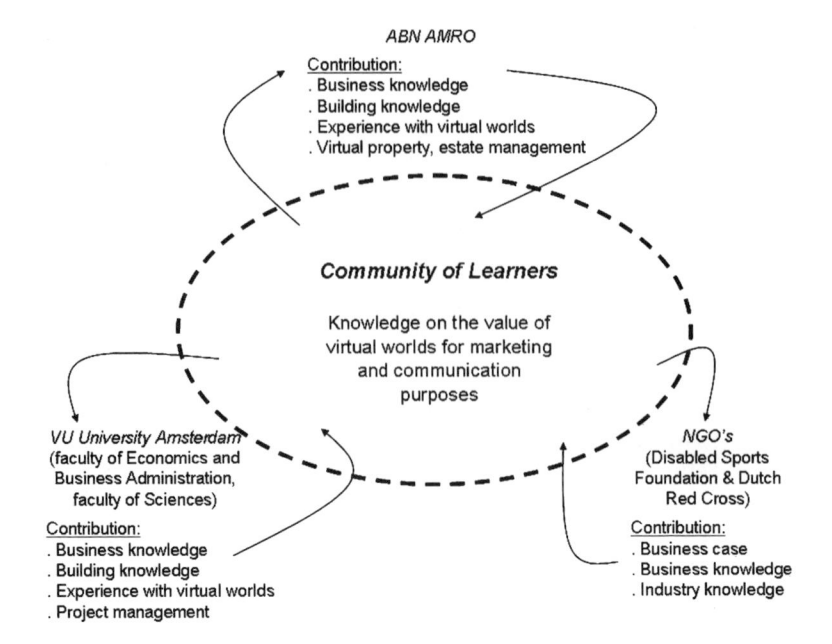

```
                          ABN AMRO
                      Contribution:
                      . Business knowledge
                      . Building knowledge
                      . Experience with virtual worlds
                      . Virtual property, estate management

                   Community of Learners

                   Knowledge on the value of
                   virtual worlds for marketing
                   and communication
                   purposes

VU University Amsterdam                          NGO's
(faculty of Economics and                        (Disabled Sports
Business Administration,                         Foundation & Dutch
faculty of Sciences)                             Red Cross)
Contribution:                                    Contribution:
. Business knowledge                             . Business case
. Building knowledge                             . Business knowledge
. Experience with virtual worlds                 . Industry knowledge
. Project management
```

Figure 3.5 Participants community of learners.

Cross[12] and the Disabled Sports Foundation (*Fonds Gehandicaptensport*[13])), worked together as a community of learners. The primary objective of this community was to investigate the role virtual worlds can play in communicating the message of charities (short-term) as well as how they can be used for fundraising purposes (long-term). ABN AMRO, one of the first commercial banks to be present in Second Life, offered the charitable institutions a piece of virtual land for free in order to help them explore the opportunities of virtual worlds for charities. Aware of the increasing attention society is giving to virtual worlds, the charities were eager to learn more about this phenomenon. The activities of the community were organized around two explicit assignments that had to be completed by the students:

1. Write a report on the value of virtual worlds for the two NGOs involved, and answer the question: Can a presence in virtual worlds contribute to the missions of the NGOs?
2. Create a presence for both NGOs in Second Life by arranging a virtual location that best fits their missions. An overview of the contributions of each party is presented in Figure 3.5.

Figure 3.4 shows the final results. After completion of the project, we interviewed the participants and asked for their opinions on the role of Second Life in support of the development of a community of learners. The most important insights are:

- Second Life appears to facilitate low-level entry for anyone who wishes to participate in the community. It should be noted that running Second Life smoothly requires a state-of-the-art personal computer and the availability of a broadband Internet connection.
- The 3D user interface positively contributed to a feeling of social presence (Walther, 1995) which, according to the participants, contributed to a sense of being a team/community.
- Participants mentioned that Second Life supported efficient and effective communications. It was very easy to organize meetings since the platform really reduces time and location barriers.
- The 3D user interface made it possible to present, visualize, and discuss relevant project results almost instantaneously, which in turn reduced development lead times and gave rise to a feeling of 'co-creation'.
- From the beginning of the project, the participants treated one another as equals and did not experience a sense of hierarchy. The participants were evaluated according to their contribution to the final results or; as one of the charities' project managers put it: 'I did not treat the students as "students", but as knowledgeable team mates from [whom] I could learn a lot'. The fact that the participants were represented by their avatars might have contributed to this process (Walther, 1995).
- The game-like experience induced a sense of involvement. According to the charities, 3D virtual worlds offer more opportunities to create involvement than 2D websites do. For example, the Disabled Sports Foundation offered visitors to their location the opportunity to participate in a wheelchair race and 'experience' how it must 'feel' to be disabled (see Figure 3.4). The charities consider involvement as an important issue, because it is positively associated with loyalty (Park, 1996).
- The Second Life tools allow for the (rapid) development of 3D prototypes. This, in combination with the presence of elementary economical principles and the opportunity to restrict access to certain areas, makes Second Life a suitable platform in which to conduct experiments.
- The number of avatars that can come together in one location without inducing serious performance problems is limited. Roughly speaking, this number is limited to 30 avatars for a single virtual island.

- Second Life appeared to be valuable in support of communication processes; however, the possibilities for interfacing and interacting with external systems are less developed, if not insufficient.
- Since Second Life is 'texture-based', it is very well suited to storing visually appealing graphical objects. However, the other side of this 'texture-based' coin is that it is very difficult to store and retrieve data and information, not to mention knowledge, in Second Life.

Aware of the limitations of our observations (single case, limited number of young participants), we nevertheless believe these preliminary insights illustrate that Second Life has the potential to contribute to the development of a community of learners, primarily through its communications support features and 3D user interface. However, owing to its limitations regarding interaction with external systems, as well as the limited opportunities it offers to store data and information, additional technological and human interventions will be needed if the activities of the community require more than communications support alone – for example, knowledge management features. In Eliëns et al. (2007) we explored the use of Web services not only as an enhancement of the functionality of our world(s), but, more importantly, also as an infrastructure for data repositories collecting information about users and their behaviour.

Implications for practice and policymaking

The first idea that comes to mind, naturally, is to use Second Life to offer courses online. But, although we organized lectures in Second Life, this approach might be considered an outdated paradigm of learning in our virtual campus, where there might be more appealing alternatives. Similarly, using the virtual laboratory for experiments might not be the best way to offer courses, although, for example, we do intend to provide a model of a living cell, allowing students to study the structure, functionality, and behaviour of organic cells in virtual space.

Considering the success of our multidisciplinary building team, it seems more worthwhile to take the cooperative effort of building as a model, and to switch to a paradigm of learning in which in-game exploration and building plays an important role. It is no secret that many students enjoy gaming, and though some might think that gaming is a waste of time, many authors, including Gee (2003) and Vorderer and Bryant (2006), think that gaming and game-related efforts provide a form of *active learning*, allowing the gamer to experience the world(s) in a new way, to form new affiliations, and to prepare for future learning in similar or even new domains.

More importantly, owing to the intense involvement and the need to analyze game challenges, according to Gee (2003), gaming even encourages *critical learning,* that is thinking about the domain at a meta-level as a complex system of interrelated parts and the conventions that govern a particular domain, which Gee (2003) characterizes as *situated cognition* (situated cognition implies that learning takes place in a context, and not, as often the case in traditional settings, detached from the situation in which the knowledge is applied) in a *semiotic domain* (semiotic domain refers to being immersed in a simulated world full of meaning, where meaning (the signified) is conveyed by elements (signifiers) specific to the game, thus, in a sense, creating a new language and new conventions, that will be learned by the player as a result of playing the game).[14]

Implications for research

In this section we discuss the relevant research implications based on combining the exploratory findings obtained during the preliminary studies presented in the previous sections of this chapter and the findings derived from established pedagogical research. In our effort to identify which direction future research should take, we are, at the same time, seeking to explore further its potential for e-learning. In doing so, we focus on the following three aspects which seem to be of particular relevance for further research on the pedagogical potential of virtual worlds, namely:

1. equality of participation,
2. involvement,
3. simulations.

1. Equality of participation

In the current body of pedagogical literature (e.g. Rogoff et al., 1996) various approaches are discussed to transmitting knowledge to students, such as 'adult-run' (top-down), 'child-run' (bottom-up), or a 'community of learners' (COL) (reciprocal) approach. Particularly the last of these, COL, is of interest in the context of virtual worlds. The characteristics of a COL are such that all participants are active, there is a shared responsibility, and no one is passive (Rogoff et al., 1996). This means that COL participation is based on equality. According to Hiltz et al. (2001), the active participation of all members in the collaboration process is necessary in order for students to deduce the lessons they had intended to learn from their studies.

In our preliminary research on Second Life's pedagogical potential, we established a COL that, besides students and researchers at our university, included ABN AMRO, the Disabled Sports Foundation, and the Red Cross. These four parties collaborated with one another in order to share knowledge and learn from one another's experiences. In this study we found that the participants did not experience any feelings of hierarchal preference and that they treated one another as equals in the virtual community. The participants were evaluated according to the contribution they had made to the final outcome. This process of equality may have been influenced by the fact that the participants were represented by their avatars and did not display visual cues that signalized social status (Walther, 1995; Berdahl and Craig, 1995).

In order to make generalizations based on these preliminary findings about a virtual world's potential for pedagogical use, it is necessary to conduct further research among a greater population to address questions such as: What determines successful 'equality of participation' of students in pedagogical projects employed in a virtual world? To what extent does the ability to control visual cues (i.e. physical appearance) in a virtual world diminish feelings that hinder equality of participation, such as hierarchy, power, and status? How do these visual controls contribute to successful learning? And, on a more technical note: To what extent does the accessibility of the Second Life medium stimulate equality of participation?

2. Involvement

To increase the success of a pedagogical project, it is important that students experience a sense of involvement. Without feeling involved, a student may not feel intrinsically motivated to do his or her best during a pedagogical project (Paas et al., 2005). In the context of e-learning, Conole and Oliver (2007) state that the concept of involvement is rather complex and is situationally dependent on whether people maintain a certain degree of involvement. In their words: 'Rather than being "types", people should be understood as having a complex profile of engagement with technology, with others and with ideas' (Conole and Oliver, 2007: p. 218). One theory that seeks to explain these underlying social psychological mechanisms of involvement is Baumeister and Leary's (1995) 'need to belong theory'. According to this theory, the 'need to belong' to a group, and therefore to feel *involved*, can be considered as a fundamental human motivation. Baumeister and Leary (1995) proclaim that this need presumably has an evolutionary basis, since some survival tasks are best accomplished by *group cooperation*.

In our preliminary research, we found that 'the game-like experience of Second Life' in fact induced such feelings of involvement. For example, the Disabled Sports Foundation offered visitors the opportunity to participate in a wheelchair race, and to 'experience' how it must 'feel' to be disabled (see Figure 3.4). Furthermore, the 3D user interface positively contributed to the feeling of social presence (Walther, 1995), which, according to the participants, contributed to a feeling of being involved in a team or community.

In order to make generalizations based on these preliminary findings, it might be interesting to conduct further research on which characteristics of 3D virtual worlds induce involvement, and to examine whether a 3D virtual context influences involvement in an e-learning setting anyway. Other interesting research issues in this context are: What personal characteristics determine the level of involvement induced by being present in virtual worlds? How can educational institutions anticipate on the underlying mechanisms of involvement in the context of virtual worlds in order to increase the success of learning? To what extent does the level of involvement in a virtual world project differ from that in a project in the real world? And how can these levels of involvement be reliably and validly measured?

3. Simulations

Simulations have been widely recognized as an efficient and effective way of teaching and learning complex dynamic systems (Parush et al., 2002; Lu et al., 1996; Plaisant et al., 1999; Rose et al., 1998). According to Wagner (2008), the ability to simulate is one of the greatest benefits of virtual worlds.

In the pedagogical literature there has been a shift from top-down content delivery towards student-centred models, with an increasing emphasis on the skills that support independent, self-motivated learning (Cullen et al., 2002; Rogoff et al., 1996). This is called the *constructivist* approach to learning (Conole and Oliver, 2007). Particularly virtual worlds offer the possibility of an alternative, constructivist perspective, to the traditional linear ways in which knowledge can be presented and understood (Doherty et al., 2006). Imagine, for instance, the concept 'apple'. In a two-dimensional (2D) world one would see a picture of an apple, whereas in a three-dimensional (3D), simulated world, such as Second Life, one would have the opportunity to view the apple as a 3D model, yet one would also have the ability to look inside the apple and observe the structure of the molecules contained in it (Doherty et al., 2006).

In other words, in a 3D environment such as Second Life, students' understanding of complex concepts can be broadened as they are able to obtain 'first-hand experience' of how one such concept relates to another. This simulative or *immersive* experience is of high pedagogical relevance (Chittaro and Ranon, 2005). Antonietti and Cantoia (2000) demonstrated that some beneficiary effects of a 3D environment cannot feasibly be obtained in a traditional 2D environment. Their study indicated that when students were asked to evaluate an unfamiliar painting in a 3D environment in comparison to a 2D environment, their conceptual comprehension increased (Antonietti and Cantoia, 2000).

Another immersive experience of virtual worlds such as Second Life is that they allow one to explore different roles, for instance in the context of MMORPGs (Knutsson et al., 2004). We have already conducted a business simulation in Second Life in which supply chain partners were supposed to play the role of the counterparts they are used to negotiate with in real life. The Waag Society[15] in the Netherlands, for instance, uses Second Life as a platform to allow socially impaired children to practise their social interaction skills. Simulations in 3D virtual worlds typically allow for the playing of different roles, and as such contribute to learning through experimenting.[16] Relevant research questions in this context are: To what extent does roleplaying in 3D virtual environments contribute to successful learning? To what extent can the activities in Second Life improve skills that can be transferred to other group work in educational and business settings? Which skills can, and which skills cannot, be transferred?

Conclusions

In this chapter we have reported on our experiences in building a virtual campus, giving our university a presence in Second Life; and we have delineated the prospects for Second Life as a platform for education and research, embodying our university's credo: to be a *community of learners*. So far, based on our observations and experiences, we can conclude that Second Life can be employed to support communication processes in the context of community development. However, support for the integration of interactive interfaces with external systems is less developed in the Second Life systems' environment, and as such we need to reflect on the technical requirements that must be met to deploy Second Life effectively as a platform for education and research in the future. And, perhaps more importantly, what paradigm of learning must be adopted in order to benefit from the full potential of virtual worlds in general and, Second Life more specifically. We propose a research agenda which has a specific focus on the influence of virtual worlds on equality of participation and involvement in educational processes, and how virtual worlds can be deployed for educational experiments.

Acknowledgement(s)

We would like thank the following students who have been involved in this project for their enthusiasm, creativity, and concerted efforts which led to this productive result: Viola van Alphen (FEWEB), Tom Bestebreurtje (FEW), Elbert-Jan Hennipman (FEW), and Bjorn de Boer (FSW).

Notes

   www.vu.nl/secondlife
1. http://secondlife.com/whatis/economy_stats.php
2. www.web3d.org/
3. www.blaxxun.com
4. www.secondlife.com
5. http://secondlife.com/whatis/economy_stats.php
6. Massively Multiplayer Online Role Playing Game
7. www.worldofwarcraft.com/index.xml
8. http://everquest.station.sony.com/
9. www.machinima.org/
10. Technology that enables one to travel from one point to another without physically crossing the distance.
11. www.abnamro.com
12. www.rodekruis.nl
13. www.fondsgehandicatensport.nl
14. A domain, that is, in which signs and symbols and their interpretation are significant.
15. The Waag Society is an internationally renowned interdisciplinary media lab located in Amsterdam, which develops creative technology for social innovation (www.waag.org).
16. More information about this project, which is called *Selfcity*, can be found on: http://www.waag.org/project/selfcity

References

Anders, P. (1999), *Envisioning Cyberspace – Designing 3D Electronic Spaces*, New York: McGraw-Hill.

Antonietti, A. and Cantoia, M. (2000), To see a painting versus to walk in a painting: An experiment on sense-making through virtual reality, *Computers and Education*, 34(3–4), 213–23.

Baumeister, R.F. and Leary, M.R. (1995), The need to belong: Desire for interpersonal attachments as a fundamental human motivation, *Psychological Bulletin*, 117(3), 497–529.

Berdahl, J.L. and Craig, K.M. (1995), Equality of participation and influence in groups: The effects of communication medium and sex composition. Computer Supported Cooperative Work, 4 (2–3), 179–201.

Bolter, J.D. and Grusin, R. (2000), *Remediation – Understanding New Media*, Cambridge, Mass.: MIT Press.

Chittaro, L. and Ranon, R. (2005), Web3D technologies in learning, education and training: Motivations, issues, opportunities, *Computers and Education*, 49(1), 3–18.

Conole, G. and Oliver, M. (2007), *Contemporary Perspectives in E-Learning Research: Themes, Methods and Impact on Practice*, The Open and Flexible Learning Series. London, UK: Routledge.

Cullen, J., Hadjivassiliou, K., Hamilton, E., Kelleher, J., Sommerlad, E. and Stern, E. (2002), Review of current pedagogic research and practice in the fields of postcompulsory education and lifelong learning. London: Tavistock Institute, 2002. http://www.tlrp.org/pub/acadpub/Tavistockreport.pdf (accessed on 8 November 2008).

Davenport, G. (2000), Your own virtual story world, *Scientific American*, November:61–4.

Doherty, P., Rothfarb, R. and Barker, D. (2006), Building an interactive science museum in Second Life. In D. Livingstone and J. Kemps (eds). Proceedings of the Second Life Education Workshop at the Second Life Community Convention, San Francisco. http://www.simteach.com/SLCC06/slcc2006-proceedings.pdf (accessed 5 November 2008).

Eliëns, A., Feldberg, F., Konijn, E. and Compter, E. (2007d), *Mashups in Second Life @ VU*. In Proc. GAME-ON 07, 20–22 November 2007, University of Bologna, M. Roccetti (ed.), 130–4, EUROSIS-ETI Publication.

Gee, J.P. (2003), *What video games have to teach us about learning and literacy*, New York: Palgrave Macmillan.

Hiltz, S., Coppola, N., Rotter, N. and Turoff, M. (2001), Measuring the importance of collaborative learning for the effectiveness of ALN: A multi-measure, multi-method approach. In J. Bourne *Online Education. Learning Effectiveness and Faculty Satisfaction*, Sloan Consortium.

Hoorn, J.F., Konijn, E.A. and Van der Veer, G.C. (2003), Virtual reality: Do not augment realism, augment relevance, *Human-Computer Interaction: Overcoming Barriers*, 4(1): 18–26.

Knutsson, B., Lu, H., Xu, W. and Hopkins, B. (2004), Peer-to-Peer support for massively multiplayer games. INFOCOM 2004. Twenty-third Annual Joint Conference of the IEEE Computer and Communications Societies, 1: 96–107.

Lu, G.B., Oveissi, M., Eckard, D. and Rubloff, G. (1996), Education in semiconductor manufacturing processes through physically-based dynamic simulation. Proc. Frontiers in Education' 96, IEEE, 250–3.

Paas, F., Tuovinen, J., Merrienboer, J. and Darabi, A. (2005), A motivational perspective on the relation between mental effort and performance: Optimizing learner involvement in instruction, *ETR&D*, 53(3): 25–34.

Park, S.H. (1996), Relationships between involvement and attitudinal loyalty constructs in adult fitness programs, *Journal of Leisure Research*, 28(4): 233–50.

Parush, A., Hamm, H. and Shtub, A. (2002), Learning histories in simulation-based teaching: The effects on self-learning and transfer, Computer and Education, 39(4): 319–32.

Plaisant, C., Rose, A., Rubloff, G., Salter, R. and Shneiderman, B. (1999), The design of history mechanisms and their use in collaborative educational simulations. Proc. of the Computer Support for Collaborative Learning, CSCL' 99, Palo Alto, CA. 348–59.

Rogoff, B., Matusov, E. and White, C. (1996), Models of teaching and learning: Participation in a community of learners. In D. Olson and N. Torrance (eds). *The Handbook of Education and Human Development*, 388–433. Oxford, UK: Blackwell Publishers.

Rose, A., Eckard, D. and Rubloff, G.W. (1998), An application framework for creating simulation-based learning environments. University of Maryland, Department of Computer Science, Technical Report CS-TR-3907, UMIACS-TR-98-32, College Park, MD.

Rymaszewski, M., Au, W.J., Wallace, M., Winters, C., Ondrejka, C. and Batstone-Cunningham, B. (2007), *Second Life – The official guide*, New York: John Wiley.

Utz, S. (2003), Social identification and interpersonal attraction in MUDs, *Swiss Journal of Psychology*, 62: 91–101.

Vorderer, P. and Bryant, J. (eds) (2006), *Playing Computer Games – Motives, Responses, and Consequences*, Mahwah, NJ: Lawrence Erlbaum Associates.

Wagner, C. (2008), Learning experience with virtual worlds, *Journal of Information Systems Education*, 19(3): 263–6.

Walther, J.B. (1995), Relational aspects of computer-mediated communication: Experimental observations over time, *Organization Science*, 6(2): 186–203.

4
Patient Preferences for Online Person–Person Support

Ray Jones, Maged N. Kamel Boulos, Inocencio Maramba, Heather Skirton, and Jennifer Freeman

Introduction

The Internet not only provides health information through 'Web pages' such as BUPA and Cancerbackup, but also offers person–person support through social networks, message boards, chat rooms, and virtual worlds. The wealth of Internet person–person support methods may benefit patients, but may be confusing. For example, some online methods offer more anonymity, some are synchronous (i.e. communication in real time), while yet others are asynchronous. Some rely on professional input, while others offer only peer–peer communication. Preference for a particular support method may vary by patient characteristics such as condition (e.g. people with depression may prefer anonymity, pregnant women may be less concerned about it), age (e.g. older people may prefer asynchronous methods that give more time to think), or stage of disease (e.g. people just diagnosed may seek professional support but longer term may prefer peer support).

The aim of this chapter is to show how patients use virtual social networks for support for health issues and to illustrate how patient preferences may vary by referring to empirical studies. We include older technologies such as discussion forums and closed environments such as 'dedicated chat rooms', as well as the massive environments of Second Life, Facebook, etc. We describe two studies in some detail but also review the published literature.

This chapter is divided into five parts.

First, we draw on applied psychology and theories of computer-mediated communication to suggest how patient preference may vary according to psychological and social characteristics as well as the health condition of patients.

Secondly, we describe opportunities for online support, illustrating the types of person–person support available. In particular we present our first case study, which describes the use of Second Life in supporting sexual health.

In the third section we describe the dilemmas in evaluating such support. We review literature which shows that there may be different preferences between individuals and at different times in the course of their condition. The heterogeneity of online communication methods and the speed with which technology changes suggest that in order to guide patients and professionals as to how best to use person–person support, we need to know more about patient preferences.

Fourthly, we argue, using illustrations from the literature, that it is unclear which aspects of support are important to patients and how preferences differ by patient characteristics. In particular, we present our second case study of motivational support for people with depression, and their expressed preferences.

Fifthly, we describe work that is needed to be able to frame policy on e-communication routes and provide guidance for users.

Finally, we review and summarize the chapter.

Theoretical background to patient preferences

Patients may have preferences for their online interactions because we all have cognitive, cultural, and personality differences that may affect how we interact with others. In addition, patients' medical, physical, or psychological states may affect how they wish to interact with others. Individual differences (cognitive, cultural, and personality) may therefore interact in different ways with the medical condition.

A large number of theories have been used in trying to explain online communication. For example, Van Dolen et al. (2007) examined online commercial group chat from a structuration theory perspective (Giddens, 1984). The basic hypothesis is that, in socially enacted environments, structures are influenced and created by the people who interact in these environments. The study of interactive technology should therefore go beyond a focus on technology and include the group as part of the structural set. Van Dolen et al. found that customer satisfaction with an online experience was influenced by perceived technology attributes (control, enjoyment, reliability, speed, and ease of use), chat group characteristics (group involvement, similarity, and receptivity), and the moderating role of an advisor's communication style. They concluded that 'structuration theory provides a sound foundation for theoretical development and empirical investigation of online group chat'. In 2005 Christopherson (2007) reviewed the theories that underpin much empirical work in computer-mediated communication (CMC), particularly in relation to online anonymity. Theory and empirical evidence relevant to particular aspects of person–person support (anonymity, social presence, etc.) are explored further in section 4. Other theories from applied psychology are relevant to patient preference for person–person support. For example, there are differences in the way individuals learn. Theories of learning styles have been developed over the last 20 to 30 years and with them various measures (Coffield et al., 2004). We might assume that people with different learning styles may have different preferences for online communication.

Much is known about patient preferences for support for particular conditions and at different times. For example, some conditions carry a stigma, influencing patients to seek anonymity. Many online and telephone services for mental health-related issues are provided anonymously and, furthermore, they can work effectively only if anonymous. The well-known Samaritans service has offered anonymous telephone support since 1953 (Samaritans, 2008). That lack of anonymity is a barrier to people with various health problems is well known and the literature on this subject is extensive. Examples of studies where lack of anonymity is a barrier to the use of mental health services include one in Australia (Boyd et al., 2007) and another in the rural United States (Rost et al., 1993). Online person–person support can overcome some face–face barriers but anonymity in online support is important. For some conditions (e.g. giving up smoking) emotional support may be most important, whereas for others (e.g. undergoing an operation) the need for informational support may predominate.

Opportunities for online person–person support for patients and carers

Online support methods range from a simple email through to virtual worlds (Kamel Boulos et al., 2007). Asynchronous methods, in which people can post messages using methods such as email or message boards and receive replies later, have been available for years and continue to thrive. Given the enormous number and 'churn' of Internet sites and methods, we can illustrate them only with a convenient sample.

Peer-only message boards: In May 2008 there were 35,000 Yahoo Groups on healthcare, alternative medicine, and medications (Yahoo, 2008). Other message boards are available through charity websites: for example, the

Cystic Fibrosis Trust (www.cftrust.org.uk/forum/index.php) has peer–peer message boards for teenagers, adults, parents and carers, partners, and others. Many boards are moderated after messages are posted. In one such organization, the Huntington's Disease Association (HDA), message-board postings (www.hda.org.uk/charity/forum.html) are reviewed regularly by authorized members of HDA, but HDA does not pre-check the content of messages before they are posted. HDA tells users that it does 'not guarantee and makes no representation as to the accuracy or quality of the content of the posts. Any user who feels that a posted message is objectionable is encouraged to contact the HDA immediately by email'. This is fairly typical of most peer–peer message boards.

Professionally focused question-and-answer message boards: Some boards are more focused on patient–professional dialogues. For example, the Multiple Sclerosis (MS) Society (www.mssociety.org.uk) runs question-and-answer sessions, normally over one month, in which stated 'experts' answer posted questions. Recent sessions include Childhood MS (May 2008) and Memory and Thinking (July 2008). Other people with MS can offer their views and the discussion is open to all registered users. The MS Society had previously run web chats (i.e. synchronous sessions) but stopped these in 2004, stating 'we now use the Q&A board because it allows more time for questions and answers'.

Live chat with expert or others with the condition: Live chat sessions, perhaps with an expert either as the main focus or as support, are held by other organizations. For example, Breast Cancer Care (www.breastcancercare.org.uk/) runs regular live chat sessions facilitated by an experienced moderator and a specialist nurse to provide sources of help and information, but mostly the dialogue is patient–patient. The melanoma section of www.cancer.com/cancer/skin_cancer.html offers live chat, message board, and question-and-answer sessions with an expert.

Social network site (home page) with email and/or instant messaging: Clearly, informal networks between friends on Facebook, MySpace, etc. can enable discussion and support for health conditions. But many, more focused groups have also been established, such as a cure diabetes group on MySpace (http://groups.myspace.com/cureDiABETES) that was established in March 2005 and had 6709 members in August 2008.

Online/phone meeting (e.g. Skype) with voice and optional webcam (VOIP): Telephone support – either as one–one or as group support – has been used for many years. Hoey et al., in a systematic review of peer support groups for people with cancer (Hoey et al., 2008) identified two papers describing one–one peer telephone support and three papers describing group telephone support. As more people start to use VOIP telephony with possible addition of webcam contact, use of this method for patient–patient and professional–patient support will grow.

Webinar by professional with text chat and questions from patients: Forums such as webcast live panel discussions, in which experts and patients discuss various health topics or conditions while participants view the expert through a 'video window' and ask questions or comment via a text chat room, have been used as a time-efficient method for educating staff, students, and patients. For example, the University of Plymouth hosts sessions which enable direct links to a wide number of National Health Service Hospitals and University Education Centres (www.plymouth.ac.uk/health/webcasts).

Virtual worlds, such as Second Life: Non-gaming, three-dimensional (3D) online social worlds such as Second Life are regularly used in the day-to-day support of people with chronic health conditions and disabilities such as MS, depression, and autistic spectrum disorders. These include scheduled synchronous meetings where people go to Second Life locations and participate in discussions as well as more informal contacts and discussions. At http://slhealthy.wetpaint.com/ a list of groups includes MS, Depression Support Group, Prostate Cancer Support, Breast Cancer Network of Strength, and Cancer Support Network, among many others. For example, the US National MS Society runs various activities; there is the MS Island VUmc, a Dutch island for MS patients run by the Vrije University Medical Centre, and many other related presences. Alice Krueger (or Gentle Heron in Second Life), who runs (with others) Virtual Ability, Inc., a non-profit corporation (http://slurl.com/secondlife/Virtual%20Ability/128/128/23), has severe MS and is unable to walk without the use of crutches. In a recent YouTube video (Krueger, 2008) featured at the 2008 San Diego Health 2.0 conference on Web 2.0 technologies in healthcare, she described how she benefits from Second Life. Other videos include a CBS News report of a woman with MS and a group of disabled adults who have created new lives in Second Life (Smith, 2008).

Other Second Life locations for depression and other conditions include Wellness Island run by the Counselling Centre (http://www.slcounseling.org/), Support for Healing Island (http://slurl.com/secondlife/Supportfor Healing/86/219/25), and Centre for Positive Mental Health (http://slurl.com/secondlife/Kkotsam/169/180/68). Second Life also offers dozens of in-world user groups dedicated to the support of people with chronic health conditions and disabilities. Figure 4.1 shows the Path of Support at HealthInfo Island in Second Life, a showcase of 60 in-world support groups for people with a wide variety of disabilities (http://slurl.com/secondlife/Healthinfo%20Island/73/88/26). Some of these are Second Life

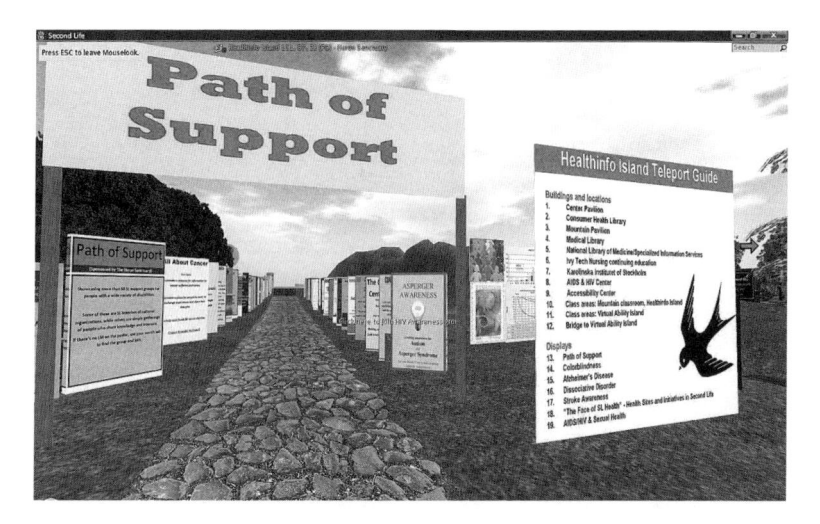

Figure 4.1 Path of support at HealthInfo Island in Second Life®.

branches of national organizations, whereas others are simply gatherings of people who share knowledge and interests. A report on providing Consumer Health outreach via HealthInfo Island is available for download (Bell, 2008). We describe one Second Life location in more detail in our first case study.

Case Study 1

What is it? The University of Plymouth Sexual Health SIM (Figure 4.2) in Second Life provides a wide variety of educational experiences about sexually transmitted infections (STIs), the prevention of unintended pregnancy, and the promotion of egualitarian sexual relationships. Visitors to the SIM are offered a wide range of 3D scripted objects and games to explore and interact with, including a virtual condom-dispensing machine offering free (virtual) male condoms, and practical information. Visitors can chat with the resident pseudo-intelligent chatterbot, 'Alice', to find out simple facts about contraception and STIs. An interactive kiosk provides an atlas illustrating STIs and ways to prevent them, and enables visitors to listen to associated voice narration or access related Web media such as a PowerPoint quiz game or Web page. An interactive 3D Earth globe offers access to current STIs/HIV/AIDS statistics and information from 53 European region countries. Visitors can also access a selection of international Web-based and in-world resources from leading organizations, including, the World Health Organization (WHO), National Health Service (NHS) in

Figure 4.2 Avatars attending a seminar on 'Sex and Disability' in Second Life®.

the United Kingdom, the Society of Obstetricians and Gynaecologists of Canada, and, from the United States, the Centres for Disease Control and Prevention, RESOLVE – the National Infertility Association – HealthInfo Island, and Ohio State University (3D tour of the testis).

Media formats include streaming video/audio, podcasts, in-world custom search engines retrieving quality sexual health results from the UK Institute database (http://www.intute.ac.uk/) and Healia (http://www.healia.com/), and a newsstand that refreshes every ten minutes to display the top two sexual health headlines on Yahoo! News. An 'AIDS-related Kaposi's Sarcoma Experience' clothing dispenser allows people wearing the clothing to see and experience on their own avatar how Kaposi's Sarcoma lesions look and feel in AIDS patients (for an image and discussion of the wider educational potential of the concept, see Huang et al., 2008). The SIM also affords visitors opportunities to test their knowledge of sexual health by participating in quizzes and other fun experiences. Live in-world seminars on sexual health topics have included domestic violence; STIs, contraception and family planning; female sexuality, and 'sex and disability'.

Before leaving the SIM, visitors are invited to provide feedback about the overall experience and specific features of the SIM via an in-world questionnaire. We monitor 24/7 traffic, including the logging of avatars' attendance at live events. A visitor counter tracks repeat as well as unique or new visitors, and emails us statistics and daily reports, including daily visitors, peak visitors, and total visitor-minutes spent on our land (an owner's minutes or visits are neither counted nor monitored). The latter statistic ('total time visiting') serves as a rough measure of visitors' interest in, and perceived utility of, our SIM, besides directly corresponding to the official Linden Lab daily traffic figures for our parcel.

The SIM received more than 4000 *unique* visitors over the past year (2007–2008). Repeat visitor figures for the same period are much higher. A mini-evaluation of the project was conducted in 2007–2008. Primary methods of evaluation consisted of a survey ($n = 135$) and traffic statistics as above. Evaluation results indicated that the Sexual Health SIM was positively viewed by its audience and fostered the development of a vibrant virtual community. Further details are given elsewhere (Kamel Boulos and Toth-Cohen, 2009 (in press)). Figure 4.2 shows avatars attending a seminar on the topic of 'Sex and Disability' (http://healthcybermap.org/slsexualhealth/). Cory Silverberg, the seminar's guest speaker, commented: 'one of the things that [was] most interesting to me was that the turnout for the talk was much higher than it would have been in real life, as getting people out to talk about sex and disability is challenging for a number of reasons'.

The potential of virtual worlds to offer anonymity allows users to be more open and honest with respect to sensitive subjects such as sexual health, alcohol and drug use. This case study confirmed that users of Second Life were able to discuss sensitive issues of sexual health and disability. What we perhaps know less about is the 'type of anonymity' and how this may vary between individuals. Second Life provides anonymity and distance through avatars but also continuity. The type of avatar may have an impact on the feeling of confidentiality and willingness to disclose. Yee and Bailenson (2007) have shown that the 'Proteus Effect' may affect users' online behaviour. For example, participants assigned to more attractive avatars were more intimate with confederates in a self-disclosure and interpersonal distance task than participants assigned to less attractive avatars. Others may find that the continuity of social networks inhibits disclosure rather than a single-event anonymous online exchange. Such preferences are discussed further in section 4.

Why do patients go online for support?

Grohol (Association, 2002) has argued that some of the factors for people going online for support were geographic issues, a lack of time, immediacy and flexibility, anonymity, and disinhibition. He argued that, owing to the well-known 'disinhibition effect', clinical issues emerge 'quicker and deeper', and also may result in people quickly finding increased access to sources of help. People accessing online health information may benefit in terms of 'being better informed', 'feeling more confident in the relationship with their physician', 'improved acceptance of the disease', 'feeling more confident about the treatment', 'enhanced self-esteem', and 'increased optimism and control', whether or not they actually post messages or just 'lurk' (Van Uden-Kraan et al., 2008a; Preece et al., 2004).

Dilemmas in online person–person support

In 2004, Eysenbach et al. (2004) systematically reviewed 38 studies that evaluated the health or social outcomes of online peer–peer communities. Most ($n = 31$) evaluated complex interventions (e.g. including psychoeducation), which made it impossible to attribute intervention effects to person–person support components. Most studies showed no effect. The use of randomized trials to evaluate person–person support has been criticized as artificial in trying to isolate its impact (Barak et al., 2004) and also because its value cannot be measured solely by using conventional measures of clinical outcome (Jadad et al., 2006). Jadad et al. have argued (2006) for innovative strategies to help understand the role that virtual communities play in helping people cope with complex health issues. We agree with Jadad et al. for the need to understand the role of virtual communities and how they work (e.g. in the self-correction and 'quality control' of information (Esquivel et al., 2006)) but also with Eysenbach that both professionals (intending to provide or recommend online resources) and patients (thinking of using such resources) would benefit from guidance.

Recent studies have explored different aspects of online communities, including identity among stigmatized (Gavin et al., 2008) or vulnerable (Hurley et al., 2007) groups, disclosure (Rier, 2007), the impact on empowerment (Van Uden-Kraan et al., 2008b), or reducing anxiety (Coulson and Buchanan, 2008), descriptions of topics discussed (e.g. problem drinkers (Cunningham et al., 2008), cancer survivors (Klemm, 2008), Huntington's disease (Coulson et al., 2007)). In 2007, Wald et al. (2007) published a discursive literature review of patients' use of the Web (including person–person support) as a guide to clinicians but there has been no detailed study of patient preferences for support.

Changing technologies

Studying online support is difficult, not only because of its complex interaction with other support, but also because technologies change rapidly. Eysenbach's review of controlled trials of the use of message boards is only four years old. The use of virtual worlds for support has risen rapidly, as described above. Eysenbach's four-year-old review did not include virtual worlds and may already be dated. Controlled trials take a long time to complete and risk being obsolete by the time a trial finishes.

Patient preferences

In addition to the difficulties already described, information and support needs are likely to be differentiated by patient characteristics such as age, gender, stage of disease, co-morbidities, information preferences, Internet experience, learning styles, attitudes to autonomy, social networks, work or occupational patterns, and educational level (Squiers et al., 2005; Boudioni et al., 2001; Rutten et al., 2005). One approach in professionally provided information has been to tailor information to individuals, for example using the patient's own medical record (Jones et al., 2006b), or online questionnaires to determine 'stage of change' or adaptation to current lifestyle (Bental et al., 1999). The recently launched Google Health provides personalized health information based on the user's health profile (Google, 2008). The 'Amazon' approach of recommendations according to 'people like you' has been adopted by www.patientslikeme.com.

Which aspects of person–person methods are important to patients?

These may be affected by the format or interface of the method or by the membership (e.g. the type of peer and whether or not there is professional membership). In this section we discuss preferences for 'method characteristics'. We illustrate by reference to published studies, in particular our second case study of motivational support for people with depression (Jones et al., 2008). We present the methods of this case study and then draw on the results in our discussion of factors that may affect patient preferences.

Case Study 2

Computerized cognitive behavioural therapy (CCBT) is recognized as an effective option in the treatment of anxiety, depression, and other mental health conditions. However, a review of self-help interventions has highlighted that contact with a therapist (guided self-help) is associated with greater effectiveness (Gellatly et al., 2007). Various technologies could provide additional motivational support to Web-based CCBT but little is known about their feasibility or user preferences. We explored the use of a 'closed' chat room with a support worker and preferences for other types of support among users of a free-to-use webCBT site for depression called Living Life To The Full (www.livinglifetothefull.com). In August 2007 we invited 525 people registering consecutively on Living Life To The Full to take part in the study. Registrants were invited to two chat-room support sessions; 37 consented, 29 booked sessions, 16 attended at least one, and 21 responded to the follow-up survey. Most participants said that the support motivated them to use other modules. Most preferred individual sessions and a female support worker, although half would still book if only group sessions were available. Finding convenient appointments was difficult for many. Preferences between alternative support methods were evenly divided between the study method, use of email only, email plus phone call, and drop-in chat room. Although this study was not of 'massive' social networks but rather of the use of a closed chat room and the preferences for support, it provides some insight into, and raises more questions about, patient preferences for person–person support. We will refer to it below in addressing preferences.

Ease of use and technical barriers: These are major factors in determining whether online support methods will be used (Hesse and Shneiderman, 2007). Computer literacy, the availability of broadband connections, the availability of modern computers, and health literacy all help to determine the accessibility of different methods. The use of all technologies decreases with age; in 2007 90 per cent of those aged 25 to 34 owned a digital TV compared to 58 per cent of those over 75; 99 per cent of those aged 16 to 19 owned a mobile phone compared to 42 per cent of those over 75, and 82 per cent of 16- to 19-year-olds had access to the Internet compared to 10 per cent of those aged over 75 (Ofcom, 2008). Access to the Internet also varies according to geography and income even within the United Kingdom (NOS, 2007). For example, 60 per cent of households in London compared to 40 per cent in Northern Ireland had a broadband connection. In 2006, 87 per cent of 16- to 30-year-olds had used a computer in the previous three months compared with 45 per cent of those aged 50 and over (see Figure 4.3) (NOS, 2006). In 2003–2004, 12 per cent of those in the worst paid decile compared to 85 per cent in the best paid decile had access to the Internet.

Amongst those who go online there is great variation in both the capacity and power of their computer and connection as well as their ability to use different software and hardware (Poynton, 2005).

Trust and relevance of information: Tools to assess the 'quality' of information on websites have been tried many times and while they may play a role for organizations developing websites (Breckons et al., 2008), their use by consumers has limited value (Eysenbach and Kohler, 2002). Assessing

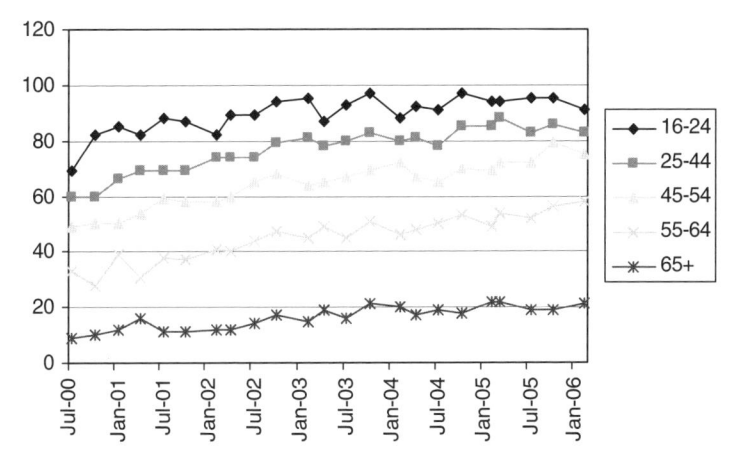

Figure 4.3 Percentage of different age groups in Great Britain who have ever used the Internet. (Constructed from NOS statistics (NOS, 2006)).

trust in person–person support is more difficult but is still likely to be important (Radin and Landzelius, 2006; Sillence and Briggs, 2008; Sarasohn-Kahn, 2008; Sillence et al., 2007). Sarasohn-Kahn argues that people are starting to use person–person support ('people like me') rather than institutional websites because trust in institutions has been diminishing in recent years. She bases her argument partly on Edelman's annual survey of trust in government and organizations between various countries (Edelman, 2006). Other work suggests that people often put more trust in peers or family than in institutions (Harris and Wathen, 2007; Green et al., 2005).

Wang et al. (2008) describe two important concepts underlying the impact of Internet communication: credibility and homophily. Credibility is the believability of a source and depends on *expertise* (a communicator's qualifications and/or ability to know the truth about a topic) and *trustworthiness* (perceptions of the communicator's motivation to tell the truth about a topic). Recipients turn to message cues to make credibility judgements when information about the source is scarce and this will be affected by homophily. Homophily is the degree of perceived similarity a receiver ascribes to a message source. Homophily affects the persuasion and perceptions of otherwise unknown individuals.

Anonymity and disclosure: Some patients may seek anonymity through unrecognizable usernames or avatars; others knowingly publish personal details. Discussion boards, though actually quite publicly visible, appear to be subjectively experienced by many as relatively private places for the exchange of intimate personal information (Seale et al., 2006). However, this may vary between individuals. Anonymity may be important for potentially socially stigmatizing conditions such as depression. In our second case study anonymity was very important. One respondent said: 'I struggle to tell people how I really feel and as it was not face to face almost enjoyed the anonymity of it'. A quarter of the respondents did not want their GP to know about their use of Web-based therapy.

Christopherson has reviewed aspects of anonymity in Internet social interactions (Christopherson, 2007) and set this within the previous literature on face–face social interaction. For example, she cited face-face studies (Pedersen, 1987; Walden et al., 1981) as showing gender differences – that men prefer solitude whereas women prefer intimacy with family and friends to escape from social situations. Such gender differences may transfer to online behaviour. She concluded from other studies (Sia et al., 2002; Short et al., 1976), that in anonymous online interaction there may be more group polarization, that is, the tendency for like-minded individuals to become more extreme in their thinking following a group discussion than in face–face interaction. She described how in CMC environments two main theories have been developed: the equalization hypothesis and the social identity model of de-individuation effects theory. The equalization hypothesis is that in the absence of physical cues, individuals who traditionally possess less power in society should have increased power in an Internet environment. The evidence to support both, however, is limited and contradictory and in particular further work is needed which takes into account the subtleties of different levels of anonymity and social cues.

Connectedness or social presence: Benthe et al. (2008) have examined the influence of avatars on social presence, interpersonal trust, perceived communication quality, nonverbal behaviour, and visual attention in Internet collaborations. They studied text chat, audio, audio-video, and avatar and found significant differences between text chat and all other communication modalities in perceived intimateness, co-presence, and emotionally based trust. They suggest that video and avatar modes are similar, both showing higher levels of exposure to the virtual other and visual attention, in particular in the initial phase of interaction, compared to text and audio. However, social presence is not defined just by technology or by the situation the person is in, but by the human perceptual response subjectively created by an interaction of situation, technology, and individual needs and expectations. People may vary in the connectedness they want with others online when talking about health and in the connectedness they feel in using different technologies.

Some people may prefer methods that give more social presence to people they communicate with, for example they like to see the real person they are communicating with (as a photograph, a live video, or an avatar); others may prefer just to read messages or hear people's voices. For example, in our second case study (Jones et al., 2008) participants expressed different views such as:

> 'Having the photo meant that the session was more personalised. I feel a little bit anxious about seeing the person over a video link for the same reason as having a phone conversation – a feeling of embarrassment about discussing my problems. But perhaps if I tried it, it would actually be quite good.
>
> Personally, I do not need that much 'intimacy' as I wish to work with the dynamics of my problem, and therefore the relationship does not need to be too therapeutic. I could see why some people would need the therapeutic presence, though.
>
> I find it easier to hear people when I can see their lips and expressions. I think you learn a lot more by seeing a person too, with facial expression, body language, etc.'
>
> Jones et al., 2008

Distance: Beyond anonymity, and in contrast to social presence, some participants may be empowered by the distance between their real and online identities to disclose and discuss difficult issues. Walther et al. (2005) have described the benefits of social distance in some situations. First, they claim that our common groups of friends often do not contain people with expertise or familiarity with specific health issues, while discussion with close friends and family members on these issues may become uncomfortable. The fact that online support providers are not part of support seekers' day-to-day physical lives makes possible the management of stigma and embarrassment. In some cases, they claim it would be more embarrassing for one's day-to-day colleagues and friends to be aware of either the problems or the lack of control implied by needing help.

Speed and style of interaction: In mobile phone research, distinct preferences for 'texting' versus 'talking' have been identified (Reid and Reid, 2007). Online, some patients may prefer asynchronous methods such as person–person email, membership of mailing lists, or message boards. For example, we stated above that the MS Society discontinued use of instant chat in favour of message boards that gave participants more time to think. Others may prefer synchronous methods such as instant messaging, desktop conferencing via webcam chat communities such as Skype or Camfrog (www.camfrog.com), through to contact in virtual worlds such as Second Life (Kamel Boulos et al., 2007).

The impact of a 'richer' environment (e.g. through synchronous methods or video rather than just text) is not always obvious. Walther (1996) has argued that in some situations relationships mediated by 'cue-lean media' where the medium of communication does not provide nonverbal information (for example, text) could be more engaging than face–face relationships because the participants are better able to control the information others gain about them and do not have physical, disconfirming information. He argued that in cue-lean media it is more likely that people's expectations of others will be met, leading people to like their interaction partners more.

Also, perhaps counter-intuitively, a richer environment does not necessarily result in more effective information acquisition. For example, Rockwell and Singleton (2007) found that participants who viewed a text-only presentation scored significantly higher in a free-recall quiz than participants who viewed the same material in a text-audio-video presentation. Nowak et al. (2005) examined the effects of synchrony and the number of cues on the person perception process in CMC. Consistent with Walther's model, those using cue-lean media felt their partners were more credible and reported more social attraction, less uncertainty, and more involvement in the interaction than those using high-cue media. However, people interacting with synchronous media reported increased social attraction, self-reported involvement, and certainty. They also felt that their conversations were more effective, although this effect appeared mainly in low-cue groups. However, preferences for asynchronous versus synchronous may vary by such obvious factors as ease of use of the technology, whether all are using their first language, and ability to type.

Support membership: Some patients may seek support from professionals, others from peers. Although these preferences may be partly explained by characteristics such as trust and anonymity, they may also remain independent factors. In some cases, such as self-harm or anorexia, participants may not wish to hear an 'expert' view even though they may trust experts for other aspects of health (Gavin et al., 2008). Johnsen et al. (2002) analysed discussion forums for (1) general psychiatry, (2) weight and eating disorders, and (3) abuse. 'Destructive' mainposts and topic threads were more than twice as common in the forum for eating disorders than in the forums for general psychiatry and abuse. Johnsen et al. argue that one reason for the destructive climate might be the homogeneous nature of participants in the eating disorder forum, which was closed and reopened with professional moderation.

To listen or to be heard: Some people may need to be 'heard' as much as they seek information or want to hear the stories of others. For example, in message boards some people just read (lurkers) while some long-standing members regularly post (elders) (Bishop, 2007). Less anonymous interfaces may be more threatening to lurkers.

Time convenience: Professionals may be willing to provide synchronous support during working hours, but less keen to see work encroaching further on their family lives, whereas patients may prefer synchronous activities at weekends and of an evening (Jones et al., 2008). Asynchronous methods may be more time convenient although they may 'score' less than other factors.

Type of support: Various questionnaire measures of social support classify support as instrumental (doing things such as shopping), informational, and emotional. Although instrumental support can be obtained online (e.g. online shopping), our focus is on informational or emotional support. Informational versus emotional support may vary by condition, gender, or other factors. For example, on cancer forums (Meier et al., 2007) emotional was less common than informational support, whereas, on other forums (e.g. recent ex-smokers (Burri et al., 2006) and HIV/AIDS (Bar-Lev, 2008)) most messages provided emotional support. Women may offer more emotional support and men more informational support (Burri et al., 2006).

Interactions between 'method characteristics': There are likely to be interactions between 'method characteristics'. For example, participants could have a social presence while remaining anonymous although there may be interaction between the need for anonymity, social presence, and ease of use. As stated above, in our second case study preferences between alternative methods were evenly divided. While we did not explore how this varied according to patient characteristics, we believe that this should be the focus of future research. Content and source of support may be related. Professionals and peers can provide both forms of support but some patients, particularly initially, may prefer informational support from professionals while using other patients' stories for continuing emotional support.

Further developments

Implications for policy and practice

People with long-term conditions are placing increasing emphasis on self-help and self-care (Zajicek et al., 2007). This is due in part to the changing relationship between service users and professionals, the increasing involvement of patient support groups, and more ready access to information by the public through Web-based media. However, studies have shown that while service users want information and support, they also wish to have guidance from health professionals regarding the use of those resources (Skirton and Barr, 2008). Increasingly, user groups are developing Web-based material or communication opportunities for people with long-term conditions; these involve the use of resources and should be targeted appropriately. Research is needed to provide:

- guidance and information to organizations wishing to provide online resources for patients so as to direct resources appropriately
- information for professionals in both the health and the charitable sectors to enable them to formulate policy on the development and use of Web-based resources
- practical guidance on the types of resource that are likely to be useful to people affected by specific conditions (both patients and their families and friends)
- information for potential users on the attributes, benefits, and disadvantages of different types of communication and information resource.

Guidance for patients and professionals

How can professionals and patients advise others on what would be useful? Various consumer guides exist on peer–peer support, often published by doctors (e.g. http://www.synspectrum.com/support.html), but these usually include only general advice rather than comparisons between different types of support or any discussion of what might suit individuals and they are rarely evidence-based.

Implications for research

We might assume a model of 'useful' online support in which (1) patient characteristics lead to (2) different preferences for 'method characteristics' of online support and that (3) these preferences will be better or worse met by different methods of person–person support from those currently available. Research is needed to help us gain a better understanding of the detailed relationships between patient characteristics, method characteristics, and different types of support. While current methods will continue to change rapidly, the relationships between patient characteristics and preferences for different online methods are likely to change more slowly.

Future research may want to deal with the following research questions. We need to:

- enhance our understanding of the importance placed by people with long-term conditions on 'method characteristics' of person–person support methods, i.e. aspects such as synchronicity, anonymity, social presence, peer or health professional membership, and similarities to and differences from other participants.
- increase our understanding of how preferences for different 'method characteristics' vary by patient characteristics, that is, how variables such as age, sex, condition, duration or stage of condition, experience of social networks, and previous computer use influence preferences.
- build a model of patient preference for 'method characteristics' of online person–person support, and
- provide guidance to patients and professionals on which online support may best suit them.

Some examples of relevant research questions are:

- Which patients prefer synchronicity, anonymity, social presence, or some other 'method characteristics'?
- Which patients prefer informational or emotional support?
- Which patients prefer peer or professional support?
- Are patient preferences in relation to these characteristics related to date/time of interaction and stage of condition?
- How do users rate trust, ease of use, speed, and style of interaction?

Research needs to take special care to get the views of all. Even in surveys where the effort is made to get a high response there is the possibility of bias due to non-response, with those who are more difficult to engage (perhaps with worse health) being less well represented (Jones et al., 2006a). Online methods such as wikis, blogs, and message boards may well miss the views of shyer, or less vocal, patients, and almost by definition those who feel less at ease using such technology. Research methods should aim to overcome such bias.

Study designs need to take into account likely differences between patient groups. For example, younger people are likely to find the Internet easier to use and may be more likely to prefer synchronous interaction than older people. People with 'stigmatizing conditions' such as depression or other mental health problems may be more likely to seek anonymity than people with cancer, for example. Women may seek more emotional than informational support than men. Other determinants of preference such as attitudes to trust and connectedness, are likely to be found in all conditions.

Factors which may affect patient preferences include: age, gender, first language, level of education, urban/rural location (Winters et al., 2006), condition (multiple sclerosis, depression etc.), stage of condition (e.g. at risk, recent diagnosis, first year, etc.), social networks and other support, IT and previous experience of online support, timing of Internet use, other technology use (e.g. whether they text using mobiles), information preferences and sources (e.g. newspaper choice) (Gatherer, 2000), learning styles (Advanogy.com, 2008) (Coffield et al., 2004; Sadler-Smith, 2001; Harris et al., 2003; Duff and Duffy, 2002), how they use the Internet for health, attitudes to self-care and autonomy, and trust in others on the Internet.

Conclusion

In this chapter we have described the range of Internet technologies which have the potential to enable users to access both information and support. We have shown that individual preferences for the type of person–person support using the Internet may differ and give some indication as to what these preferences may be. However, the current state of our knowledge does not enable providers either to offer evidence-based guidance or to tailor services to potential user groups. Further research is required to maximize the use of these resources for the benefit of the population.

References

Advanogy.com (2008) Learning Styles Online (Memletics.com).
Association, A.P. (2002) 110th Convention Chicago, 22–25 August 2002. Chicago.
Barak, A., Grohol, J.M. & Pector, E. (2004) Methodology, Validity, and Applicability: A Critique on Eysenbach et al. (Rapid response). *British Medical Journal*, 328.
Bar-Lev, S. (2008) "We are here to give you emotional support": performing emotions in an online HIV/AIDS support group. *Qualitative Health Research*, 18: 509–21.
Bell, L. (2008) Providing Consumer Health Outreach and Library Programs to Virtual World Residents in Second Life.
Bental, D.S., Cawsey, A. & Jones, R. (1999) Patient information systems that tailor to the individual. *Patient Education and Counseling*, 36: 171–80.
Bente, G., Ruggenberg, S., Kramer, N.C. & Eschenburg, F. (2008) Avatar-mediated networking: Increasing social presence and interpersonal trust in net-based collaborations. *Human Communication Research*, 34: 287-U30.

Bishop, J. (2007) Increasing participation in online communities: A framework for human-computer interaction. *Computers in Human Behavior,* 23: 1881–93.
Boudioni, M., McPherson, K., Moynihan, C., Melia, J., Boulton, M., Leydon, G. and Mossman, J. (2001) Do men with prostate or colorectal cancer seek different information and support from women with cancer? *British Journal of Cancer,* 85: 641–8.
Boyd, C., Francis, K., Alsbett, D., Newnham, K., Sewell, J., Dawes, G. & Nurse, S. (2007) Australian rural adolescents' experiences of accessing psychological help for a mental health problem. *Australian Journal of Rural Health,* 15: 196–200.
Breckons, M., Jones, R., Morris, J. & Richardson, J. (2008) What do evaluation instruments tell us about the quality of complementary medicine information on the internet? *Journal of Medical Internet Research,* 10: e3-e3.
Burri, M., Baujard, V. & Etter, J.F. (2006) A qualitative analysis of an Internet discussion forum for recent ex-smokers. *Nicotine & Tobacco Research,* 8: S13–S19.
Christopherson, K.M. (2007) The positive and negative implications of anonymity in Internet social interactions: "On the Internet, Nobody Knows You're a Dog". *Computers in Human Behavior,* 23: 3038–56.
Coffield, F., Moseley, D., Hall, E. & Ecclestone, K. (2004) Should we be using learning styles? What research has to say to practice. Learning and Skills Research Centre. www.LSRC.ac.uk
Coulson, N.S. & Buchanan, H. (2008) Self-reported efficacy of an online dental anxiety support group: a pilot study. *Community Dentistry And Oral Epidemiology,* 36: 43–6.
Coulson, N.S., Buchanan, H. & Aubeeluck, A. (2007) Social support in cyberspace: a content analysis of communication within a Huntington's disease online support group. *Patient Education and Counseling,* 68: 173–8.
Cunningham, J.A., Van Mierlo, T. & Fournier, R. (2008) An online support group for problem drinkers: AlcoholHelpCenter.net. *Patient Education and Counseling,* 70: 193–8.
Duff, A. & Duffy, T. (2002) Psychometric properties of Honey & Mumford's Learning Styles Questionnaire (LSQ). *Personality and Individual Differences,* 33: 147–63.
Edelman (2006) Annual Edelman Trust Barometer.
Esquivel, A., Meric-Bernstam, F. & Bernstam, E.V. (2006) Accuracy and self correction of information received from an internet breast cancer list: content analysis. *British Medical Journal,* 332: 939–42.
Eysenbach, G. & Kohler, C. (2002) How do consumers search for and appraise health information on the world wide web? Qualitative study using focus groups, usability tests, and in-depth interviews. *BMJ (Clinical research ed.),* 324: 573–7.
Eysenbach, G., Powell, J., Englesakis, M., Rizo, C. & Stern, A. (2004) Health-related virtual communities and electronic support groups: systematic review of the effects of online peer to peer interactions. *British Medical Journal,* 328: 1166–70A.
Gatherer, L. (2000) Patient information on cancer – Newspaper read is good predictor of information needs. *British Medical Journal,* 321: 48.
Gavin, J., Rodham, K. & Poyer, H. (2008) The presentation of "pro-anorexia" in online group interactions. *Qualitative Health Research,* 18: 325–33.
Gellatly, J., Bower, P., Hennessy, S., Richards, D., Gilbody, S. & Lovell, K. (2007) What makes self-help interventions effective in the management of depressive symptoms? Meta-analysis and meta-regression. *Psychological Medicine,* 11: 1–24.

Giddens, A. (1984) *The Constitution of Society: Outline of the Theory of Structuration*, Berkely, University of California Press.

Google (2008) Google Health.

Green, J.M., Draper, A.K., Dowler, E.A., Fele, G., Hagenhoff, V., Rusanen, M. & Rusanen, T. (2005) Public understanding of food risks in four European countries: a qualitative study. *European Journal of Public Health*, 15: 523–7.

Harris, R. & Wathen, N. (2007) "If my mother was alive I'd probably have called her:" Women's search for health information in rural Canada. *Reference & User Services Quarterly*, 47: 67–79.

Harris, R.N., Dwyer, W.O. & Leeming, F.C. (2003) Are learning styles relevant in web-based instruction? *Journal of Educational Computing Research*, 29: 13–28.

Hesse, B.W. & Shneiderman, B. (2007) eHealth research from the user's perspective. *American Journal of Preventive Medicine*, 32: S97–S103.

Hoey, L.M., Ieropoli, S.C., White, V.M. & Jefford, M. (2008) Systematic review of peer-support programs for people with cancer. *Patient Education and Counseling*, 70: 315–37.

Huang, S.T., Kamel Boulos, M.N. & Dellavalle, R.P. (2008) Scientific discourse 2.0. Will your next poster session be in Second Life ®? *EMBO Reports*, 9: 496–9.

Hurley, A.L., Sullivan, P. & McCarthy, J. (2007) The construction of self in online support groups for victims of domestic violence. *The British Journal of Social Psychology/The British Psychological Society*, 46: 859–74.

Jadad, A.R., Enkin, M.W., Glouberman, S., Groff, P. & Stern, A. (2006) Are virtual communities good for our health? They seem to be good at managing chaotic information – and may have other virtues too. *British Medical Journal*, 332: 925–26.

Johnsen, J.A.K., Rosenvinge, J.H. & Gammon, D. (2002) Online group interaction and mental health: An analysis of three online discussion forums. *Scandinavian Journal of Psychology*, 43: 445–9.

Jones, A.M., Koolman, X. & Rice, N. (2006a) Health-related non-response in the British household panel survey and European community household panel: using inverse-probability-weighted estimators in non-linear models. *Journal of the Royal Statistical Society Series a-Statistics in Society*, 169: 543–69.

Jones, R.B., Martinez, R., Maramba, I., Prestwich, J., McCauley, M., Farrand, P. & Williams, C. (2008) Exploratory study of chat room motivational support for users of an Internet-based cognitive behavioural therapy for the treatment of depression. In S. Kay (ed.) *Healthcare computing 2008*. Harrogate, BJHC Books.

Jones, R.B., Pearson, J., Cawsey, A.J., Bental, D., Barrett, A., White, J., White, C.A. and Gilmour, W.H. (2006b) Effect of different forms of information produced for cancer patients on their use of the information, social support, and anxiety: randomised trial. *British Medical Journal*, 332: 942–6A.

Kamel Boulos, M.N., Hetherington, L. & Wheeler, S. (2007) Second Life: an overview of the potential of 3-D virtual worlds in medical and health education. *Health Information and Libraries Journal*, 24: 233–45.

Kamel Boulos, M.N. & Toth-Cohen, S. (2009 in press) The University of Plymouth Sexual Health SIM experience in Second Life®: evaluation and reflections after one year. *Health Information and Libraries Journal*, 26.

Klemm, P. (2008) Late effects of treatment for long-term cancer survivors: qualitative analysis of an online support group. *Computers, Informatics, Nursing: CIN*, 26: 49–58.

Krueger, A. (2008) A second life on Second Life. (YouTube video featured at the Health 2.0 conference on Web 2.0 technologies in healthcare on 3–4 March 2008 in San Diego, USA in which Alice Krueger who has severe MS describes how she is benefiting from Second Life).
Meier, A., Lyons, E.J., Frydman, G., Forlenza, M. & Rimer, B.K. (2007) How cancer survivors provide support on cancer-related internet mailing lists. *Journal of Medical Internet Research*, 9: 59.
NOS (2006) Adults who have ever used the Internet by sex/age (Great Britain): Individual Internet Access. National Statistics.
NOS (2007) Households with access to the Internet, GB. National Office of Statistics.
Nowak, K.L., Watt, J. & Walther, J.B. (2005) The influence of synchrony and sensory modality on the person perception process in computer-mediated groups. *Journal of Computer-Mediated Communication*, 10: 28.
OFCOM (2008) Media Literacy Report.
Pedersen, D.M. (1987) Sex differences in privacy preferences. *Perceptual and Motor skills*, 64: 1239–42.
Poynton, T.A. (2005) Computer literacy across the lifespan: a review with implications for educators. *Computers in Human Behavior*, 21: 861–72.
Preece, J., Nonnecke, B. & Andrews, D. (2004) The top five reasons for lurking: improving community experiences for everyone. *Computers in Human Behavior*, 20: 201–23.
Radin, P. & Landzelius, K. (2006) "To me, it's my life": Medical communication, trust, and activism in cyberspace. *Social Science & Medicine*, 62: 591–601.
Reid, D.J. & Reid, F.J.M. (2007) Text or talk? Social anxiety, loneliness, and divergent preferences for cell phone use. *Cyberpsychology & Behavior: The Impact of the Internet, Multimedia and Virtual Reality on Behavior and Society*, 10: 424–35.
Rier, D.A. (2007) Internet social support groups as moral agents: the ethical dynamics of HIV+ status disclosure. *Sociology Of Health & Illness*, 29: 1043–58.
Rockwell, S.C. & Singleton, L.A. (2007) The effect of the modality of presentation of streaming multimedia on information acquisition. *Media Psychology*, 9: 179–91.
Rost, K., Smith, G.R. & Taylor, J.L. (1993) Rural-urban differences in stigma and the use of care for depressive disorders. *J Rural Health*, 9: 57–62.
Rutten, L.J.F., Arora, N.K., Bakos, A.D., Aziz, N. & Rowland, J. (2005) Information needs and sources of information among cancer patients: a systematic review of research (1980–2003). *Patient Education and Counseling*, 57: 250–61.
Sadler-Smith, E. (2001) Does the Learning Styles Questionnaire Measure Style or Process? A Reply to Swailes and Senior (1999).
Samaritans (2008) Samaritans Information Resource Pack 2008.
Sarasohn-Kahn, J. (2008) Trust Driving People to Web Social Networks for Health Info. iHealthBeat. California HealthCare Foundation.
Seale, C., Ziebland, S. & Charteris-Black, J. (2006) Gender, cancer experience and internet use: A comparative keyword analysis of interviews and online cancer support groups. *Social Science & Medicine*, 62: 2577–90.
Short, J., Williams, B. & Christie, B. (1976) *The social psychology of telecommunication*, New York, John Wiley.
Sia, C., Tan, B.C.Y. & Wei, K. (2002) Group polarization and computer-mediated communications: effects of communication cues, social presence, and anonymity. *Information Systems Research*, 13: 70–90.

Sillence, E. & Briggs, P. (2008) Ubiquitous computing trust issues for a "Healthy" society. *Social Science Computer Review*, 26: 6–12.

Sillence, E., Briggs, P., Harris, P. & Fishwick, L. (2007) Going online for health advice: Changes in usage and trust practices over the last five years. *Interacting with Computers*, 19: 397–406.

Skirton, H. & Barr, O. (2008) Antenatal screening: Informed choice and parental consent. . Foundation for People with Learning Disabilities.

Smith, T. (2008) Live a Second Life Online. *CBS News*.

Squiers, L., Rutten, L.J.F., Treiman, K., Bright, M.A. & Hesse, B. (2005) Cancer patients' information needs across the cancer care continuum: Evidence from the cancer information service. *Journal of Health Communication*, 10: 15–34.

Van Dolen, W.M., Dabholkar, P.A. & De Ruyter, K. (2007) Satisfaction with online commercial group chat: The influence of perceived technology attributes, chat group characteristics, and advisor communication style. *Journal of Retailing*, 83: 339–58.

Van Uden-Kraan, C.F., Drossaert, C.H.C., Taal, E., Seydel, E.R. & Van de Laar, M.A.F.J. (2008a) Self-reported differences in empowerment between lurkers and posters in online patient support groups. *Journal of Medical Internet Research*, 10: e18-e18.

Van Uden-Kraan, C.F., Drossaert, C.H.C., Taal, E., Shaw, B.R., Seydel, E.R. & Van de Laar, M.A.F.J. (2008b) Empowering processes and outcomes of participation in online support groups for patients with breast cancer, arthritis, or fibromyalgia. *Qualitative Health Research*, 18: 405–17.

Wald, H.S., Dube, C. & Anthony, D.C. (2007) Untangling the Web—the impact of Internet use on health care and the physician-patient relationship. *Patient Education And Counseling*, 68: 218–24.

Walden, T.A., Nelson, P.A. & Smith, D.E. (1981) Crowding, privacy, and coping. *Environment and Behavior*, 13: 205–24.

Walther, J.B. (1996) Computer-mediated communication: Impersonal, interpersonal, and hyperpersonal interaction. *Communication Research*, 23: 3–43.

Walther, J.B., Pingree, S., Hawkins, R.P. & Buller, D.B. (2005) Attributes of interactive online health information systems. *Journal of Medical Internet Research*, 7: e33-e33.

Wang, Z., Walther, J.B., Pingree, S. & Hawkins, R.P. (2008) Health information, credibility, homophily, and influence via the Internet: Web sites versus discussion groups. *Health Commun*, 23: 358–68.

Winters, C.A., Cudney, S.A., Sullivan, T. & Thuesen, A. (2006) The rural context and women's self-management of chronic health conditions. *Chronic Illness*, 2: 273–89.

Yahoo (2008) Yahoo Health Groups.

Yee, N. & Bailenson, J. (2007) The Proteus Effect: The Effect of Transformed Self-Representation on Behavior. *Human Communication Research*, 33: 271–90.

Zajicek, J., Freeman, J. & Porter, B. (2007) *Multiple Sclerosis Care: a practical manual*, Oxford: Oxford University Press.

5
The Social Impact of Online Games: The Case of Germany

Thorsten Quandt and Jeffrey Wimmer

Introduction: Collective gaming in virtual worlds

The increasing uptake of broadband Internet connections not only involves a growing number of Internet users; increasing numbers of computer gamers are also using the Internet for online gaming. In addition to the continual increase in Internet use, the impact of the 'breakthrough hit' (Ducheneaut et al., 2006) of the massively multiplayer online role-playing game (MMORPG), *World of Warcraft* (*WoW*), which made online gaming a mass phenomenon, can be considered a major factor in this development of online gaming. In spring 2008, *WoW* was reported to have ten million paying subscribers.

In fact, the history of online games is much older than *WoW*, extending back to the late 1970s. Group-based gaming on computer networks began with MUDs (multi-user dungeons/dimensions, see Keegan, 1997), played on university networks as a hobby of 'early adopters'. A large part of the fascination with these early games lay in the possibility of users communicating or interacting among themselves. Likewise, the success of modern online role-playing games such as *WoW* is largely based on their strong communicative component. The main attraction of such games is the negotiation of social rules and standards, and the differentiation of individual 'characters' based on real-time interactions in the game (Götzenbrucker, 2001: p. 39). Although these sophisticated aspects are a key feature of online games, current MMORPGs are so user-friendly that they can be played by 'normal' users.

Much less is known about 'normal' users of online role-playing games than might be suggested by the long history of the game genre and its apparently widespread use. Previous studies have focused on highly specific aspects of the topic (see the following section on the status quo of research), yet there exists a lack of overview studies that outline this field in its full complexity.

In any event, online role-playing games remain the best-researched genre of online gaming: little information is available regarding online strategy games, or sports and racing games. Furthermore, the online modes of game consoles are poorly researched compared with their counterparts in the computer gaming world, even though most game consoles also provide Internet functionality (e.g. Xbox 360, Wii, and PlayStation 3). In contrast to strategy, sports, and racing games, online action games have been heavily discussed in the public domain, particularly in recent years, and generally after instances of adolescents running amok: several school shootings have been linked to online action games such as *Counter-Strike* (*CS*). This negative discussion about the 'damage' done by computer games is not restricted to action games: with the continuing growth in popularity of MMORPGs, there is a growing suspicion that such games can impart systematic damage to users because they take up all of their spare time, ultimately making them 'addicted'. There are many reports of users whose 'virtual life' had a dramatic effect on their 'real life' structures (e.g. Castranova, 2005; Yee, 2002a). Despite the publicity such reactions have attracted, it is important to note that only a handful of studies have demonstrated a clear dependency on the part of the user. In fact, there is a lack of reliable studies on gamers' intensity of usage of diverse genre games that could be transferred to the general population.

Given the social relevance of online gaming and the somewhat limited knowledge within this field, it is important to collect general data on the users of online games. The present study seeks to address this need and presents general data on the users of online games in Germany, based on a paper-and-pencil survey of approximately 700 online gamers (quota sample, according to *Die Allensbacher Computer- und Technik-Analyse* (ACTA) 2006).[1]

The remainder of the chapter is organized as follows. In the next section, the status quo of research is systematized and analysed in detail to identify the most important research questions. A description of the methodological process adopted in this study is presented in the third section. The results, including basic data about all gamers and comparisons between different groups of gamers, are discussed in section 4. Finally, the last section considers the limitations of the present study and outlines further research objectives and possible future studies.

Status quo of research on online games: Data, types, and risks

It is unlikely that anybody could have imagined the broad impact that would eventually unfold when the first online games appeared, mainly as the activity of 'nerds' in computer-related university institutes. In the early years, research on the players themselves was of peripheral interest – after all, this was an insider community whose composition was believed to be known, especially within the community itself. Research efforts were extremely limited at that time.

Richard Bartle, co-developer of the first online game (MUD), was one of the first to develop a typology of MUD-gamers (see Bartle, 1996). In his classification scheme, Bartle, as senior administrator, structured and summarized the results of a long discussion thread on a bulletin board where MUD-players discussed various approaches to playing MUDs. Although the classification of types did not follow the rules of systematic work in social sciences, it turned out to be extremely durable and remains frequently quoted. Bartle distinguished four player types: the success-oriented 'Achiever'; the 'Explorer', who specializes in discovery and plays via trial and error; the communicative 'Socializer'; and the 'Killer', who aims to kill other players in the virtual world.[2] Critics of Bartle's work claim that the typology is primarily based on the game mechanics of MUDs (e.g. the 'Explorer' type), although the types could be partially applied to completely different kinds of game (e.g. the success-oriented action of the 'Achievers'). In response to this criticism, Yee (2002c) compiled a five-factor model of the basic motivations for playing MMORPGs. In several further studies, Yee analysed other peculiarities of online roleplayers (2002b, 2005) and identified, for example, factors related to gaming addiction in MMORPGs (2002a).

Studies that deal with the motivations of online gaming are also closely related to the typologies proposed by Yee and Bartle (see above). In an early work, based mainly on 40 partially standardized interviews with online players, Götzenbrucker (2001) identified the development of social networks as one of the main motivating factors behind online gaming. Fritz (2003: p. 1), who has dealt with online players using a variety of methods over a series of research works, highlights the factors of power, control, and contest: 'Playing computer games also means looking for success'. Fritz supposes that this is the actual reason for the selection of specific games. Accordingly, players select the game type most likely to correspond to their abilities. In this respect, player typologies could also be based on success-oriented genre preferences.

While the basic motivations for gaming appear to be unproblematic in themselves, there appear to be certain conditions under which they might lead to excessive gaming. As mentioned above, research projects on addiction and online games have appeared in recent years (e.g. Yee, 2002a). This development was probably promoted by the success of *WoW*, which soon after its appearance was identified in public discussion as being highly addictive. However, as in the works on gamer typologies, it must be noted that these studies are mostly based on samples that are non-representative or even 'anecdotal', and that their results are not always coherent. Nevertheless, indicators of damage (see the introductory section) need to be pursued, because press reports are a sign of the growing social impact of the phenomenon – although a 'damage discussion' could be applied to all forms of excessive media consumption. Excessive online gaming is probably also seen to be threatening because it is a comparatively new phenomenon and because the number of related press reports is increasing. In contrast, the phenomenon of the 'heavy user' in relation to other media (e.g. the excessive TV viewer) is long established.

To estimate the extent of addiction problems in regard to online players, and in comparison with similar problems related to other media, it would be necessary to collect overview data of online game use as well as basic data on the composition and socio-demographic properties of the players. There exist several works within communication studies, especially with respect to online role-playing games, which already supply some relevant data. For example, Kolo and Baur (2004) interviewed 104 *Ultima* online players, using a multi-method design, and Griffiths and Davies (2003, 2004a, 2004b) performed similar studies on *Everquest* players. Yee (2003) provided comparable information on online role-playing gamers and the popular *WoW*, and Cypra (2005) administered an online survey of more than 11,000 participants in Germany; this latter study was based on a self-selective sample.

Without going into the details of these individual studies, it is safe to say that they largely agree in their main results (despite their differences in quality and barely comparable databases): men dominate the group of online role-playing gamers. Female gamers account for as little as several percent of the samples in most studies (and a similar proportion of the expected base population). Findings on the age distribution of users indicate that most do not belong to the group of underage, male core gamers, as perhaps would be assumed based on the usual stereotypes; instead, 'twens' (people in their twenties) appear to be the most active group in online role-playing games.

Because past research has concentrated on online role-playing games, comparable data are missing for other game genres. General information on computer and online gaming can be collected from representative surveys on media consumption, such as the ACTA study in Germany, which confirms the age distribution suggested by the non-representative studies mentioned above. The average (online) computer player is aged 20–29 years. However, ACTA disagrees with previous studies regarding gender distribution: it reports that about one-third of online gamers are female (see the next section).

Overall, it is important to note that existing scientific knowledge on online gaming is based on somewhat unreliable, and sometimes contradictory, data material. The present study therfore is a first step towards a more reliable database on the use of online games.

Methodology

Basic problems of previous empirical analyses and conception of the present study

As outlined above, some knowledge already exists regarding online players. However, this knowledge has mostly been gathered within studies that can raise a claim neither to representativity nor to the selection of well-balanced samples. One might accept these approaches in the absence of other possibilities for certain questions (e.g. intergroup comparisons); however, the inherent distortions are serious, and barely allow conclusions to be drawn regarding a relevant basic population: many such studies are based on samples almost exclusively composed of young males (e.g. Cypra, 2005). One could assume that such samples match the profile of the searched group of persons; however, general studies of representative populations that enquire into (online) games (e.g. ACTA) refer to a clearly different composition. Such studies consistently identify much higher numbers of elderly and female players. One might suppose therefore that the outlined method of unchecked, online data collection results in systematic distortions (e.g. because young males spend more time in the relevant forums than females and persons aged 40 years or older; the latter two groups are rarely recruited, if at all, in such forums).

As a result of the problems stated above, two central demands became apparent for the present study: first, a sensible method of sampling should be developed that enables conclusions to be drawn regarding the basic population of online players. Secondly, basic data about this group should be collected on a large scale, which has not been attempted until now. This intention was realized in the form of paper-and-pencil questionnaires (a controlled filing of written questionnaires rather than freely accessible online questionnaires) based on a quota sample (referring to the data of ACTA collected in 2006). The study itself does not test any given, highly specialized hypotheses: it is more of a broad descriptive survey. The relevant fields of interest are briefly outlined in the following section. Of course, certain theses of coherency could be tested based on the accumulated data.

Study design

According to the state of research described above and the intention to design the study as a survey, we compiled a number of central questions and demands for the present study. A review of the relevant research literature has revealed that the variety of different network games is too large to enable a study focusing on online gaming as a whole; specific game genres were therefore identified in order to structure the questionnaire. An ad hoc list of game genres was established based on the previous research works described above and other studies on game varieties. This list was checked against a recent German sales chart and matched against classifications of common genres employed by magazines concerned with computer games (which are considered to be known by the majority of the respondents). Based on pre-tests and the need for a pragmatic study design, four main online genres were ultimately identified: (1) role-playing games, (2) action games, (3) strategy games, and (4) sports and racing games. The respondents were able to handle this classification in the pre-tests without major difficulties.

Considering the above basic conditions for the questionnaire, we developed three central fields of interest and respective items:[3]

- basic data about the general use of computer games (time spent playing per week, length of game sessions, genre and frequency of gaming, additional gaming action);
- basic data about online gaming (time spent playing per week, length of game sessions, interconnection between real life and the virtual game world, played genres, genre preferences);
- information about the played games (experience with the genre and – if so, since when, played games per genre as an open item, time spent playing per week, length of game sessions, clan membership, financial expenses, characteristics, evaluations and motives regarding the specific genre, style of playing).

The questionnaire was designed to accord with existing studies on computer game use and diverse studies on general media use. The questions regarding game motivation and playing type were oriented towards previous approaches (Asgari, 2005 and the works of Bartle, Cypra, Griffiths, Fritz, and Yee, among others). During pre-tests, all the questions were again optimised. The final version of the questionnaire contained 50 questions, not all of which were to be answered, depending on the respondents' combination of played genres.

The quota arrangement within the study refers to ACTA 2006. ACTA is a representative study on computer and technology used by the German-speaking population aged between 14 and 64 years and is administered annually by the Institut für Demoskopie Allensbach. The study conducted during the first half of 2006 involved interviews with 10,008 individuals, of whom 19.9 per cent (1993 respondents) stated that they had already played online. Because ACTA consists of a sufficiently large sample, this subgroup of respondents can be subdivided again to extract a quota specification from the data.

The present study requires a quota arranged along three combined variables: age (four groups), gender, and education (with/without high-school-leaving exam, the German *Abitur*).[4] This subdivision resulted in a quota-matrix with 16 fields, representing a useful compromise between the practical feasibility of conducting the research, on the one hand, and the wish for a differentiated subdivision, on the other (see Table 5.1).

This 'quota-matrix' already provides an interesting insight into the composition of the searched group. As expected, men, especially younger men aged between 14 and 29 years, form the biggest part of the gaming community. Nevertheless, about one-third of online players are women,

Table 5.1 Distribution of online gamers/Quota matrix

Sex	Men (%)		Women (%)		Total (%)
Education	Without high-school-leaving exam	With high-school-leaving exam	Without high-school-leaving exam	With high-school-leaving exam	
Age group					
14–19 years	13.3	5.9	6.1	4.2	29.4
20–29 years	12.7	7.0	5.5	2.6	27.8
30–39 years	9.4	5.4	5.5	1.9	22.2
40–64 years	9.2	4.6	5.3	1.6	20.6
Total	44.6	22.8	22.4	10.2	100.0

N = 1993.
Source: ACTA 2006.

and older people make a surprisingly large contribution: around 20 per cent of online players are aged 40 to 64 years.[5] This composition contradicts the usual bias towards the computer-gameplaying male teenager, and suggests a much more varied composition of the gaming community. To reach all of these groups, we designed a multi-level recruitment procedure that helped to maximize the number of respondents and, above all, ensured the homogeneous composition of each group.

The different means of contact were spread as wide as possible to avoid biases that might arise by emphasizing a certain route of access to the players. Four different methods of contact were adopted:[6] (1) recruitment via computer magazines and their websites. We identified the most important computer magazines and asked for their cooperation (we received support from *GamePro*, *PC Praxis*, and *PC Welt*, among others); (2) recruitment via gaming portals and forums: here we contacted (via their websites) the developers of the most important commercially distributed online games for the years 2004–2007, as listed by the German Media Control Charts; (3) recruitment via the Games Convention 2006 held in Leipzig, one of the largest gaming tradeshows in the world. Here, all ages and gamer groups can be found on days open to the public, when part of the data collection was undertaken in the present study; (4) social networks: the adoption of a paper-and-pencil questionnaire made possible the use of a large number of interviewers all over Germany. As a result, social networks were used to cover certain groups of users.

The participants were informed about the nature of the study, and different forms of cooperation were offered (electronic ePaper or print questionnaire). The participants were provided with our contact details, enabling them to request the questionnaire. In contrast to online questionnaires, this form of participant selection provided better control of who took part, thereby avoiding those who might deliberately seek to mark incorrect items for their own amusement. This approach therefore served as a means to improve the quality of the collected data.

Data were collected in the summer of 2006 and the winter of 2006–2007. The rate of return of the sent questionnaires, over all periods, was 76 per cent. However, several questionnaires had to be discarded because of incorrect or contradictory statements, or because they fell outside of the searched quota limits. Ultimately, 688 out of 792 (i.e. 87 per cent) received questionnaires were included in the analysis. Despite the efforts made to cover all groups according to ACTA, a comparison with the quota specifications reveals biases in the data collection (see Table 5.2).

There are two central reasons that might explain this result. First, because older persons rarely visit the relevant websites or events

Table 5.2 Quota sample, arrangement before weighting, absolute numbers, and proportion

Sex	Men		Women		Total
Education	Without high-school-leaving exam	With high-school-leaving exam	Without high-school-leaving exam	With high-school-leaving exam	
Age group					
14–19 years	117 (17.0%)	35 (5.1%)	20 (2.9%)	10 (1.5%)	182 (26.5%)
20–29 years	86 (12.5%)	164 (23.8%)	28 (4.1%)	53 (7.7%)	331 (48.1%)
30–39 years	45 (6.5%)	62 (9.0%)	9 (1.3%)	10 (1.5%)	126 (18.3%)
40–64 years	19 (2.8%)	15 (2.2%)	9 (1.3%)	6 (0.9%)	49 (7.1%)
Total	267 (38.8%)	276 (40.1%)	66 (9.6%)	79 (11.5%)	688 (100%)

N = 688.

(e.g. the Games Convention) some of the contact methods employed would be less successful in reaching them than in reaching younger players. This also applies to female gamers. In other words, these groups engage in gaming, but their playing behaviour is less commonly connected with secondary 'supplementary actions' (e.g. visiting websites for playing) that might be used in their recruitment.[7]

Secondly, drawing conclusions based on the online gamers included in the ACTA database raises certain problems. Although the ACTA sample is representative, the quota specification described above is based on specific questions; comprehension of these questions is crucial in this respect. However, the somewhat misleading nature of certain item groups raises the possibility of the respondents' systematically misunderstanding the questions. Less-experienced individuals might encounter difficulties in understanding the meaning of 'playing online' and hence mistakenly affirm the relevant item.[8]

Despite the sampling difficulties mentioned above, the adoption of the quota specification according to ACTA is preferred over self-selective surveys in discussion forums. To balance the inequalities that exist between the quota and the as-is state of the enquiry, the data were weighted according to ACTA (cells were assigned weights such that the weighted quota was exactly consistent with Table 5.1). In this respect, the weighted tables used below reflect the particular prerequisites within the basic totality according to ACTA, and are therefore expected to deliver a useful representation of German online players aged between 14 and 64 years in the autumn/winter of 2006–2007.

Findings: Usage, social aspects, and comparisons

Overview of online gaming

To cover the complexity of online gaming, the present study not only collected general data of usage, but analysed the four main genres individually: role-playing games, action games, strategy games, and sports and racing games. Based on a list of the played game genres, one can obtain a first impression of the most popular types of online game (see Table 5.3).

Online role-playing games, which are played by almost 70 per cent of the interviewees, are clearly the dominant genre. In contrast, action games constitute part of the games repertoire of less than 50 per cent of the gaming community, strategy games are mentioned by only 35 per cent, and just 14 per cent of the interviewees play sports and racing games online.

The preference for role-playing games reflects the phenomenal success of *WoW*. In this respect, it is no surprise that *WoW* ranks first (by a clear margin) among the named favourite games (Table 5.4), with about 46 per cent of online players citing this popular game as their favourite. *Guild Wars* follows a distant second in the role-playing sector (7 per cent); all the remaining nominations rank less than 5 per cent.

Some action games were frequently named as favourite titles, headed by the much-discussed *CS* series, which more than 20 per cent of the interviewees regard as a favourite game. The *Battlefield* series, another action series, ranks second (11.1 per cent), followed by *Unreal* games (5.3 per cent). There are two remarkable aspects that emerge from these data. First, although highly controversial and having been on the market for many years, the *CS* series enjoys an unbroken popularity. Secondly, young interviewees commonly nominated age-restricted games as their favourite titles, despite being under age (which could actually represent an additional game incentive for them; see the section on Group comparisons below).

Table 5.3 Played online genres (multiple answers were permitted, weighted)

Genre	N	Proportion (%)
Role-playing games	470	68.3
Action games	315	45.8
Strategy games	244	35.4
Sports and racing games	96	13.9
Total	688	100.0

Table 5.4 Top favourite games, main title per genre (multiple answers possible)

Game	N	Proportion (%)
Role-playing games	(562 nominations, 59 games)	
WoW	316	45.9
Guild Wars	48	7.0
Diablo series	23	3.4
EverQuest	13	1.9
Dark Age of Camelot	12	1.7
Final Fantasy XI	12	1.7
Action games	(406 nominations, 41 games)	
CS series	158	22.9
Battlefield series	77	11.1
Unreal series	36	5.3
CoD series	22	3.2
DoD	14	2.0
Strategy games	(263 nominations, 71 games)	
Warcraft series	47	6.8
C&C series	25	3.6
AoE series	18	2.7
Ogame	18	2.7
Earthlost	18	2.6*
Sports and racing games	(90 nominations, 28 games)	
NfS series	18	2.6
GTR	12	1.8
Pro Evolution Soccer	8	1.1
FIFA series	5	0.8

N = 688.
* The occurrence of different percentage values, despite an equal number of cases, arises because of rounding differences due to the employed weightings.

Finally, few favourites were identified in the sports and racing game sector. Even the main titles in this sector were rarely mentioned. In contrast to other genres, it appears that the sports and racing games are played only occasionally, with less time invested in them. This assumption is supported by data describing the average weekly playing time per genre (see Table 5.5), in which sports and racing games rank last. Gamers who play sports and racing games spend an average of just 3.7 hours per week on this activity.

More time is invested in action games (9 hours per week) than in sports and racing games; however, strategy games are even more time-consuming (13 hours per week). The most frequently played genre, and that with the most time invested, is online role-playing games (20 hours

Table 5.5 Time spent playing per week on each online genre (weighted, multiple genre profiles per person possible)

	N	M (h)	max (h)	s (h)
Online games in general[9]	680	19.8	105.0	17.6
Role-playing games	441	20.5	100.0	17.2
Action games	271	9.3	45.0	8.6
Strategy games	193	13.1	105.0	19.0
Sports and racing games	51	3.7	21.0	4.3

per week). For this genre, many players reported up to 100 hours playing time per week (as did players of strategy titles). On closer examination, this finding points to the special living situations of these players, who spend almost all of their waking time on gaming (except for time taken with essential activities). Other information given by such players is congruent with the finding of extreme gaming consumption, including the duration of individual gaming sessions, other leisure activities, and working activity. Finally, the game seems to be the explicit centre of the players' lives. Of course, this information needs to be considered in a more differentiated manner. On average, the interviewed online players spend much less time on online gaming than the 'extreme gamers': approximately 20 hours a week.

In considering the played genres, a number of other intra-genre differences attract our attention. Again, online role-playing games stand out in terms of the number of years that players of different genres have been using computer games. Although online role-playing games have existed for many years, they are relatively new as a mainstream gaming phenomenon. This insight is confirmed by the available data: 72.0 per cent of the players of online role-playing games claim to have been using this genre for less than three years (N = 450). The equivalent percentages for action games, strategy games, and sports and racing games are 43.3 per cent (N = 273), 58.6 per cent (N = 194), and 66.6 per cent (N = 58), respectively. Only about 11.1 per cent of role-playing gamers have spent five years or more on online gaming. Larger proportions of players of action games (37.9 per cent), strategy games (22.3 per cent), and sports and racing games (13.8 per cent) are long-term players (>5 years). The high number of experienced action-game players also shows that network games, as a larger phenomenon, originate mainly from the area of ego-shooters. In this regard, LAN parties can probably be considered as an evolutional nucleus that has subsequently been transferred to larger player groups via the online versions of action games.

However, online role-playing games became a mass phenomenon only with the success of *WoW*. Previously, few game-lovers dedicated themselves to the genre, although today it clearly leads the online games market.

Online games and everyday life: Social games between real life and the virtual world

The data reported above already provide a first impression of the preferred games of German online gamers, as well as of the scope of gaming. However, they provide little information regarding the intensity of activity and its integration into everyday life. The adoption and integration of gaming into everyday life can take on a variety of forms. Thus, various activities are connected with the game with the aim of improving or maintaining the gaming experience. At least 51.1 per cent of the interviewees frequently or very frequently look for updates to their preferred games (N = 688). Many players also search for additional information on the respective computer games (39.2 per cent frequently or very frequently, N = 686), such as cheat tips. Likewise, about one-third of the interviewees frequently or very frequently participate in game forum discussions (36.9 per cent, N = 687). Game extensions (expansion sets) are frequently or very frequently bought by 28.7 per cent of the interviewees (N = 688), enabling the user, for example, to extend the gaming experience after reaching the end of the original game. Fewer interviewees name other supporting activities frequently or very frequently. Game fan-art is mentioned in a quarter of cases (24.0 per cent, N = 685), whereas gamers are rarely involved in the trading of special game items (2.0 per cent, N = 688). In this respect, it is also worth noting that at least 73.3 per cent of players have actually bought fan-art, although 80.7 per cent of the interviewed gamers have never traded game items in real life. This finding can probably be explained by the fact that many games do not support this possibility, and that it is largely restricted to role-playing games. In addition, various game manufacturers strictly forbid any trade in games items as part of their terms of use, which is apparently largely successful in the prevention of trading.

However, the social importance of virtual game worlds also appears in other aspects, such as durable networking with other players, whether on- or offline. Intense players and professionals frequently unite in clans. These clans, like sports clubs, arrange game contests, form organizational structures and rules, and, by doing this, ultimately institutionalize the game experience. Moreover, the game structure of online role-playing games commonly provides for the possibility of grouping. Certain aims and game strategies can therefore only be achieved with the help of others (e.g. 'raids'), and others are substantially simplified by common actions. Many role-playing games offer options for the formation of groups or persistent guilds that consist of players who, as in a clan, get together for online gaming on a regular basis. The degree of obligation differs among groups, varying from short-term commitments to long-term affiliations that involve social engagements (e.g. scheduled gaming sessions, providing technical, personal, and game support to guild members). In fact, 75.0 per cent of the interviewees (N = 688) declare themselves to be a member of a clan or guild. Taking account of genre, however, it becomes obvious that the strength of team formation also depends on the game type: only 17.9 per cent of players of online sports and racing games belong to a clan (N = 55), whereas 44.0 per cent of online strategy players (N = 195), 51.1 per cent of online action players (N = 272) and 79.3 per cent of online roleplayers (N = 452) tend to connect within groups. Again, the latter figure is undoubtedly related to the success of *WoW*, in which it is comparatively simple to form groups (and guilds) to take part in 'quests' or 'raids'. Together with dedicated game servers for different gaming orientations (such as 'role-playing servers' or 'player vs player' servers), these different forms of grouping possibilities help the player to engage with individual interests within a chosen virtual–social group and thereby to meet other individuals with similar (game) interests. In short: those who play *WoW* are usually guild members. This applies to an even greater degree to the second most popular role-playing game, *Guild Wars*, in which cooperative gaming in groups is an integral part of the game. These are social games directed at interaction, both communicative and acting.

Belonging to a guild, clan, or a similar group of players can lead to an obligation that exceeds the actual gaming sessions. On the one hand, the game worlds are persistent; that is, they exist even if the players are not online. On the other, these worlds can change, either induced by the game (e.g. by changes in the story of the game, the evolution of the game elements or the game mechanics, or the extension of the playable worlds) or by the inter-action of the players (e.g. the advancement of fellow players to a higher level, changes in guilds or player groups, or, more generally, changes in the social network). In this way, the virtual gaming sometimes produces authentically felt necessities and obligations (such as the compulsion to go online frequently and to play for a long time to 'keep up' with one's guild, the commitment to participate in a 'raid'), or being preoccupied with what might happen to colleagues in the guild when offline.

The questionnaire administered in the present study contained several items intended to explore such interconnections between the 'real life' and the virtual game world. About half of the interviewees (45.7 per cent, N = 678) rather agreed or completely agreed with the statement regarding 'looking forward to contact with their fellow players while being offline'. Even more players expressed the desire not to let other players down during a game session, even if actually wanting to finish the game or being concerned with some unrelated matter in 'real life' (60.5 per cent, N = 680). The social commitment in this regard seems to be much more important than the competitive character of the game: only 12.4 per cent of the interviewees (N = 681) rather agreed or completely agreed with the statement that they not keeping up with fellow players when offline. Very little support was found for the idea that the virtual game occupies the 'mindset' of the 'real life'. Only 11.8 per cent of the interviewees (N = 684) claimed to think about what happens in the game world when offline, and only 18.1 per cent (N = 682) stated that they missed the game when not playing. About one-third of the respondents, however, self-critically noted experiencing the feeling that they neglected other parts of their life when gaming (29.2 per cent, N = 683). These findings are consistent with those of previous studies which highlight the possibility of collisions between the virtual and real worlds (e.g. if a conflict of interest arises because of time spent online).

Group comparisons I: Gender differentiation

The previous sections examined the totality of online players in view of general usage data and the interrelation of 'real life' and virtual world. In addition to this general consideration, it is interesting that a more differentiated view appears in certain groups, which is repeatedly focused upon in public discussion. Women, for example, were recently discovered as a 'new' target group of the game industry. Differences are proposed with respect to the previous 'standard' player in terms of both genre preferences and style of play. The known 'stereotyped' (Griffiths et al., 2003) (mostly young) male gamer can be seen as a counter-model here.

In fact, our data also reveal differences between men and women. Overall, women, consistent with their image constituting a 'new' player group (see Table 5.6), have been engaged in online gaming for a shorter period of time than men. Nearly 18 per cent of female players are 'newbies' who have been playing for less than one year, more than twice the proportion of their male counterparts. More than 70 per cent of the interviewed women have played online for less than three years, compared with less than 50 per cent of men. Compared with female

Table 5.6 Online gaming experience, differentiated by gender (weighted)

Sex	Experience in online gaming			
	<1 year	1–3 years	3–5 years	>5 years
Men	8.2%	39.9%	21.6%	30.4%
Women	17.8%	54.7%	17.8%	9.8%
Total	11.3%	44.7%	20.3%	23.7%

χ^2-Test: $p<0.0005$; $N=688$.

Table 5.7 Played online genres, differentiated by sex (weighted)

Sex	Men (%)	Women (%)	Total (%)
Genre			
Role-playing games**	62.9	79.5	68.3
Action games**	57.8	21.0	45.8
Strategy games***	37.1	32.1	35.5*
Sports and racing games**	16.4	8.9	14.0*

* Different from the data in Table 5.3 because of weighting and rounding differences in the χ^2-Test.
** χ^2-Test: $p<0.01$; ***n.s., $p=0.2$; $N=688$ ($N_m=464$, $N_w=224$).

gamers, more than three times as many men have more than five years of online gaming experience (more than 30 per cent of men vs less than 10 per cent of women).

In this respect, the data confirm existing assumptions. However, a closer look at the data regarding average weekly playing time reveals some interesting and somewhat counter-intuitive points. Female players, with 22.9 hours' average playing time per week, are clearly ahead of men, with 18.3 hours.[10] At first glance, this appears to contradict the stereotypes of the male 'hardcore gamer' and the female 'casual gamer'. However, it is important to bear in mind the different usage data obtained for different genres. In fact, the different playing times of men and women indicate markedly different genre preferences (see Table 5.7).

Particularly striking in this respect are online role-playing games and online action games. The former are much more popular among women than among men. Almost 80 per cent of the questioned female gamers play this genre, compared to only about 60 per cent of men. In addition, whereas 60 per cent of the male participants play action games online, little more than 20 per cent of women do the same. Because women constitute a much smaller group of players than men, in absolute numbers the latter difference is even more pronounced. In this respect, one can say that action games, especially the favoured ego-shooters such as *CS* or *Battlefield*, are a domain almost exclusively occupied by men.

In contrast, strategy games are almost equally accepted by both genders (differences are not significant). In considering sports games, men are again predominant, although the database of women players is comparatively small (i.e. the results should be treated with caution, despite the significant χ^2-Test, given the low number of cases in the relevant cells).

While the observed differences in genre preferences were somewhat expected, the analyses on interrelations between 'real life' and virtual game yielded a number of surprises. The data barely indicate any gender-specific differences in the intensity of entering into virtual worlds and thereby the development of dependencies. In fact, no significant difference was observed between men and women in many other items either. In view of the number of cases under analysis, this result is remarkable. Only two items ('the anticipation to gaming' and 'not letting down fellow players') produce differences among males and females at a high level of significance ($p \leq 0.001$). Nevertheless, the measured effects are low. On average, the degree of agreement with the statement is slightly higher among women (in the first item, $M = 2.14$ vs 2.49; in the second, $M = 2.45$ vs 2.76). This result could tentatively be interpreted as indicating a slightly higher social orientation among women. Nevertheless, and speaking generally, the responses of men and women to these items show barely any significant differences.

In summary, it is possible to state that on average women select different games from those selected by men. This can, for example, lead to differences in the extent of game use. However, if one considers the effects of gaming on everyday life, these seem to be evaluated somewhat similarly by male and female players, despite the differences in their genre preferences.

Group comparisons II: Age differentiation

As explained above, the description of computer players is commonly connected with the stereotype of the adolescent gamer, whereas ACTA data demonstrate that older players make up a substantial proportion of the gaming community. To date, few studies have considered older players (e.g. Quandt et al., 2009). In the present study, we obtained data on older players, thereby enabling group comparisons with younger players. The comparisons yield few differences. For example, there is no clear difference in playing time: the group of oldest players (40 years

Table 5.8 Played online genres, differentiating adults vs adolescents (weighted)

Age group	Adults (18+ years) (%)	Adolescents (14–17 years) (%)	Total (%)
Genre			
Role-playing games**	68.7	65.3	68.3
Action games**	44.0	60.0	45.8
Strategy games**	35.1	37.3	35.4
Sports and racing games**	14.2	11.8	14.0*

Differences compared with Table 5.3 occur because of weighting and rounding differences in the χ^2-Test.
* χ^2-Test: p = 0.009; **n.s., p > 0.5; N = 687/8, N_{adults} = 612/13, $N_{adolescents}$ = 75/6, (varying N is due to case weights and rounding).

and above) might spend marginally less time on gaming than other groups (i.e. 40+ years: 17.6 hours; 14–19 years: 19.0 hours; 20–29 years: 19.8 hours; 30–39 years: 23.0 hours), but there exists no clear, linear relation between age and playing time when considering the weighted data. The differences are not significant.[11]

A more detailed age differentiation (e.g. distinguishing between adult and adolescent players) does not change the picture at first: few differences arise. This applies to both playing time and most other variable groups, such as items regarding the connection between the real world and the game world.[12] Even when considering game preferences, we find fewer differences with age than might be expected (see Table 5.8). Clear and significant differences between young people and adults are observed only for action games. Within the questioned groups, there are proportionately more action players among the 14- to 17-year-olds than among the adults. Thus, 60 per cent of young persons play online action games compared with just 44 per cent of adults.

This aberration in genre preferences is also reflected in data regarding favourite games (see Table 5.4). A total of 43.4 per cent of adolescent gamers name *CS* as one of their favourite games, followed by *WoW* (33.7 per cent), the *Warcraft Strategy* series (22.8 per cent), and the action role-playing game, *Guild Wars* (17.4 per cent). One must add, however, that although almost all of the titles in the *CS* series are restricted to those aged 16 years or over, the games is often played by younger gamers. Moreover, some of the adolescents mentioned titles that they are not legally old enough to play. It is valid to ask whether the heated debate concerning the prohibition of *CS* is somewhat counterproductive, contributing to the popularity of the series among young players. It is clear that existing age restrictions are largely ineffective, either because young people are still able to buy the titles in shops or, for example, because they can obtain them illegally over peer-to-peer networks.

Discussion: Ways of playing online

Online computer games such as the showcase role-playing game, *WoW*, the much-discussed Second Life, and the controversial shooter *CS* have generated a seemingly never-ending discussion within the news media. Public discussion is increasingly realising that network-based multiplayer games are not a niche phenomenon for nerds, but a widely used leisure activity. User data (e.g. ACTA data) reveal that considerable segments of the population already play online games. Moreover, some of the stereotypes about online gamers need to be discarded: according to ACTA, one-third of online players are female, and older players are making an increasing contribution to the online gaming community.

The significance of online gaming does not solely result from the scale of the respective user groups. The present survey shows that online playing is time-consuming. With an average of nearly 18 hours per week, the time spent on online games exceeds that spent in many other forms of media use. Moreover, in many respects the social activity within online gaming creates stronger user loyalty than do other forms of media use. The results of the present survey provide a diverse range of indications of social inclusion within online games. Players organize themselves within groups (e.g. clans or guilds) that are similar to clubs. They feel socially engaged to their fellow players and look forward to the virtual game world and their 'friends' when not playing. This clearly shows that online games are social games that draw their attraction from their interpersonal interactivity. On the other hand, this leads to an increasing engagement within the gaming world that can interfere with engagements in the 'real world'. Thus, frequent players, who spend a considerable part of their free time playing, are not isolated cases.

Considering such excessive ways of playing, it seems legitimate to discuss possible forms of gaming addiction. However, one must bear in mind that quite a number of the frequent players are unemployed and hence occupy their unused time with gaming. Some of the respondents stated that they regretted having so much free time and that they preferred doing something other than online gaming (in response to the qualitative items in the questionnaire). In this respect, one can assume that excessive gaming is not the primary cause of problematic life conditions; instead, the opposite is true: people try to compensate for their living situation by playing games. Excessive gaming has the potential to become a permanent problem because it is extremely time-consuming and thereby inhibits any improvements in the real life situation (as no time is available for other activities).

There exist other remarkable differences between the different player groups. For example, men and women differ in terms of a diverse range of gaming parameters. These differences can basically be traced back to contrasting genre preferences: while women prefer role-playing games, men prefer network-based shooters and online action games. Age also plays a role here, as younger players prefer action games. This trend creates problems, as many age-restricted games, especially in the action genre, are inappropriate to adolescents.

Despite these differences, we note that overall, the identified groups of online players are somewhat homogeneous. Even with the large sample size, many items showed no significant differences between subgroups, perhaps reflecting the fact that online gaming allows for only a specific set of possibilities. In many cases, the players must yield to a specific game logic. For example, role-playing games are extremely time-consuming, so one needs to spend a certain amount of time online to obtain a joyful and successful game experience. However, the overview data presented above provide only the first indications of 'ways of playing' online games.

Conclusion and implications

The overview data presented in this study provide the first indications of different types of online gamer. To identify types of player independently of game genre, increasingly differentiated analyses are required. The data at hand certainly enable more detailed analyses. The available basic data also encourage further investigations of online gaming. Profitable areas of study would be the phenomenon of 'extreme' players (based on the time spent playing per week), and groups of action players, who are also clearly deviants in their socio-demographical parameters. Moreover, it would seem plausible that a time-consuming and involving activity such as online gaming, in combination with the social engagement of its players referred to above, would have an impact on players' lives. In this respect, it would be beneficial to focus more intensely on the interconnections between real life and the virtual world.

The present study sheds no light on whether the consequences of excessive gaming on the players' lives are limited to the individual her- or himself or can be viewed as being positive or negative for families, peer groups, and society at large. However, when considering a mass phenomenon such as online gaming, society – and indeed those in communication studies – is well advised to undertake additional investigations in this field.

Notes

1. ACTA is a representative study, "Allensbacher Computer- und Telekommunikations- Analyse" [Computer and Telecommunications Analysis of Allensbach].
2. MMORPGs such as *WoW* include complex control systems that sanction or stigmatize certain forms of killing. These norms are partially programmed into the game, and in part arise from the social contexts in the virtual worlds themselves (e.g. there are frequent reports of 'police troops' chasing 'player-killers' in online role-playing games). In contrast, the killing of opponents is not only allowed but strongly supported by the game rules in PvP (Player versus Player) modes (in *WoW*, dedicated PvP servers exist for users who wish to play the game according to such a rule set).
3. We would like to thank our students – Carolin Friedel, Manuel Futterer, Martin Haldenmair, Thomas Liesch, and Ilona Momot – for their support in performing this task.
4. For persons under the age of 18, the variable 'with/without school-leaving exam' is (in almost all cases) no criterion for differentiation. However, an alternative additional differentiation (e.g. via school type) was not included for pragmatic reasons and because of theoretical considerations (being a different construct; furthermore, the meaning is different for adults and adolescents).
5. However, we should not be misled by the overall percentages in the different age groups. When the quota groups were formed, we followed the ACTA distribution. The older age segments have a much larger age range than the younger ones, so this partially explains the high percentage of older players.
6. We thank Ilse Johnen, Florian Schneider, and Sven Jöckel and his team for their support in carrying out the survey. We would also like to thank the relevant magazines, online publications and forums, as well as the management of the Games Convention, who made it possible for us to reach large groups of gamers.
7. An alternative option would have been to recruit the players (gamers) via their primary activity (i.e. the gaming itself); i.e., to get in touch with the gamers online, in *WoW*. This method has been successfully implemented by other researchers (e.g. Kolo and Baur, 2004), although for the purposes of a survey-based study this approach appears excessively time-consuming.
8. Indeed, our study revealed that several (especially older) gamers initially mistakenly assumed that they were playing online, based on the fact that their PC had Internet access. However, they soon discovered their mistake when completing the questionnaire. These persons, or rather their questionnaires, were of course excluded from the analysis.
9. This indication was collected separately, in a different part of the questionnaire to that in which data were collected concerning individual genres. Also, the 'general' data should not be viewed as a sum of the individual genres: because gamers play partly in multiple genres in different compositions, the

values for individual genres can be higher than those for online gaming in general.
10. These differences are highly significant, which however is to be expected given the number of cases ($N_m = 456$, $N_w = 224$; Welch's t-Test: p = .004).
11. ANOVA, Welch and Games-Howell post-hoc tests (as the Levene test was significant after applying the case weights). The p values were above the 5% level in all cases, also in the pairwise Games-Howell post-hoc tests.
12. No significant differences were found, apart from a single exception: when asked if one is still occupied with the gaming world when not gaming, the agreement from adolescents is significantly higher than that from adults. (M = 3.46 vs. 3.82, p = .006); however, the strength of the effect is rather small, insofar it should be emphasized just how similar the two groups are.

References

Asgari, M. (2005): A three-factor model of motivation and game design. http://www.gamesconference.org/digra2005/viewabstract.php?id = 269 (accessed on 15 November 2008).
Bartle, R.A. (1996): Hearts, clubs, diamonds, spades – players who suit MUDs. http://www.mud.co.uk/richard/hcds.htm (accessed on 15 November 2008).
Castranova, E. (2005): Synthetic worlds: The business and culture of online games. Chicago: The University of Chicago Press.
Cypra, O. (2005): Warum spielen Menschen in virtuellen Welten? Eine empirische Untersuchung zu Online-Rollenspielen und ihren Nutzern. University of Mainz, Germany, unpublished M.A. thesis.
Ducheneaut, N., Yee, N., Nickell, E. & Moore, R.J. (2006): 'Alone together?' Exploring the social dynamics of massively multiplayer online games. In: Conference Proceedings on Human Factors in Computing Systems CHI 2006, 22–27 April 2006, Montreal, PQ, Canada, 407–16. http://www.nickyee.com/pubs/Ducheneaut,%20Yee,%20Nickell,%20Moore%20-%20Alone%20Together%20(2006).pdf (accessed on 15 November 2008).
Fritz, J. (2003): Computerspiele, logisch einfach, technisch verwirrend, sozial komplex. Was unter Computerspielen verstanden und wie man mit ihnen umgehen wird. In: J. Fritz & W. Fehr (Hrsg.): Computerspiele - Virtuelle Spiel- und Lernwelten. Medienpädagogik. Bonn: Bundeszentrale für politische Bildung.
Götzenbrucker, G. (2001): Soziale Netzwerke und Internet-Spielewelten. Eine empirische Analyse der Transformation virtueller in realweltliche Gemeinschaften. Opladen/Wiesbaden: Westdeutscher Verlag.
Griffiths, M.D., Davies, M. & Chappell, D. (2003): Breaking the stereotype: The case of online gaming. *CyberPsychology and Behavior*, 6(1): 81–96.
Griffiths, M.D., Davies, M. & Chappell, D. (2004a): Online computer gaming: a comparison of adolescent and adult gamers. *Journal of Adolescence*, 27: 87–96.
Griffiths, M.D., Davies, M. & Chappell, D. (2004b): Demographic factors and playing variables in online computer gaming. *CyberPsychology and Behavior*, 7(4): 479–87.
Keegan, M. (1997): A classification of MUDs. *Journal of MUD Research*, 2(2). http://www.brandeis.edu/pubs/jove/HTML/v2/keegan.html (accessed on 15 November 2008).

Kolo, C. & Bauer, T. (2004): Living a virtual life: Social dynamics of online gaming. *Gamestudies*, 4(1). http://www.gamestudies.org/0401/kolo/ (accessed on 15 November 2007).

Quandt, T., Grüninger, H. & Wimmer, J. (2009): The grey haired gaming generation: Findings from an explorative interview study on older computer gamers. *Games and Culture*, 4(1): 27–46.

Yee, N. (2002a): Ariadne. Understanding MMORPG addiction. http://www.nickyee.com/hub/addiction/home.html (accessed on 15 November 2008).

Yee, N. (2002b): Codename blue: An ongoing study of MMORPG players. http://www.nickyee.com/codeblue/Report.PDF (accessed on 15 November 2008).

Yee, N. (2002c): Five motivation factors for why people play MMORPGs. http://www.nickyee.com/facets/home.html (accessed on 15 November 2008).

Yee, N. (2003): Gender and age distribution. http://www.nickyee.com/daedalus/archives/000194.php (accessed on 15 November 2008).

Yee, N. (2005): Motivations of play in MMORPGs. http://www.gamesconference.org/digra2005/viewabstrac (accessed on 15 November 2008).

6
The Sexi(e)st of All: Avatars, Gender, and Online Games

Mia Consalvo and Todd Harper

Introduction

Chain-mail bikinis, boob sliders, and Barbie-like physiques. Female avatars in MMO games would seem to be the equivalent of pinup Playboy bunnies, constructed solely for male players' pleasure. Yet women players choose female avatars almost exclusively, and regularly talk of their joy in creating powerful, creative, dangerous characters. Those joys are not temporary either: other researchers have found that among heavy MMO players, women tend to play more hours than men do, and they are less likely than men to plan to quit playing (Williams, Consalvo, Caplan, and Yee, 2008). But do women enjoy such representations, or merely tolerate them as a flawed part of their gameplay experience? Perhaps different groups of women feel differently, with factors such as play style, player type, MMO experience, and demographic differences such as age or sexuality playing a role. And what of the gear that games provide for avatars, in all its multiple representations? Is it simply a stat-enhancing tool, or something more? These are some of the questions that drove us to explore more deeply how and why women choose their avatars and the ways in which they can now customize them, including avatar creation options, in-game barber shops, and increasingly through gear.

Women are an increasingly important part of the gameplaying demographic. In some areas, such as in casual games, they dominate the player base, while in others they have achieved parity, such as in the number of active Nintendo DS owners (Dromgoole, 2008). Women have always played MMO games, historically representing 10 to 20 per cent of players. That proportion continues in contemporary MMOs, which tend to draw older players with more education (as compared to traditional console gamers) to their spaces (Yee, 2006).

This chapter focuses on the players of two such fantasy-themed MMO games which were released in the past four years. We chose those games for their popularity, in the first case, and the extensive level of avatar customization offered, in the second. The first, *World of Warcraft* (*WoW*), was released in 2004, and surpassed all sales expectations, currently boasting more than 11 million players globally (Smith, 2008). Featuring a heavily stylized, colourful world with perpetual strife between the Horde and the Alliance, *WoW* offers players an array of potential avatars, including humans, elves, orcs, trolls, and gnomes, among others. All avatars can either be male or female, and feature no sex-based differences in terms of skills, playable classes, or starting abilities or traits. With the recent release of its expansion pack *Wrath of the Lich King*, players can level avatars to 80, explore increasingly expansive regions, participate in epic raids, duel with other players, and generally enjoy the lore of the world.

Age of Conan (*AoC*) was heavily promoted as the first 'adult-themed' MMO prior to its 2008 release, earning an M-rating for its gore as well as its nudity. Based on the fictional world of Hyboria and drawing from the lore of the Conan novels, the game initially sold quite well, shipping more than 700,000 copies. Yet the game's many glitches and bugs, as well as extremely demanding hardware requirements, have resulted in mergers of some game servers to consolidate smaller than expected player populations, with some sources speculating that only 10 per cent of original sales have resulted in ongoing subscribers (Johnson, 2008). Stylistically, the game is more realistic in terms of its design – avatars all resemble real-life humans, differing only in skin tones and body markings. An early difference in attack damage by male and female avatars has been designated a bug, with no other differences apparent. Players can create characters that are one of four archetypes – priest, soldier, rogue, and mage. The world of Hyboria is less cartoon-like and grittier than *WoW*, with character and world designs that are much more detailed in appearance.

In terms of this research project, an important point of comparison between the two games lies in their character creation screens. Players of *WoW* can choose whether their avatars are male or female, what race and class combination they would like, and then can customize appearance with various hair styles, skin tone, faces, and limited other options depending on race; for example, night elf females choose facial markings, while the minotaur-like tauren can alter the size and shape of their horns. Players of *AoC* can likewise choose gender, race, and class, but then they are given multiple customization options for features such as eye shape and colour, skin colour, skin markings, hair style, hair colour, body type, height, relative weight, bust size, facial shape, and limb length.

Naturally, avatar creation options are critical areas of study, but there has been little work on their importance relative to other factors, such as how appearance relates to in-game accomplishments or what players think of options to modify avatars when starting a game or throughout the course of their gameplay. So far, we know that avatars are important to players, and female players are somewhat different in how they design and play their avatars compared to male players. For example, Yee reports that men are four times as likely as women to create a character of the opposite gender, suggesting women prefer to play female avatars. Women are also more likely to devote the majority of their time to one character, and (perhaps as a result) they are more likely than male players to have at least one avatar at the maximum level. However, women do not focus solely on one character – they also have more characters on average than male players (Yee, 2008).

Past research such as Taylor's study of *Everquest* players (2006) has also found that women enjoy playing MMO games, but that enjoyment often occurred in spite of the character design – hypersexualized avatars wearing the stereotypical plate-mail bikini. Yet most research on this topic has not accounted for how players might feel about their avatars relative to *both* avatar and gear design. To explore that duality, this study examines players' reactions to representations of female and male avatars in *WoW* and *AoC*. We focus not only on avatar design, but gear design and function as well. Gear carries multiple meanings: it is a stat-enhancing device that gives a player a material advantage in combat, it advertises the achievements of a player to others in the game world, and it is also (potentially) aesthetically pleasing. Yet we know little of how players react to gear, or negotiate those multiple meanings in their gameplay, particularly when gear is also designed to appear differently on male and female avatars. To do so, we interviewed players from each game about their avatars, including the visual presentations of their bodies, armour and clothes. This is the first study to do a cross-MMO comparison of avatars, as well as to focus on both avatar bodies and gear, giving us better insights into how MMO games construct the feminine and masculine forms in different fantasy worlds.

Relevant literature

Several issues are at play in the present study, and we must therefore look at different bodies of work related to gender and games. Past work addressing representations of game characters has mostly focused on single-player and offline games, and has not addressed the issue of how gear with gameplay-related statistics is related to character appearance, or how male or female appearance could change when wearing the same outfit or gear. But, overall, content analyses of videogame characters have painted a fairly consistent picture of the differences between male and female characters. In her study of gender stereotyping in games, Dietz found that when women characters were present, they were usually sexualized through clothing or appearance (1998: pp. 434–5). Beasley and Collins-Standley likewise found that if women were present at all, there was a significant sex bias in how male and female characters were portrayed (2002). In a study specifically addressing hyper-sexuality in videogame characters, Downs and Smith found females to be significantly more likely to be depicted as partially nude, shown wearing sexually revealing clothing, and with an unrealistic body image (2004). Finally, Jansz and Martis performed a content analysis on the introductory movies in a dozen popular games, finding that, again, female characters were portrayed as hyper-sexualized and sex objects, even if a few were portrayed in leadership roles (2007).

Qualitative studies have similarly addressed the issue of gender, with analyses of game content focusing on particular videogame heroines such as Lara Croft of the *Tomb Raider* series (Kennedy, 2002; Mikula, 2003; Pretzsch, 2000) and games involving the television heroine, Buffy the Vampire Slayer (Krzywinska, 2003; Labre and Duke, 2004). That work draws many of the same conclusions as content analyses do, pointing to hyper-sexualized avatars, yet researchers do also point out how the performativity of the player changes the dynamic of play as the avatar moves from static object to dynamic agent. Thus, while Lara resembles a pin-up model, it is her agency that carries the game forward, and players can take pleasure and gain a sense of mastery as they drive the game onwards as Lara. However, even as some work points to the agency of the player, there is little or no discussion of how gear, clothing, or fashion might be related to gameplay considerations.

How female players themselves feel about portrayals of their avatars and characters is also important to note. Taylor's early work on adult female players of MMOs is a useful starting point for exploring how women feel about various aspects of MMO gameplay in particular, as opposed to single-player games (2006). Seeking to focus on players of *EverQuest*, Taylor wrote about the women's 'multiple pleasures' in the game. Thus, far from being solely concerned with socializing, the women she talked to also enjoyed the power and mastery associated with levelling their avatars, engaging in high-level end-game activities, and achieving various goals they had set for themselves. Taylor writes that these women appeared to enjoy the game despite sexist imagery they acknowledged was present, as they felt they were not the target audience for the game.

Kerr's study of women players in Ireland reported similar findings, as women enjoyed playing a variety of genres of game, going beyond the stereotypical puzzle or casual games ascribed to female gamers (2003). Likewise, women said they enjoyed the freedom afforded to them by games, and those who were committed players were also likely to be technologically proficient, and not to view games as part of masculine culture. Lucas and Sherry (2004) examined gaming and gender from a uses and gratifications perspective, arguing that women gamers may avoid gameplay because available games don't offer experiences that give them a feeling of control and efficacy in play.

Royse, Lee, Undrahbuyan, Hopson, and Consalvo also found that adult female gamers of all types enjoyed the feelings of mastery and control they experienced while playing games, yet for women who did not play at all, games were thought of as a masculine domain, of little interest to them (2007). Finally, a recent survey of *EverQuest 2* players by Williams, Consalvo, Caplan, and Yee (2008) found conflicting results – that for women being social was a primary motivator for playing, yet the 'hardest of the hardcore' – that is, the people who play the most – were women, who were also more likely than male players to underestimate how much time they spent playing the game. But again, no one has explored the feelings and attitudes of women gamers in relation to avatar appearance beyond basic representations, even as gear in MMOs has become a critical element for avatar advancement as well as a mark of status in most game worlds.

Method

To explore women players' experiences with gender and avatars directly, we interviewed a number of players of both *WoW* and *AoC*. Respondents were recruited on the Web, from posts on the official forums for both games, from womengamers.com, from a Livejournal community for women *WoW* players (wow_ladies), and through the forums of online feminist gaming magazine, *Cerise*. Our initial call for players of either game aged 18 to 69 resulted in a large pool, from which 14 were selected for interviewing. Respondents ranged in age from 20 to 45, and their average age was 28.

Interviews were primarily conducted via the Internet, using voice-over-IP (VoIP) technologies such as Skype and Ventrilo. A small number were conducted by standard telephone, and two were text conversations (one instant messenger, one email). Voice interviews were recorded for transcription and review purposes, while the Instant Messaging (IM) conversation was logged and stored. Each respondent was assigned a pseudonym to maintain confidentiality. In addition, respondents were asked to provide a screenshot of their 'main' (primary avatar), which most opted to do.

Respondents came from a variety of backgrounds, with a number living outside the United States, including players from the United Kingdom and Germany. For the most part, the response pool favoured *WoW* players, though *AoC* had some representation. In addition, respondents brought experiences from a number of other MMOs to the table as well, including *Guild Wars, Star Wars Galaxies, Final Fantasy XI, City of Heroes*, and *Ultima Online*.[1]

Findings

Our findings support a growing body of research that suggests women gamers are decidedly not monolithic in their desires and activities, and that many of the early differences found between male and female gameplayers were probably due to length of time playing games rather than to gender-based differences in their styles or interests. However, there are some differences that seem to persist, which we discuss next. It is important to note, though, that while we have found that women do appear to pick same-sex avatars more frequently than men do, no research has yet examined male players' attitudes toward gear or fashion in MMO games. In general, then, our findings focus on two aspects of the in-game avatar: the creation and selection of the body, and managing the appearance of the character, be it through equipment/gear or other avenues.

As stated, the majority of our interviewees played *WoW*, with two of them also having tried *AoC*. Another interviewee had played *WoW* for two years and then quit *WoW* to play *AoC* full time, which she had played for five months at the time of the interview. Most had been playing MMO games for at least a year, with the shortest time being four months and the longest over two years. Playing time ranged from 5 to 40 hours a week, with most players reporting 8 to 15 hours a week on average. Almost everyone we talked to had at least one character at the maximum level (at the time of the interviews, 70 for *WoW*, 80 for *AoC*), if not more. Players cited many routes into the game, including heterosexual partners, friends, and their own research about the game. None had immediate plans to quit, although some players acknowledged that their playing schedules could change in the future, due to various life changes.

Body creation and selection

In relation to the selection of avatars, one commonality was evident among those we interviewed: everyone across both games had a female main avatar. Those mains took many different forms, including almost equal distributions of Horde and Alliance characters in *WoW* and the three races (Stygian, Aquilonian, Cimmerian) in *AoC*, as well as a variety of classes that cut across fighting, casting, support, and stealth jobs. The diversity alone is noteworthy, as women chose avatar bodies that ranged from the conventionally beautiful to the decidedly unfeminine, and likewise played classes that ranged from front-line fighters, through casters, to support and solo jobs. Players reported a variety of reasons for choosing their particular avatars, which were sometimes at odds with the rationalizations of other players. For example, players who chose Horde races or stereotypically less feminine avatars reported wanting to create 'different'- or 'strong'-looking characters who would be truly distinct from 'real life' representations of women. Alternatively, some respondents felt that most players preferred 'pretty avatars', evinced by the fact that races such as blood and night elves were so popular, while female troll and orc avatars were quite rare in the game world. Overall, in both games, women related their enjoyment to being able to experiment with different types of character, either for how different races and job classes looked or functioned or for their roleplaying potential, or simply to serve as 'bank alts' that looked interesting. In addition to their mains, women had created a multiplicity of characters (numbers varied across respondents), the majority of those alt characters being female too, although several respondents did say they had some male characters on their accounts.

Women offered different reasons for their choice of female mains as well as their predominantly female alt characters. Several women explained, as Clara did, that 'I really identify more with them [female characters] than I do [with] the males'. Likewise, Kyouran added: 'If I'm able to choose the gender and appearance of the character I'll be living through vicariously, it might as well be one that I would actually like to embody in one way or another'. One player of *WoW*, Noelove, mentioned that she chose one of the more fantasy-like races available – a tauren female – because she felt that body was like hers: 'I picked a tauren after looking at all the other characters, because I found her body style to be incredibly similar to my own. I'm...a...38-30-38 built woman, so I'm very curvaceous,

I'm tall... I thought that she kind of represented me best'. Interestingly, Noelove also mentioned that when she plays other characters – such as her male orc shaman – she feels an increasing level of distance between her and the avatar; in a way, the less like her the avatar became, the more like a puppet it was.

Of course, not all the players felt strongly about identifying with their avatars, citing instead the ugliness of male character designs as reasons for not choosing them. This appeared to be a common complaint, whether or not players felt strongly about playing female characters. This was most evident with players of *WoW* – where designs were more fantastic and races were often not 'traditional' humans in appearance. Players described male character designs as 'odd', 'horrible', 'too beefy', 'ugly', and 'too comic book stereotypical'. This held across various races, with different players voicing their particular displeasures with certain designs – such as human males being too beefy, or male orcs looking too stereotypically designed. One player wondered why the less fantastic races in *WoW* – humans, night and blood elves, and dwarves – were all Caucasians, leaving only the more esoteric-looking races (dranei, orcs, trolls, undead, tauren) marked as non-white. Interestingly, an *AoC* player cited the diversity of races in the game as a draw, where all races are humanoid yet offer a variety of skin tones.

Equipment and avatar customization

Another point of convergence among women was a consensus that the options presented in *WoW* in terms of character design were too limited. Players wanted greater options for hairstyles and hair colour, facial design as well as additional elements such as skin tone and character animations (including dances, gestures, and movements). Several women reported playing with the recently added 'barbershop' function in *WoW*, which allows players to change a character's hairstyle and some race-specific markings, for a small fee. However, some players complained the choices were merely reworked designs from other races, or were not extensive enough to make a real difference. As Zzora explained, 'all the hairstyles for Trolls look very weird. They are short hair, and I just generally don't like them. I think there should just be more... I think there's eight blood elf faces but only four troll faces. So I don't know if I ever wanted to create a second female troll I'd probably be stumped on how to design her'.

Most respondents also identified a desire to be able to shift body types: taller/shorter, broader/thinner, less/more muscular, etc. A few people identified that this was especially problematic in terms of class; for example, a bulky warrior is believable but a super-muscled mage or priest seems out of place. Sarita, for example, expressed a desire for physically active classes (such as warriors) to 'build up muscle' as they advanced, as compared to casters, who would stay relatively slim, based on their more cerebral choice of profession. Audri expressed a similar sentiment: 'If I could add a customization option in general to *WoW*, I would add the ability to change your character's build, so that if you were a tank, and you were a warrior, you could get that more muscle-y, macho-looking build. But if you were going to play a mage, you could choose an aesthetic more typical to a mage'. Itsy Bitsy made the comparison to *Oblivion*, another favourite game of hers: 'If you play *WoW* and you play, you know, an orc, then you're a big, burly, beefy orc. If you play an undead you're skinny and skeletal, and if you play a blood elf you're an anorexic heroin chick. Doesn't matter, it's what you play'. She then described the many ways in which *Oblivion* lets the player customize his or her avatar, down to minutiae such as facial bone structure. However, she notes that technological limitations in *WoW* might make that scale of customization impossible.

Reactions to avatar designs in *AoC* were mixed. Those who didn't like the game cited darker designs and less variety offered; all races in *AoC* are human, with no fantasy races. Yet for those who did actively play and enjoy the game, the level of customization was a clear draw. Kyouran talked of 'drooling all over again when I saw the degree to which I was able to customize my characters – 26 sliders just for facial adjustments; ability to change the height, voice, body type, etc. This was something I had always wanted in a game, and I spent hours fiddling with it'. Players who had stopped playing other games such as *City of Heroes* and *Second Life* in order to concentrate on *WoW* ironically cited those past experiences as offering better choices for avatar creation. However, unlike Kyouran, the opportunity to customize was clearly not a deal-breaker; while missed, a more limited offering of character designs was simply not a good enough reason to quit playing *WoW*. Even Kyouran cited her growing dissatisfaction with *WoW*'s gameplay elements as a central reason for leaving, just as Clara, who explored Second Life, said she disliked the virtual world for its lack of clear goals.

Likewise, Raven is also a player of *Guild Wars*, and spoke about that game's more enjoyable system of armour and clothing – 'You buy armour sets, not individual pieces' – that let her create outfits that matched. The tendency of *WoW* to produce avatars wearing mismatched colours or textures was of concern to many respondents. However, players of *WoW* noted that mismatched armour was sometimes just part of the game, a consequence of levelling up that happens to everyone; Itsy Bitsy commented that upon reaching a certain area in *WoW*, all the players who wear cloth armour effectively look like 'a hobo wearing a clown suit'. In response, some expressed a desire that characters with crafting professions such as tailoring be given the ability to have their clothing altered; Raven in particular was a proponent of the dye system used in *Guild Wars* to change the colour of armour so that sets would match.

Participants also talked of the differences between male and female characters comparatively, referencing both avatar design and how gear was designed to look on both types of character. One issue in particular was how various pieces of armour in *WoW* might look different depending on the gender of the wearer; for example, how a full breastplate on a male avatar might be no more than a metal bikini top on a female one. For example, Zzora remarked that 'I'm not repressed or anything like that, but I think it's a little sexist'. However, Zzora also laughed while saying so, indicating that the matter was perhaps not as problematic as other aspects of the game.

Indeed, a number of players interviewed were not troubled. The reasons why are varied; some cite the fantasy milieu and its tropes as an unavoidable cause of such things, while others recognize that they enjoy the sexy appearance and want their characters to be attractive. Audri notes: 'I know a lot of people have issues with the way that, say, a shirt will be a full breastplate on a male and it'll only cover...the boobs on the female. But that doesn't really bother me so much, because...if you're really bothered by it, put a shirt on under it and a tabard over it. But it's a high-fantasy game, and if you look at high-fantasy art and you know anything about it, the women are always skimpily dressed. That's just how it is. It's never bothered me'.

Yet it is important to note that while respondents claimed not to care, they were also quick to note that they perceived they 'should care' in some way. Raven, for example, said that *WoW* was probably designed with a male audience in mind, 'but on the other hand, like I said, I kind of like playing characters that I think look sexy as well...I dunno. It...I sort of feel like it should bother me. But it doesn't'. Speculation on reasons why follow in the conclusions. Overall, however, the responses of those interviewed suggest they believe that the sexualized content is simply an inevitable consequence of the games' genre and origin, as well as a perception of a male target audience. While gendered and sexualized avatar appearance was something to which they've given thought, these players appear to accept it as part of the experience.

For some, there are far larger issues of misogyny or sexism than of equipment. Rachel expressed concerns about popular stereotypes of female players and a desire not to be 'that girl': a player of a female night elf who uses the 'dance' emote while standing on top of an in-game mailbox is her example. Audri spoke of a similar problem with the idea of the 'guild princess' stereotype: '[they are] using their femaleness, and the fact that they are female, to flirt around and convince everyone to fawn all over them, and give them gold and give them gear, and they never have to work for anything, and they always get given all of the good loot just because they're female'. For her, this is linked to the common stereotype that women don't have gaming skill – 'not only are you substandard at it, but you're using your feminine wiles to get ahead' – and these two stereotypes are both prevalent and far more troubling to her than differences in equipment. In contrast, Sarita mentioned how the less feminine avatars, such as orc and dwarf females, can be looked down upon by other players, indicating that perhaps 'someone's not comfortable [with] being female if they don't have the more fem characters'. Thus, while some avatars may receive too much attention for their feminine attributes, others receive another sort of attention for displaying too little femininity.

What is clear from most interviews, however, is that, in terms of equipment, gameplay and factors such as in-game statistics are ultimately more important than appearance. This was most clear when speaking with *WoW* 'raiders': players who engage in coordinated group play content, typically in groups of 10 or 25. A number of the players interviewed are either members of – or in a few cases leadership of – high-end raiding guilds, game-based social networks focused on high-level raid content. For those players, making a decision on which equipment to wear based on appearance was almost unthinkable. Itsy Bitsy was quite emphatic, when asked if she'd ever choose a statistically inferior piece of equipment because she liked the look more, that she would not: 'Never for raids. There're times when I've just endlessly bitched and moaned about things that looked horrible, like the Hood of Hexing, but I'm not going to wear something that's going to be statistically and performance-wise inferior to something else...it's like wearing gym clothes to the gym, and work clothes to work'. Other raiders were less emphatic but agreed that in a raiding environment statistics came first. The concept of different outfits for different play activities, as Itsy Bitsy suggested with the parallel to work clothing, did play out, however; most players said that they have a silly or pretty outfit that they wear during 'off time' when they're engaged primarily in social play rather than combat. Similarly, Red explained how, prior to raids, when groups were still gathering, 'I wear like an elegant pant suit and a hat that has what looks like a satellite dish on it, so yeah, we do dumb stuff like that'. Noelove described one such outfit in detail: 'My outfitter [an equipment-changing mod] would automatically switch me into a...level 20-something purple dress, with level 20-something purple shoulders, and a purple hat, and in my offhand I carried a bunch of wild flowers'. However, all made it clear that such outfits were something done for fun, outside of the more 'serious' play of raid content.

Finally, players expressed pride in certain pieces of gear, equating them to a badge of honour or accomplishment. That happened in several ways – raiders would point to equipment or sets that they wore which announced their success in participating in extremely difficult battles. The powerful equipment they won from raids showed to other players that they were highly accomplished; how it looked was less important than where it came from. In fact, one of Audri's primary complaints about equipment stemmed from just such a belief: 'The high-end arena gear and the high-end raiding gear looks the same. That bothers me, because I think they're two different skill sets, and they're two different types of accomplishment, and I think both the people who arena and the people who raid would be happy to have distinctive-looking sets, so that you look at somebody and [think], "Oh, they must have been 2000 rating in the last bracket"'. Noelove also drew great pride from being the first of her class on her server to complete a 'tier set' (a full set of themed/named armour) unique to her class. Likewise, crafters talked about the joy of fashioning their own gear and being able to wear something they had themselves created. Louise, for example, talked of being able to broadcast her accomplishments through what her avatar is wearing, even if she is not high-level: 'I take...satisfaction in wearing something that I was able to make or obtain through some amazing feat of skill'.

Conclusions and implications

Women who play MMO games such as *WoW* and *AoC* are clearly invested in their avatars, both in bodily appearance and in gear and clothing choices. Confirming trends that Yee (2006, 2008) has also reported, we found that women continue to prefer having female main avatars, although they can and do have male avatars in their extended roster of characters. The reasons for doing so were affirmative (wanting to play an avatar that resembled them in some way) as well as negative (disliking the design of male avatars). Yet the prevalence of such a choice is striking and notable, given that men still choose to play many male avatars, despite their 'ugly' or 'too stereotypical' appearances. Women do seem to be continually drawn to playing female avatars, across time and various MMO games. Thus game designers should be careful to include a range of such avatar types if they wish to continue to attract female MMO players.

Even though women regularly choose female avatars, their choices are not unproblematic, nor free of limitations. Several women expressed frustration at both the gear and the bodily design differences between male and female avatars, noting the fairly distinct sexual dimorphism of what are supposed to be fantasy races. At the same time, many players were careful to point out that such differences did not bother them, or that they didn't bother them to a large degree. It is difficult to know exactly how to interpret such statements, especially given past research indicating women players do not like hypersexual female avatars. It could be that women have grown to accept – if not welcome – such designs, which are now a familiar part of practically every fantasy-themed MMO game. Alternatively, women could be uncomfortable with such representations, yet feel that such dissatisfaction might be read as overly critical or 'too feminist' for them to identify with. For example, players often laughed when making such comments, or would qualify their statements with phrases such as 'maybe it's just me' or 'I'm far from a prude, but'. It could also be that women were happy (or happy enough) with the representations, but felt while talking to academic researchers about the topic that they should express some discontent with images that are popularly stereotyped as overly sexual. We cannot know for certain what the exact reasoning (or, more likely, multiple reasonings) is, but can only point to the potential for multiple interpretations of such findings.

Although players did find fault with game avatars, they also expressed great pride and interest in their creations, often creating histories and justifications for their characters that they sometimes attempted to imbue with a sense of personality over and above their own. As part of that, women also, as a group, wanted more customization options, to be able to create avatars more in line with their own desires. However, customization was not a deal-breaker – it was never something that a player said she would leave *WoW* over, and several players reported having left virtual worlds (*City of Heroes*, *Second Life*, *Guild Wars*) where greater customization was offered. Thus, such an element is an important part of gameplay, with at least some basic level of customization deemed necessary. However, beyond that level it became a discretionary aspect of the game world: desirable, but not a requirement.

In talking with players about gear, interesting distinctions emerged. It was something that players definitely noticed, and had given a great deal of thought to. Players were divided, however, in how they thought about gear. For those who were more inclined to raid or engage in competitive group-based activities, gear certainly had an aesthetic component, but first and foremost it was considered for its stat-enhancements: it might be ugly, but it was functionality that ultimately counted. In contrast, players who were not so invested in competitive aspects of gameplay could be more circumspect about their gear choices, sometimes choosing to ignore certain items because of their aesthetic. Yet no one admitted to preferring consistently suboptimal gear simply because it looked better. Clearly, gear might be less than pleasing to look at, especially in various combinations, but the women we talked to expressed clearly that *gear was gear* – equating it to work or gym clothes that were worn in order to get a particular job done. Interestingly, several women also confided that some of their male friends were just as, if not more, concerned with the look of gear as they were. We know of no studies which have talked to male players about fashion and gear in MMO games (or any digital games) and this would be an area ripe for analysis.

Finally, it is difficult, if not impossible, to make comparisons between the two games we drew players from for analysis, mainly because of the very small sample of *AoC* players we could recruit. But that number is in itself telling, as well as the comments of those few who did try *AoC* and did not like it. Thus, for example, we can say that even though *AoC* offered players far more detailed options for avatar customization and a world that is not 'cartoony' in any sense, players could not see past the sexism that was marketed as part of the experience of *AoC*. Even for players who might find *WoW*'s avatars acceptable or not too stereotypical, then a line was drawn between acceptable and unacceptable depictions of avatars and sexuality in MMOs. For those who tried but rejected *AoC*, the nudity, realism and gore were turn-offs, blocking them from further explorations of the game's potential. Yet, at the same time, the cartoonishness and avatar limitations of *WoW* were *not* enough to keep them from moving across. Of course, there will always be greater incentives to stay in a game than to leave and start all over somewhere new, but it is instructive to know that even if players wish for something, or wish for another practice to stop, they will often not take action to change their circumstances, unless and until they are thoroughly dissatisfied with their gameplay experiences.

Perhaps one of the more salient takeaways from this research is that the sexism or gendered nature of content is of less importance to the players interviewed than the ability to control characters and avatars that they saw as extensions of themselves. Certainly, this reflects much of what the literature considered above suggests: an avatar is definitely iconic, a potentially sexualized symbol, but part of it is also performance on the part of the player. Ultimately, what MMO game designers should consider is how best to give players the tools to make the experience their own, and it may be that players use their desire for customization as a way of managing and navigating a world of unavoidably sexualized content.

Note

1. We tried recruiting on forums geared especially to *Age of Conan* players as well as forums geared specifically to women players in order to find women who played *AoC*. However, our low yield rate in this regard mirrors player demographics for the game. Statistics released by game administrators on the *AoC* forums report that the player base is approximately 92 per cent male, in both the United States and Europe (Age of Conan Survey, 2008).

References

Age of Conan Survey. (2008). http://forums.ageofconan.com/showthread.php?t=176240

Beasley, B. & Collins-Standley, T. (2002). Shirts vs. Skins: Clothing as an indicator of gender role stereotyping in video games. *Mass Communication and Society*, 5(3): 279–93.

Dietz, T.L. (1998). An examination of violence and gender role portrayals in video games: Implications for gender socialization and aggressive behavior. *Sex Roles*, 38(5–6): 425–42.

Downs, E.P. & Smith, S. (2004). Keep abreast of hypersexuality: A video game character content analysis. Paper presented at the International Communication Association, New York.

Dromgoole, S. (August, 2008). Who are playing what games, where, and why. Paper presented at the EIF 2008, Edinburgh, Scotland.

Jansz, J. & Martis, R. (2007). The Lara phenomenon: Powerful female characters in video games. *Sex Roles*, 56: 141–8.

Johnson, B. (2008). *Age of Conan* desperate for subscribers. *Wowriot*. http://wowriot.gameriot.com/blogs/Epidemic-Obesity/Age-of-Conan-Desperate-for-Subscribers

Kennedy, H. (2002). Lara Croft: Feminist icon or cyberbimbo? On the limits of textual analysis. *Game Studies* 2: 2. http://www.gamestudies.org/0202/kennedy/

Kerr, A. (2003). (Girls) Women just want to have fun: A study of adult female players of digital games. Paper presented at the Level up: Digital Games Research Conference Utrecht, The Netherlands.

Krzywinska, T. (2003). Playing Buffy: Remediation, Occulted Meta-game-Physics and the Dynamics of Agency in the Videogame Version of Buffy the Vampire

Slayer. *Slayage: The Online International Journal of Buffy Studies*, 8(March). http://www.slayage.tv/essays/slayage8/Krzywinska.htm.

Labre, M. & Duke, L. (2004). Nothing like a brisk walk and a spot of demon slaughter to make a girl's night: The construction of the female hero in the Buffy video game. *Journal of Communication Inquire*, 28(2): 138–56.

Lucas, K. & Sherry, J. (2004). Sex differences in video game play: a communication-based explanation. *Communication Research*, 31(5): 499–523.

Mikula, M. (2003). Gender and videogames: The political valency of Lara Croft. *Continuum: Journal of Media & Cultural Studies*, 17(1): 79–87.

Pretzsch, B. (2000). *A Postmodern Analysis of Lara Croft: Body, Identity, Reality*. http://www.frauenuni.de/students/gendering/lara/LaraCompleteTextWOPics.html

Royse, P., Lee, J., Undrahbuyan, B., Hopson, M. & Consalvo, M. (2007). Women and games: technologies of the gendered self. *New Media & Society*, 9(4): 555–76.

Smith, M. (2008). WoW: The world's biggest game is about to get bigger. *Yahoo! Games*.

Taylor, T.L. (2006). *Play between worlds: Exploring online game culture*. Cambridge, Mass.: The MIT Press.

Williams, D., Consalvo, M., Caplan, S. & Yee, N. (2008). Women and Men at Play: Gender Differences in Motivations, Practices, and Intimate Relationships Among MMO Players. Association of Internet Researchers Conference, 15–18 October 2008, Copenhagen, Denmark.

Yee, N. (2006). The Demographics, Motivations and Derived Experiences of Users of Massively-Multiuser Online Graphical Environments. *PRESENCE: Teleoperators and Virtual Environments*, 15: 309–29.

Yee, N. (2008). Characters and 'main' character. *The Daedalus project*. http://www.nickyee.com/daedalus/archives/001634.php

7
What Users of Virtual Social Networks Value about Social Interaction: The Case of GreyPath

Oliver K. Burmeister

Introduction

The emphasis of this chapter is on social interaction, with a particular focus on one sector of society, namely seniors. Around the world there is an emphasis on helping people to age well, to enjoy old age and be productive in retirement. One way that this can be aided is by helping seniors make new connections with their peers, helping them to contribute in meaningful ways to society, and giving them a feeling of belonging and purpose. The social capital depicted by the strength of informal social networks in regional communities has been described as the glue that holds aged care communities together (Sappey, Bone, and Duncan, 2007). Virtual social networks can be a significant tool in making use of such social capital. This is a case study about one such network, called GreyPath.com.au.

GreyPath is a virtual social network that in July 2006 claimed a membership of 45,000 seniors, mostly in Australia, with participants in 61 countries. It then made significant changes to its Web interface, which initially caused a reduction in its membership base. That base has been steadily rebuilt, with 5 to 15 new members signing up daily in April 2008 (Lewis, 2008b). Over a period of two months to June 2008, it was rated consistently in the top 5 per cent of world websites by traffic (Alexa, 2008). In December 2007 GreyPath had over 30,000 discreet visits and more than 1 million hits (Lewis, 2008a), rising to almost 1.5 million hits per month by April 2008 (Lewis, 2008b). GreyPath enables members to learn new skills, to find e-pals, to engage in house swaps and house-sitting, it presents information on many topics important to seniors, such as forums, a member photo gallery, and much more. The great variety available to seniors on the site is one of its main appeals.

Seniors are a growing market in the virtual arena. Around the world the numbers of retiring baby boomers is expected to increase dramatically in coming years (Belsky, 1999). While many researchers have sought to discover the varying needs of seniors, this study is uniquely seeking to understand their *values*, that is, the things that are important to them individually and as a social group as they interact online. This has not previously been attempted anywhere. To date, an attempt to develop an understanding of values in design in the Australian context has occurred only once – in the context of electronic voting technology (Bowern, 2005). The project followed the Value Sensitive Design (VSD) approach, a complementary approach to VAP (see section below) for exploring the role of values in the design process. There has also only been one other attempt to explore values in the design of an online community, this being in the context of schoolchildren in the United States, again following the VSD approach.

Understanding what is important to members of the social network

Arising from gaming technology is a human computer interaction (HCI) design methodology known as Values at Play (VAP). While initially applied only to the design of games, it has been more widely used in recent years. One new application for VAP is reported here, where it has been used to discover what Australian seniors value about interacting in the GreyPath community.

VAP researchers have identified a gap in the literature which they refer to as the need for a 'library of analysis'. This chapter reports on the application of VAP to discover user values, and in the process suggests one tool that should be in such a library of analysis, namely a categorization of values which goes beyond the categories previously considered in VAP research.

Well-established approaches within user-centred design (UCD), such as participatory design and contextual design, have led HCI researchers to consider the role values should play in technology design. VAP is a relatively new design methodology in the field of HCI (Flanagan and Nissenbaum, 2007). There are still many aspects of the methodology that need refining so that it can be used effectively in the design process. Though a great deal of work has already been undertaken, in the main this has been 'proof of concept' work, with projects having been designed and developed from the ground up (Flanagan, Howe, and Nissenbaum, 2007; Flanagan and Nissenbaum, 2007; Friedman, Kahn, and Borning, 2005). In other words, until now HCI values researchers have set out to develop systems that incorporate values to prove that such design is possible. For example, in their 'cookies in the Web browser' project, Friedman, Kahn, and Borning (2005) began their project knowing which values to include. Similarly Flanagan, Howe, and Nissenbaum (2007) determined values for the RAPUNSEL project (a game to teach young girls to program) at its inception.

To gain wider acceptance, VAP also needs to be applied in situations requiring the redesign of legacy systems. The study discussed in this chapter attempts to do this by examining an existing virtual social network. It sought to discover stakeholder values and the extent to which the current system interfaces support or hinders those values. Therefore, unlike previous VAP research, there was no preconceived notion of what stakeholder values should or might be. In the current study, field observations of online community members are the starting point for value identification. That is, the study was an empirical investigation which began with structured observation, followed by interviews. It was a study that engaged in contextual enquiry, as part of a discovery process involving both conceptual and empirical enquiry (Flanagan et al., 2007). Only the observation phase of the study is reported in this chapter, though some insights from early interview data are drawn on too.

This chapter begins by briefly exploring the concept of values in design.[1] The ethnographic approach adopted in this study is also discussed, as well as the particular techniques used to gather the data. The chapter then goes on to discuss the particular online community where this study is based, placing this in the context of current theories of ageing, and, in particular, how our present understanding of ageing influences studies such as this one. The chapter then concludes with a discussion of suggested shortcomings that currently exist in values research and suggests a possible way forward with a categorization system.

Values in design

This study sought to answer the question: 'What do seniors value about online social interaction?' The initial work involved identifying stakeholder values, through observation. The next part of the study was to interview GreyPath members to confirm or deny findings from the observation phase as well as to extend the understanding of seniors' values and the meanings they attach to them.

What are values? Values are things that are important. They can be things that are important to an individual or to a group. For many people they are linked to their sense of identity and are often things to which the individual or group has an emotional attachment. Values can address issues of usability (such as ease of use), they can be commercial in orientation (such as profitability), and they can be moral (such as trust). Values researchers restrict their definition to 'values with moral import' (Friedman and Kahn, 2003) or to 'important social values' (Flanagan and Nissenbaum, 2007). That is, in the context of values in design, the focus is not on commercial, market penetration, or usability considerations per se. Values researchers do not seek to replace conventional design approaches and researchers in both areas advocate that their approaches to incorporating values in design complement conventional approaches. That is, both methodologies are to be used in addition to conventional HCI design methods in order to create effective systems. There is therefore is no need to focus on issues of profitability and usability, because such considerations are already dealt with by conventional approaches. Instead, both approaches advocate the additional considerations of moral and social values, in social contexts involving technology.

VSD and VAP are built on a foundation of participatory design and contextual design. In participatory design users are co-designers, equal partners in the design process together with the developers of the ICT; users play active roles in many design activities (Muller, 2003). Unlike other UCD techniques, participatory design requires that users come out of the work situation to collaborate with designers (Dix, Finlay, Abowd, and Beale, 2004). While this is described as an ethnographic technique, it differs from most other ethnographic approaches in that participatory design approaches are not situated in the context of ICT use.

Another variant of UCD that is drawn upon by values researchers, is that of contextual design (Beyer and Holtzblatt, 1998). Contextual design starts with gathering data about users in the field. It involves recognition that the environment of the user influences the way they see their world of work and their own role within it. Like participatory design, a central notion of contextual design is that of partnership, partnership between the user and the developers (Dix et al., 2004). Dix et al. describe contextual design as employing ethnographic techniques that seek to view the user in context. It is about collecting unbiased views of the user's work practice, including the organizational culture.

According to contextual design proponents, end-users develop a mental model, a world-view of how their organization and the tasks they perform within it operate. To understand users properly, designers should attempt to see the world as the users see it, by taking the context into account. In this way contextual variables that cannot be learned any other way can be observed and incorporated into the design of the ICT. The focus is on what people do, as discovered through observation and interviewing (Holtzblatt, 2003). Beyer and Holtzblatt (1998) describe it as a means of gathering the ongoing experience of users rather than than summary experiences brought by users to a participatory design session. Holtzblatt (2003) says that, without knowing user practice, it is likely designers will miss achieving the goal of a usable product.

VSD is not only built on participatory and contextual design, but also draws on concepts such as design for universal usability (a common term to describe making technology artifacts accessible to all people) (Schneiderman, 2001, 2002) as well as philosophical and sociological research for the development of technical artifacts. VSD is concerned with value considerations throughout the entire system development life cycle, with a particular focus on the early stages in design. VSD captures the moral values of users, centring on values such as human well-being, human dignity, justice, welfare, and human rights (such as equality of access) in a principled and comprehensive manner as part of the design process. This broadens the criteria for judging the quality of socio-technical information systems to include ethical considerations in terms of user values.

VAP is both complementary to VSD and builds on it. In addition, it draws on two other theories, Reflective Practice and Critical Technical Practice (Flanagan and Nissenbaum, 2007). Flanagan, Howe, and Nissenbaum (2007) describe VAP as the systematic application of three activities: discovery, translation, and verification. During discovery the focus is on developing a list of values by examining sources of values and defining which values are important in the particular context of the information system to be designed. The discovered values are then translated into design features. Finally, verification is concerned with assessing whether the project successfully implemented values in a way that enhanced and did not detract from the design goals.

Library of analysis

One area of potential confusion for designers who have little or no training in philosophy derives from the fact that the values research to date has poorly articulated what values are and what they are not. Some researchers list values they have discovered in their research and many share a common set of values. Schneiderman (2002) and Flanagan, Howe, and Nissenbaum (2007) give examples such as human well-being, human dignity, justice, welfare, and human rights (such as equality of access). In some cases the lists of values are identical, in other cases the lists vary. Aside from supposedly universal values, other values that have been identified in the literature include the following: privacy (Ackerman and Cranor, 1999; Bowern, 2005), ownership and property (Lipinski and Britz, 2000), physical welfare (Leveson, 1991), freedom from bias (Friedman and Nissenbaum, 1996), universal usability (Schneiderman, 2001, 2002), autonomy (Suchman, 1994), informed consent (Millet, Friedman, and Felten, 2001), accountability (Friedman and Kahn, 1992), courtesy (Wynne and Ryan, 1993), identity and identity management (Bers, Gonzalez-Heydrich, and DeMaso, 2001; Bowern, 2005), calmness (Friedman and Kahn, 2003), environmental sustainability (Brundtland, 1987), and trust (Fogg and Tseng, 1999).

One observation that Flanagan, Howe, and Nissenbaum (2007) made was that designers could be aided through a *library of analysis*. They envisaged this as a way of relieving the burden on designers to carry out philosophical enquiry, when often this was out of their field of expertise. If instead of having to grapple with abstract conceptions of values designers were able to refer to a library of concrete definitions that would help them significantly in the task of design.

Similarly, Bowern (2005) critiqued values research because of the added burden it lays on developers. He argued that developers were burdened by existing methods of developing systems and that there would be resistance to adopting yet further requirements, especially when value considerations are outside the expertise of many developers. These views echo those of Muller (2003) described in the participatory design discussion above. Muller said that designers experience difficulty understanding the needs of users. Values researchers argue this is true for designers' understanding of user values too.

One tool such a library of analysis should include is a way of categorising values. As shown above, values researchers do not hold that all values are equal. Some are more important that others, some are temporally bound, some yet are contextually bound and others are universal. This chapter brings together (below) what VAP, VSD and values researchers in non-technological fields have found to be categories that are meaningful, using examples from observations of the GreyPath community to illustrate the categories.

Interpretivist methodology

Both VSD and VAP ethnographic enquiries are useful for drawing out the contextual influences necessary to understanding stakeholder values. The particular approach adopted for this study is a twofold interpretivist one involving first an eight-month period of observing the GreyPath community, and then interviews with GreyPath members. This is effectively what VSD describes as the 'conceptual phase' and what VAP describes as the 'discovery process'.

The observation phase was twofold, in both cases following a systematic approach to theory building. Observations took place 'periodically' (weekly, and in a few instances more than once during a given week), with the researcher making notes about the observation while it was happening and after it occurred (Bow, 2002). The initial three months involved unstructured observation, looking for events, activities, and behaviours that were salient, guided by concepts developed in the available literature on virtual social networks (Al-Saggaf, 2003; Al-Saggaf and Williamson, 2004). This stage enabled the researcher to become aware of the nature of the activities, the characteristics of participation and the general behaviour of the participants of the GreyPath community. One aim of this stage was for the researcher to become 'familiar with the online culture of the community, its vocabulary, history, and people' (Al-Saggaf, 2003: p. 67). The following five months involved structured observation, during which the expressions of values were specifically sought. The observations took place from July 2006 to March 2007. All these observations were restricted to public spaces in the online community that could be visited by any observer. That is, some parts of the online community were restricted to registered members only, while many parts were freely available to the general public. It is only the latter that were part of the observation. In this way no members were aware that they were being observed. (Ethics approval for the observation phase of this research required only that GreyPath management give permission for this research to proceed.)

Observations involved all publicly available community interaction. These included the various forums (these were threaded email discussions, one on issues important to members, another on jokes, another on daily life issues), online learning initiatives, message boards, online community editorials, information on jobs for seniors, the types of advertising permitted on the site, site statistics, arts and crafts, links to related areas, house swaps, e-Pals, question-and-answer segments (such as computer help, gardening tips, exchange of recipes, and travel advice), messages from GreyPath management, site policies, and more. Unlike the interviews, for which participants were selected, the observation involved the whole GreyPath community interaction.

Values were identified in various ways. Some arose from forum discussions. For instance, when a new member introduces him- or herself and asks a question. The discussion typically shows care, concern, a willingness to help others, respectful language (profanity on GreyPath is rare), and considered responses (seen in their length and the fact that abbreviations that are common in other communities (such as lol for 'laugh out loud') are rarely used). The rapidity and number of responses to such requests shows that new members are made to feel welcome. From such observations values can be inferred. Further observations and later the interviews with members sought to confirm or deny inferred values.

Initially the structured observation sought to identify all values. Only through later reflection was it possible to isolate those values that have moral import or are important socially. For example, one could prematurely dismiss certain values as being concerned only with usability if one were only on the lookout for values with moral import. However, some values cross boundaries and can be both socially important and usable (e.g. an aspect of HCI is accessible interfaces, which, socially and morally, is also an issue of equitable access), or important commercially and morally (such as some aspects of security). Therefore it was important in the first instance to identify many values and only later to engage in the task of reducing the list to those that were morally and socially important.

The interpretivist philosophy employed studied social interaction on GreyPath in its natural settings. The philosophy seeks to produce descriptive analyses that emphasize deep, interpretive understanding of the meanings within the social phenomenon under study (Williamson, 2002). To understand a particular social action (such as online friendship or mutual support) the enquirer must grasp the meanings that constitute that action. The work presented here is part of a larger ongoing study to discover what seniors value about their online social interaction. Given that this is an interpretive study, the results cannot be used to say that all seniors share these values. However, the study will help us to understand user values, particularly those of seniors interacting in a virtual network.

Seniors

GreyPath is a not-for-profit organization which manages the portal greypath.com.au. Membership is restricted to seniors, which it defines as anyone over 50. Most members reside in Australia, though some reside overseas and many Australian residents travel overseas yet maintain contact with their friends through this virtual network. In sociological terms, participation is not spatially determined, as traditional communities have been (Wellman and Leighton, 1979), but ubiquitous (Wellman, 2004). It was created and is managed by a particular family. GreyPath has 35 senior volunteers, who freely give of their time and skills to maintain the site.

Understanding the needs of seniors has grown in importance in recent years. One worldwide demographic trend that needs to be considered is the worldwide phenomenon that the proportion of the population defined as old is increasing and is forecast to increase further. Belsky (1999) has said that only 4 per cent of Americans were elderly in 1900, whereas by 1999 that figure had risen to 13 per cent. In 1999 the proportion of elderly Americans was one in eight (12.5 per cent), and was forecast to rise to one in five (20 per cent) by 2030. This phenomenon, said Belsky, is the result of a significant rise in birth rates following the Second World War among a group of people known as the 'baby boomers', who were people born between 1946 and 1964. The baby boomers do not alone account for the increase in the number of people forecast to be among the aged in years to come. Another common trend in developing countries is that of decreasing fertility and decreasing mortality rates. That is, people are living longer and because they are having fewer babies, the proportion of older people is forecast to increase further.

The online social interaction and social networking aspects of the study draw on understandings from sociological and psychological models of ageing. That is, while particular behaviours of seniors are not being studied, psychological studies about cognitive processes may shed light on the value systems of seniors.

At the turn of this century, a theory of ageing that gained credibility was that of selective optimization with compensation (SOC) (Baltes and Carstensen, 1996; Baltes and Baltes, 1990; Baltes and Smith, 2002; Marsiske, Lang, and Baltes, 1995). It is a theory which focuses on maintaining function in a restricted period of one's life. SOC arose out of attempts by Baltes to develop a meta-theoretical framework which combined ageing research in biological-evolutionary as well as lifespan psychological perspectives (Baltes, 1997; Baltes and Smith, 2002). The evolutionary perspective shows that selection pressures have operated in the first half of an individual's lifespan to ensure reproductive fitness as well as effective parenting behaviours. According to this theory, progression to successful ageing means one has to go beyond reliance on evolutionary biology, to cultural influences. Successful ageing is less a function of biology and more one of increasing the culturally based resources available to people to help them find supportive compensations for biological losses. SOC proceeds 'from the assumption that the life course consists of a changing script in the means and goals of life' (Baltes and Smith, 2002: p. 20). In order to achieve these changes, changes need to occur in the allocation of resources. Early in the lifespan, resources are allocated to growth; later in the lifespan, resources are allocated to maintenance and repair.

SOC is a theory which takes an integrative approach to multiple factors affecting people in their Third and Fourth Age, combining individual, social, and institutional perspectives. It distinguishes optimization in the Third Age (what is commonly understood as old age) and Fourth Age (the very old). For example, Baltes and Smith (2002) argue that the Fourth Age (85 and over) presents unique challenges which comparatively little research has yet addressed. They argue that the Fourth Age is categorized by pathology much more than the earlier age groups, and that this means the way people in the Fourth Age are to be understood differs considerably from that for people in other age groups.

Baltes and Smith (2002) also say that the process of optimization is more difficult for people in the Fourth Age than it is for the younger old (old age). They argue that in developed countries people maintain mental achievement levels until about age 70. However, for those in the Fourth Age new learning is severely impaired. They argue that 'the Fourth Age tests the boundaries of human adaptability' (Baltes and Smith, 2002: p. 13). To illustrate SOC, Baltes and Smith (2002: p. 21) cite an example of an 80-year-old pianist, whom they interviewed in the course of their research, called Rubinstein.

> 'When Rubinstein was asked how he continued to be such an excellent concert pianist, he named three reasons. He played fewer pieces, but practiced them more often, and he used contrasts in tempo to simulate faster playing than he in the meantime could muster. Rubinstein reduced his repertoire (i.e. selection). This allowed him the opportunity to practice each piece more (i.e. optimization). And, finally, he used contrasts in speed to hide his loss in mechanical finger speed, a case of compensation.'

This understanding of seniors, especially those in the Fourth Age, has implications for technology design, which will be further explored in another section below.

Categorizing values: The GreyPath community

A library of analysis can be one means of helping designers to incorporate values into their designs. A step towards this is to categorize values. The closest values researchers have come to this has been discussions of value trade-offs (Flanagan et al., 2007; Friedman and Kahn, 2003; Friedman et al., 2005).

The structured observation of GreyPath initially yielded a long list of values. Flanagan, Howe, and Nissenbaum (2007) advocate culling the initial list to a shorter one of those values that are socially important. However, designers should not simply be given a list of values and expected to somehow incorporate those into their designs. Better would be some form of guidelines for thinking systematically through values issues. One way of achieving this is with a categorization scheme for the values identified. That is, values can be grouped along themes, or identified as belonging to certain groupings. Current literature says to look through one's list of values for the important ones. However, when one categorizes values, a further distinction is possible: it becomes possible to identify those values within certain categories which are more important than others. This in turn is helpful for value-related trade-off considerations.

In the literature, it is apparent that some researchers do think in terms of categories of value, though not in consistent and systematic ways. They use terms such as 'dimensions' or 'factors', or they use descriptors that suggest temporal relationships or some form of abstraction, or higher and lower levels of value. Table 7.1 attempts to capture the disparate aspects of value definitions in the literature.

Table 7.1 Value categories

Descriptor	Definition
Direction	Towards and away-from values.
Expression	Some values are explicit in the way a system operates. Other values are less obvious, but are implicitly inherent in the design of a system.
Order	Higher and lower orders allow for abstraction hierarchies of values.
Purpose	Means and ends values.
Scope	Scope can be thin or thick. Thin is for the current user group, thick for the wider group.
Temporal	Descriptions of immediate effects of values, and of longer-term effects.
Type	Two types of value need to be considered: those of the stakeholders, and those of the designers.

The following discussion gives examples of each of the descriptors from the literature and this study of seniors online in order to illustrate what each category is about.

Direction: Robbins (1996) describes values in terms of their direction. Towards values are those people strive to fulfil, whereas away-from values are those people attempt to avoid. Examples of towards values in GreyPath include human dignity, which was seen in such things as open calls for respectful language and the fact that the use of profanity on the site is very rare; the exceptions tend to be in the jokes forum, where profanity can be what makes the joke funny. Examples of privacy are seen in that some social interaction takes place in publicly open forums, while other interaction takes place in moderated chat rooms only available to registered members. However, away-from values are more difficult to discover through observation. It was the interview phase that revealed these in greater detail. These are values such as avoiding being embarrassed. Such values can be inferred, such as by observing how supportive the online community is, and how participants avoid hurtful, put-down comments. It is acceptable to ask 'dumb questions', because the questioner will not be put in an embarrassing position, but will instead be supported through the learning process. This is particularly evident in observations about learning to work with computers – an important learning activity for people wanting to participate in a virtual network, which by definition requires certain minimum computing skills.

Expression: Some values are *expressed* explicitly and others implicitly. Explicit values, such as privacy protection, can be seen in the form of a (now discontinued) chat room for seniors suffering from depression, that restricted entry to registered members and was carefully moderated. Other values are less obvious, but are implicitly inherent in the design of a system. Anonymity is explicit in the GreyPath design, in that anyone can read forum postings; and equally explicit is that the ability to post messages is restricted to members, to people who belong to that community. Recently, GreyPath has introduced a bell sound to alert members to a new entrant to their chat room. This is useful for the many members who have their computer running all the time. One lady I interviewed keeps her computer on all day as she cleans her house and prepares meals in her kitchen, checking from time to time what is happening online. The bell initiative is an explicit design implementation that assists people in her situation. Also explicit in this design is that one cannot enter the chat room without others currently online becoming aware of the new entrant.

An example of implicit design values arises from an interview with a 'young' member of GreyPath, a lady in her late 50s. GreyPath has an events section where members can advertise social events in their region that other members of GreyPath might be able to attend. The entrance to that events section has for some time had a photo of several ladies at what appears to be some sort of fête. The interviewee said of this:

> What you see first is this picture of a bunch of old women with hand crafts and artsy-craftsy, and I thought, well that's certainly not me...put on an older couple on a bicycle somewhere in the countryside, or in a camper van, not this...And you look at the women and they're all in their seventies, all little grey haired old ladies in their seventies, and long tables of Rotary, RSL type knitted tea-cosies, and artsy-craftsy – and I find that very off putting.

Order: Order allows for hierarchies of value to be abstracted. Flanagan, Howe, and Nissenbaum (2007: p. 12) use the term 'higher order' for values such as equity, autonomy, and liberation, and (2007: p. 14) cooperation and fair representation. Bowern (2005) sees trust as an 'overarching' value which has related (lower-order) values associated with it. This could be limiting and perhaps a better view of trust is of the degree of trust. For instance, parts of GreyPath require authentication and moderation: other parts require only a username, which could be fictitious. This appears to indicate different levels of trust. Interview data suggests that GreyPath members use chat facilities for discussions with trusted others, whereas they are less trusting of discussions in the public forums. The least trusted are the anonymous observers who are not willing to reveal their presence. There is limited trust of people participating in forums, more in chat rooms and then beyond that several members, having met through GreyPath, chat using webcam and other facilities, using services not currently provided by GreyPath. Such webcam interaction is described by interviewees as involving their highest level of trust.

Purpose: Robbins (1996) addresses *purpose* when he distinguishes between means values and ends values. An example he uses to illustrate this distinction is that a person may say they value their car, but when pressed it is the freedom that driving the car affords them that the person really values. The car, then, is the means value and freedom is the end value. An example of this on GreyPath is the use of usernames. Some seniors sign their postings with their first or full name. Most, however, do not sign their postings, so only their username is shown. The username is therefore a 'means' employed to achieve an 'end' of limited self-revelation. Though inferred from observations, this was borne out in later interviews, where GreyPath members expressed their desire for privacy and stated that using a non-identifying username helped achieve that. Another example is the end value of GreyPath management to restrict membership to seniors, where the means is registration. Similarly, GreyPath management have an end value of protecting members from unsolicited advertising, again achieved through the means of requiring registration for posting messages. Another example is what is generally referred to as 'lurking'. Several interviewees have told me they will not post a message for days or even a week, even though they feel they are present in GreyPath daily and for hours each day. They have a sense of 'presence' and like to keep themselves informed about community activity. Their means is anonymous observation without logging in; the end value is the achievement of this sense of belonging to a group of peers, of being present (even silently) in their community.

Scope: Thick values include those described as universal; their scope encompasses a larger group. In the context of this study, thick values include values generally held by most Australians. Thin values are those held by a particular group or certain individuals that either conflict with thick values or are redefinitions of those values. Further differentiations may be necessary too. Early interview data suggest that GreyPath members over 80, though sharing many (thick) values with other GreyPath members, have unique (thin) values distinctive to them. These were people born before the Great Depression who were adults during the Second World War, as opposed to younger GreyPath members, who were children at the time of the Second World War.

Another example from interview data has to do with heated discussions. The thick value of the GreyPath community is the desire to avoid argumentation and heated discussions. A comment repeatedly heard in interviews is 'life is too short' to engage in this type of debate. When some members repeatedly sought to push their own views to the point of putting down other members, GreyPath management asked them to leave the virtual network. However, recognizing that a few people in the community do wish to engage in deeper thinking on certain types of issue, and to debate those issues, two forums (the Think Tank and the Senate) were created specifically for engagement in this way. The few members who make use of these two forums are therefore expressing thin values, values that are not generally held by the wider group, yet which are acceptable enough to the wider group to allow the participation of this subgroup.

Temporal: Another way of conceptualizing values is to think of their *temporal* nature. Flanagan, Howe, and Nissenbaum (2007) describe some values as 'emergent', such as gameplayers developing a value of subversion in which they deliberately break the rules of the game. Other values are experienced immediately. Bowern (2005) sees identity management in temporal terms, as people's self-understanding changes over time. Online identity can also be seen as a value in the GreyPath community, where over time people form relationships online that they consider important; those relationships are with online identities such as Koko, Jennywren, Gaspresser, Jean4, Pam/QLD – user names first adopted for perhaps no great reason which become their online persona, the way they are identified within the community. Friedman, Kahn, and Borning (2005) also use temporal terms to describe VSD as an approach concerned with designing systems that account for 'enduring' values.

One woman emailed me some time after the interview to say that her computer had not worked at all the day before and that she had really missed having contact with her friends on GreyPath. It is not that she necessarily posts something every day, but rather that she has a need to be 'present' in the community, observing what is going on with her virtual friends.

One design example related to temporal values is raised by the chat room bell (discussed above), which has recently been introduced. Several websites have a time-out facility, where users are disconnected when the computer is not used for a set period. That would be counterproductive for a network such as GreyPath. In order to feel present in the community, to have a sense of connection without necessarily participating actively, members should not be (and in the case of GreyPath, are not) timed out. GreyPath chat rooms can at times be very active and at other times there is very little interaction. The bell is a temporal alert that aids social interaction.

Type: Type distinguishes the values of stakeholders and designers. A possible shortcoming of VAP is that the purpose of the discovery phase of the values research is to discover the values of stakeholders, not including those of the designers. The consideration of value type addresses this shortcoming. Flanagan, Howe, and Nissenbaum (2007) give an example from the RAPUNSEL game, for eleven, 13-year-old girls in which the users (the girls) wanted sexy character representations, but the designers refused to accommodate this, because they felt it would reinforce negative stereotypical views of girls. Effectively they mounted an argument in favour of being able to veto user values discovered. This suggests that the professional judgment of the designers should be allowed to override user value choices; user-centred design does not mean the user's views dominate design choices. In this instance, the designers iterated from geometric shapes that users didn't want to agents that, while looking like young girls, were not stereotypical sexy depictions; in other words, a compromise was reached between the designers and this particular group of stakeholders.

Implications for practice/policymaking

In the discussion above it was seen that for seniors, the older they are, the more difficult it becomes to cope with change. Given the model of ageing described, selective optimization with compensation (SOC), it is likely that new participants joining the online community will be people in a range of age groups up to age 85. Given the learning impairment experienced by people in the Fourth Age, few new participants in the community are likely to come from that cohort. Instead, Fourth Age participants in the study are likely to be members long standing of the GreyPath community, people who have learnt to navigate the online structures and the processes involved in online social interaction. From a digital divide point of view, it is also likely that changes in online interaction technologies (hardware and/or software) alienate Fourth Age participants due to the new learning involved.

One significant advantage for seniors with a virtual social network is that it can provide them with social capital in the form of cultural and social resources needed to age successfully, particularly so when the network is one involving other seniors. In the case of GreyPath, it is a network created and maintained by seniors and is exclusively for the use of seniors. Therefore new members come into a more tolerant and understanding environment when they voice their requirements for resourcing their age-related needs.

Baltes and Smith (2002: p. 22) argue that cultures which 'offer older persons ways of selecting, optimizing, and compensating are the cultures which assist best in maximizing the gains of older age'. They link this to the value of human dignity. That is, society is showing older people greater dignity, when it provides resources that enable people to maximize the gains of older age. From the perspective of Human–Computer Interaction, designers might achieve this by permitting the continuation of previous navigational structures when new ones are introduced so that older participants are not forced to engage in (for them) difficult new learning. Given that with increasing age people experience increasing difficulty in coping with new learning, this may be a significant reason for the dramatic decline in the membership of

GreyPath following the major site upgrade in October 2006. For instance, in 2005 GreyPath management told this author that the majority of GreyPath members were in their late 70s and early 80s, whereas at the time of writing this chapter the average membership age was in the late 60s. This suggests that many members approaching or in their Fourth Age at the time of the change-over to the new website ceased their membership.

Implications for research

This categorization of values is an attempt to address the need for a library of analysis. Equipped with a library of analysis, which needs to be much more than just a categorization of values, designers will be in a better position to understand how to incorporate values into their designs. Further research may reveal the need to add more categories, or to redefine the category choices in Table 7.1 above. For example, anonymity is an example of both expression and purpose. Explicit (expression) in the GreyPath design is that non-members can lurk anonymously. Similarly, members can achieve the end (purpose) of feeling present in the community through anonymous lurking.

Flanagan, Howe, and Nissenbaum (2007: p. 1) have said that 'we are still at the shaky beginnings of thinking systematically about the practice of designing with values in mind'. Similarly, Friedman, Kahn, and Borning (2005) saw research into values in design prior to the mid-1990s as piecemeal. Both VSD and VAP are relatively new approaches in the design space and significant research is still needed to help us understand better how design can incorporate values.

What remains to be seen through future research is whether there are certain universal values or whether these are all culturally or contextually bound.

Conclusion

Research into the GreyPath community is ongoing. Following the interpretive approach of this study, defining values discovered during observation will result from obtaining user interpretations of their meanings through indepth interviews with GreyPath members.

The focus of this study is on what VAP refers to as 'discovery'. In system life cycle terms, the focus is on analysis, not design. VAP advocates that following discovery is the process of translation, that is, of incorporating discovered values into the design process. That, however is beyond the scope of the study reported here.

Work to date on this project has highlighted the need to be able to think in terms of value categories. Previous values research has shown the need to help designers, who frequently have no expertise in philosophy, to think through the issues involved in incorporating values into the design process. It has been suggested that what is needed is the creation of a library of analysis. Such a library would be a tool to help analyse how values can be incorporated in design. Table 7.1 above is a step in that direction. Rather than arbitrarily attempting somehow to incorporate a value that has been identified as important, designers can use the categories table to help them analyse ways to incorporate that value. For instance, should the value be explicitly expressed in a technology artifact or should it be implicitly present in the system as a whole? Should the value be a one-time expression or is it an enduring value?

Note

1. A more detailed description of the theoretical underpinnings of this research can be found in Burmeister (2008).

References

Ackerman, M.S. and Cranor, L. (1999). *Privacy critics: UI components to safeguard users' privacy*. Paper presented at the CHI 1999.
Alexa. (2008). Alexa The Wed Information Company. http://www.alexa.com/ (accessed on 1 June 2008).
Al-Saggaf, Y. (2003). *Online Communities in Saudi Arabia: an ethnographic study*. Unpublished PhD Thesis, Charles Sturt University, Wagga Wagga.
Al-Saggaf, Y. and Williamson, K. (2004). Online Communities in Saudi Arabia: Evaluating the Impact on Culture through Online Semi-Structured Interviews. *FQS*, 5(3).
Baltes, P.B. (1997). On the incomplete architecture of human ontogeny: Selection, optimization, and compensation as foundation of developmental theory. In P.B. Baltes and O.G.J. Brim (eds.), *Life-span development and behavior*. New York: Academic Press, 255–79.
Baltes, P.B. and Baltes, M.M. (1990). *Successful aging: Perspectives from the behavioral sciences*. New York: Cambridge University Press.
Baltes, M.M. and Carstensen, L.L. (1996). The process of successful aging. *Aging and Society*, 16: 397–422.
Baltes, P.B. and Smith, J. (2002, April 1–4). *New frontiers in the future of ageing: From successful ageing of the young old to the dilemmas of the fourth age*. Paper presented at the Valencia Forum Valencia, Spain.
Belsky, J.K. (1999). *The Psychology of Ageing: Theory, Research, and Interventions* (3 ed.). Melbourne: ITP.
Bers, M.U., Gonzalez-Heydrich, J. and DeMaso, D.R. (2001). *Identity construction environments: Supporting a virtual therapeutic community of pediatric patients*

undergoing dialysis. Paper presented at the Conference of Human Factors in Computing Systems, CHI 2001.

Beyer, H. and Holtzblatt, K. (1998). *Contextual Design. Defining Customer-Centered Systems*. San Francisco, CA: Morgan Kaufmann Publishers, Inc.

Bow, A. (2002). Ethnographic techniques. In K. Williamson (ed.), *Research Methods for students, academics and professionals* (2 ed.). Wagga Wagga: CIS, CSU, 265–80.

Bowern, M. (2005). An ethical method for developing electronic voting systems. *MANUSYA: Journal of Humanities on Computer Ethics*.

Brundtland, G.H. (1987). *Our Common Future*. Retrieved. from.

Burmeister, O.K. (2008). *What 45,000 seniors value about online social interaction*. Paper presented at the IFIP WG9.5 Conference on Massive Virtual Communities, Luneburg, Germany.

Dix, A., Finlay, J., Abowd, G.D. and Beale, R. (2004). *Human-Computer Interaction* (3 ed.). Sydney: Pearson.

Flanagan, M., Howe, D. and Nissenbaum, H. (2007). Values in Design: Theory and Practice. In J. van Den Hoven and J. Weckert (eds.), *Information Technology and Moral Philosophy*. Cambridge: Cambridge University Press.

Flanagan, M. and Nissenbaum, H. (2007). *A Game Design Methodology to Incorporate Activist Themes*. Paper presented at the CHI 2007.

Fogg, B.J. and Tseng, H. (1999). *The elements of computer credibility*. Paper presented at the CHI 1999.

Friedman, B. and Kahn, P.H.J. (1992). Human agency and responsible computing: Implications for computer systems design. *Journal of Systems Software*, 17: 7–14.

Friedman, B. and Kahn, P.H.J. (2003). Human values, ethics, and design. In J. Jacko and A. Sears (eds.), *The Human-Computer Interaction Handbook*. Mahwah, NJ: Lawrence Erlbaum Associates.

Friedman, B., Kahn, P.H.J. and Borning, A. (2005). Value Sensitive Design and Information Systems. In P. Zhang and D. Galletta (eds.), *Human Computer Interaction in Management Information Systems: Foundations*. New York: M.E. Sharpe.

Friedman, B. and Nissenbaum, H. (1996). Bias in computer systems. *ACM Transactions on Information Systems*, 14(3): 330–47.

Holtzblatt, K. (2003). Contextual Design. In J.A. Jacko and A. Sears (eds.), *The Human-Computer Interaction Handbook*. Mahwah, New Jersey: Lawrence Erlbaum Associates, 941–63.

Leveson, N.G. (1991). Software safety in embedded computer systems. *Communications of the ACM*, 34(2): 34–6.

Lewis, R. (2008a). About Greypath. http://greypath.com/taxonomy_menu/30 (accessed 1 June 2008).

Lewis, R. (2008b). Greypath Usage Stats. In O.K. Burmeister (ed.). Melbourne, 1.

Lipinski, T.A. and Britz, J.J. (2000). Rethinking the ownership of information in the 21st century: Ethical implications. *Ethics and Information Technology*, 2(1): 49–71.

Marsiske, M., Lang, F.R. and Baltes, P.B. (1995). Selective optimization with compensation: Life-span perspectives on successful human development. In R.A. Dixon and L. Baeckman (eds.), *Compensation for psychological defects and declines: Managing losses and promoting gains*. Hillsdale, NJ: Erlbaum, 35–79.

Millet, L.I., Friedman, B. and Felten, E. (2001). *Cookies and Web Browser Design: Toward Realizing Informed Consent Online.* Paper presented at the CHI, 31 March–5 April 2001.

Muller, M.J. (2003). Participatory Design: The Third Space in HCI. In J.A. Jacko and A. Sears (eds.), *The Human-Computer Interaction Handbook.* Mahwah, New Jersey: Lawrence Erlbaum Associates, 1051–68.

Robbins, A. (1996). *Personal Power II.* San Diego: Guthy-Renker Corporation.

Sappey, J., Bone, Z. and Duncan, R. (2007). *The Aged Care Industry in Regional Australia: Will it cope with the tsunami to come?* Paper presented at the 21st Australian and New Zealand Academy of Management, 4–7 December 2007, Sydney, Australia.

Schneiderman, B. (2001). CUU: bridging the digital divide with universal usability. *ACM Interactions,* 8(2): 11–15.

Schneiderman, B. (2002). *Leonardo's Laptop.* Cambridge: MIT Press.

Suchman, L. (1994). Do categories have politics? The language/action perspective reconsidered. *CSCW Journal,* 2(3): 177–90.

Wellman, B. (2004). The three ages of internet studies: ten, five and zero year ago. *New Media and Society,* 6(1): 123–9.

Wellman, B. and Leighton, B. (1979). Networks, Neighborhoods, and Communities: Approaches to the Study of the Community Question. *Urban Affairs Quarterly,* 14(3): 363–90.

Williamson, K. (2002). The two major traditions of research. In K. Williamson (ed.) *Research methods for students, academics and professionals* (2 ed.). Wagga Wagga, CIS.

Wynne, E.A. and Ryan, K. (1993). *Reclaiming our schools: A handbook on teaching character, academics, and discipline.* New York: Macmillan.

8
Labour's Second Life: From a Virtual Strike to Union Island
Bruce Robinson

Introduction

An everyday event taking place in an unusual environment can throw a sharp light on things usually taken for granted while at the same time showing the difference a shift in location can make. When the new environment is cyberspace, it can illuminate the relationship between the real and the virtual as well as the broader social relations within which such an event is anchored.

This chapter examines one such event and its consequences: the 'virtual strike' and mass picket held in the virtual world Second Life on 27 September 2007 in support of workers at IBM Italy. The transfer of conflictual industrial relations to the virtual realm enables us to consider the similarities between the virtual and real worlds and the differences between cyberspace from other forms of space; the extent to which unions as an oppositional force can transform space in pursuit of their aims; and the overall value of the Internet for labour as a means of organization and intervention. The strike also acted as a catalyst for a collaborative project to create Union Island, a long-term trade union presence in Second Life. The strike as a one-off event will be contrasted with this project in terms of its implications for theorizing the production of space and for the fruitful use of virtual worlds by the unions.

The author participated in the 27 September action and has since then taken part in other labour-oriented activity in Second Life, joining the Union Island users' group and interviewing several of the central organizers of the IBM strike and Union Island. In line with Kendall's (1999) recommendation that research on the Internet requires experience of using the technology, the main research method used has been that of participant observation, which has also enabled closer consideration of the social processes at work in Second Life. Direct experience is of particular value in research into virtual worlds as assumptions about the givens of everyday real-world life do not necessarily apply.

The paper first examines a number of themes relevant to analysing union use of Second Life; then describes the IBM virtual strike and the setting up of Union Island before revisiting the theoretical framework in the light of the shift from a one off event to a permanent presence in Second Life and discussing the implications of the use of Second Life for trade unions.

Second Life and the production of (cyber)space

The spatial dimension is explicit in and central to the virtual world of Second Life. It appears on the computer screen as a physical landscape 'that looks a lot like the real world' (Ondrejka, 2007). Location in Second Life is mapped onto a grid which reproduces the conceptualization of the Earth as a space defined by three-dimensional (3D) coordinates and embodying the points of the compass we take for granted as a means of orientation. This defines what Harvey (2006) calls 'absolute space...usually represented as a pre-existing and immoveable grid amenable to standardized measurement and open to calculation'.

Yet awareness of the landscape of Second Life as a totally human product, a graphical representation in software, and its location in cyberspace leads us beyond this commonsense reading of Second Life as an absolute physical space. One of Second Life's founders claims it is 'collapsing geography' (Ondrejka, 2007): it enables the power of place to be harnessed by distant participants in the world and it lays claim to embodying the space–time compression considered central to understanding the impact of globalizing capital. Second Life is more than simply a landscape one can move through; instead, it presents an explicitly social space of communication, co-presence and shared activity. Second Life is thus a 'technology of spatiality...implicated in the operation and emergence of [spatial] logics and the forms of collective encounters with space' (Dourish, 2006).

The nature of Second Life therefore leads us to consider not merely what light established theories of space can throw on a virtual world but also whether what we encounter there confounds those theories. The self-proclaimed nature of Second Life as a social space leads us to Marxist theorists of space such as Henri Lefebvre, David Harvey, and Andrew Herod, who see 'space [as] not merely an inert stage on which social life simply plays itself out, but rather a social product' (Herod, 2001: p. 507). This does not mean that space is somehow immaterial or unreal nor that physical space as such does not exist, being simply a social construction.

Rather, 'processes do not occur in space but define their own spatial frame. The concept of space is embedded in or internal to process' (Harvey, 2006: p. 121). This enables us to consider physical space as overlaid by social space, which both creates and is created by a range of social and spatial practices. Hence the 'production of space'.

This, in Lefebvre's (1991: p. 33) understanding, has three dimensions:

- Space as perceived, the particular locations and spatial sets characteristic of each social formation encountered through human interaction with the material.
- Space as conceived and usually implemented through particular representations (e.g. maps).
- Space as lived experience: 'The space of "inhabitants" and "users". The dominated space which the imagination seeks to change and appropriate'.

Space as perceived and conceived serves for Lefebvre as a means of reproducing the dominant social order through its structuring of spatial and social practice. However, space as experienced allows the social order to be subverted through the creation of 'counter-spaces'.

Nunes (2006) maps Lefebvre's concepts onto the world of ICT-based networks in order to answer the question 'Where is cyberspace?' Resisting the reduction of cyberspace to either an immaterial world of ideas, language and communication or to the materiality of its underlying technology and the associated human–computer interaction, Nunes instead sees cyberspace as an implementation of Lefebvre's triad:

> 'a dynamic relation of material form, conceptual representation and dispositional practice that produces networked social space...enacted and articulated in the relational interactions of individuals involved in computer-mediated communication (CMC) and mapped as a nexus of material and semiotic processes...an event articulated in various contexts'.

Space in this sense is

> 'multiple, relational and produced...the interaction that occurs between language, bodies, material and experience [...] maps the spatiality of cyberspace – or rather *cyberspaces*...always structured as an event, and as such, a dialectical emergence of several processes, not reducible to any one thing' (pp. 12 and 24).

Labour and the remaking of spatial relations

If the making of space is a social process, then social inequalities and class divisions remain present in that process. These social locations play a part in how 'different actors engage with the economic landscape to ensure their "geographical vision" is inscribed in that landscape'(Herod et al., 2007). There has been discussion about whether labour can effectively remake the spatial relations created by globalization for its own ends or whether it merely responds to the remaking of those relations by capital. Herod (2001) has argued that the remaking of space by labour has tended to be downplayed by critical geographers. He has given a number of examples of labour remaking space, including the use of CMC to redefine the spatial scope of action (1998a; 2001).

For Herod, labour solidarity is part of this remaking of spatial relations: 'The practice of labor solidarity is an inherently geographical one...a process of opening up the landscape and making the connections between workers in different parts of the globe visible' (Herod, 2003: p. 509). In the 'virtual strike' this takes place explicitly and in very graphic forms, which enable us to consider the potential for and means by which trade unions can make a space conducive to practical solidarity and the pursuit of their demands.

The forms and effectiveness of Internet-mediated labour solidarity

The 'virtual strike' is one example of what we call 'cybersolidarity' – Internet-mediated action in support of trade unions or groups of workers involved in disputes with employers or the state (Robinson, 2006, 2008). Of the different forms of cybersolidarity – including email campaigns, boycott campaigns, and the collection of funds – the IBM strike most closely approximates 'info war' or 'hacktivism', where the information assets of a target are attacked over the net (Walker, 2002), though the action also involved an online petition which could be emailed to IBM Italy management. However, the insertion of this action into a virtual world suggests a new form of cybersolidarity in which aspirations to a 'Cyber Picket Line' (the title of an early labour website) takes on a direct force by virtue of its telepresence in a virtual world. From this there emerge similarities and differences between Second Life and other actions which affect the viability of Second Life actions as a form of cybersolidarity.

Collectivity, co-location and co-presence in Second Life

Second Life embodies a particular set of social relations in a virtual space. Within this space avatars – software representations of humans controlled by real-world actors – can exist and act, subject to a set of evolving rules governing acceptable behaviour, economic relations and political governance decided on by the owners of the real world company Linden Labs. The spatial and social relations of capitalism are inscribed in Second Life but the degree of freedom of action permitted means that they remain open to subversion.

Any strike requires the creation of a collective actor pursuing its shared goals. Collectivity can emerge from common action in pursuit of a shared goal as well as more structurally determined causes such as membership of a union or working for the same employer. It can occur as a result of solidarity action, which may take place through spatial dispersion of the participants. In Second Life they can be brought together at a location in the virtual world that allows not merely a shared goal but the emergence of deeper forms of interaction and collectivity.

Zhao and Elesh's (2008) distinction between co-location and co-presence explains why the possibility of social interaction often remains unfulfilled when people are at the same location and therefore why technologies such as the Internet that potentially connect people do not necessarily lead to deeper social relationships. Co-location is a spatial relationship, 'being in' a place, mutually present and within range. Co-presence is a social relationship, 'being with' someone, mutually accessible and 'in touch'. Both are possible virtually in Second Life.

Generally co-location is constrained from becoming co-presence by social norms such as those regarding politeness, privacy, and appropriate behaviour. Although these rules are somewhat looser in Second Life, they remain a constraint. However, Shah-Shuja (2008), in a study of demonstrations and riots, argues that in such situations of collective action and shared goals, these restrictions of everyday life can break down, creating a situation where mutual learning and informal sociability are possible. Such situations of co-presence occurred in the course of the IBM strike.

The initial event

Background

IBM has been a major investor in Second Life, spending $10 million on buying land and developing virtual built environments. Some IBM areas in the Second Life world are public and function as sales and marketing tools; others are restricted to IBM employees for internal purposes such as international meetings. IBM has recently announced that is will host Second Life software on its own computers with seamless access to and from the public Second Life grid run by Linden Labs. More than 6000

IBM employees spend some or all of their time in Second Life (Barillari, 2008a) and the company has sought to control its employees' activities in Second Life by issuing a code of conduct enforceable through internal disciplinary measures (McDougall, 2007).

IBM has traditionally been a paternalistic and anti-union employer. The dispute with its Italian workforce arose when IBM Italy rejected a claim for a small pay rise, cancelled a performance bonus worth €1000 and refused to talk to representatives of the 9000-strong Italian workforce, organized in the Rappresentenza Sindacale Unitaria (RSU) union.

The initiative for the Second Life action came from RSU, who approached the international union federation, Union Network International (UNI), at the time the only union organization with a presence in Second Life (Revkin, 2008). For the RSU the Second Life strike was a response on which the authority of the union depended after other attempts to resolve the dispute had failed (Barillari, 2008a). Publicity went out in advance through unions and labour portals such as Labour Start. The action also received considerable media attention, with the result that more than 900 people had registered to take part in the action beforehand (Barillari, 2008a). Its precise timing remained secret until shortly before it started, when those who had registered received email details on when and how to take part. It took place over 12 hours to enable supporters across a range of time zones to take part. The Second Life protest was also coordinated with Real Life pickets outside the IBM offices in Italy. (All online materials relating to the action, including the blog of the action and instructions to participants, can be found at http://ibmslprotest.blogspot.com.)

On the day

RSU and UNI had taken considerable steps to prepare the action in Second Life, including setting up a UNI site to which protesters were advised to report initially. There the avatars could pick up placards and put on T-shirts so that they were clearly identified with the strike. Helpers speaking several languages were on hand to provide information on what to do and how to do it. A central platform had buttons to enable the avatars to 'teleport' (move instantly) to a number of IBM installations in Second Life, where further helpers were on hand. They carried banners both to inform passers-by of what was going on and to suggest how they might take part by signing an online petition; they also offered advice for protesters on what they could do.

For the early part of the day, protesters could wander in and out of largely deserted IBM locations. As the action became more focused and the protesters became more numerous, IBM reacted by closing down its Business

Figure 8.1 Protester excluded from IBM space.

Centre to the public, despite the boast in its publicity that 'the business center is staffed 24 hours per day, five days per week, with global access from Los Angeles to Paris to Sydney'. Anyone trying to enter without a password bounced off an invisible barrier (see Figure 8.1). The protest therefore brought about the closure of a public space 'open for business' and its transformation into a private territory open only to those who could be trusted by IBM. Here a shift in spatial and social relations coincided directly. The rights of the owners of the space were asserted against those seeking to transform the space into a site of protest – a function that in Real Life would be carried out by police or security guards.

However, this technical solution failed to work as an anonymous contributor to the UNI blog (open for protesters to describe their experiences) reported:

'Remember the IBM Business Center I was telling you about? The one that closed down some parts so protesters couldn't enter anymore? Well I don't know what miracle happened, but my avatar got in...to a real staff meeting!

'They were discussing the corporate website's new functionalities, it seems. So since I managed to get in, why not call some of my protester friends? Minutes later, some 20 participants and staff teleported to literally crash the meeting. We had people saying slogans, some beeping sounds, horns and again, the jumping up and down with our banners and flying fish...It was the most disrupting event I've witnessed so far!

Figure 8.2 Pickets gatecrash an IBM meeting.

'The poor IBM staff were quite confused and asked us to go protest outside. We, in return, demanded to speak to IBM management to put forward our requests.

'They ended up canceling their meeting'. (See Figure 8.2.)

In this scenario, two claims to control the space for conflicting purposes clashed literally (well, virtually) face–face. For the IBM executives, their business meeting was disrupted by the presence of the pickets, for whom their telepresence, in turn, marked an assertion of their control over the space and its transformation into what Lefebvre calls a 'counter-space'.

This went beyond a mere presence or protest. According to one of the organizers,

> 'When we planned the IBM Protest in [Second life (SL)], we had not thought of the fact we'd be blocking real IBM work in SL that day. The number of avatars allowed on IBM sims (islands) was around 70 – which we reached for more than 12 hours in a row. No IBM staff could get to their island nor could their customers' (Revkin, 2008).

How different is this from the way a picket line might operate in real life? Another participant wrote on the UNI blog:

'I don't know about you, but this is my first virtual protest! Surprising to **notice how close to [Real Life] it really is.**

'I'm in a virtual world, protesting outside IBM offices, but I'm still hungry, my fingers are getting cold (my office is in Switzerland) and people in Second Life are exactly as you'd expect them to be in the streets: SHOUTING slogans, jumping up and down, picketing and mingling. You have the quiet ones who sit on a bench and watch, the really original ones with funny outfits (I met a French-speaking Banana today), and the ones playing music and talking too.

'**Yet, nothing's normal:** no one I meet 'has' a real name, I have no idea if they are all IBM workers, trade unionists or spies, if they are from Canada or India! But they all showed up, speaking many languages, demonstrating with the banners, all wearing coloured IBM T-shirts.

'*Nothing's normal*, except that IBM management hasn't met with us in SL and still hasn't offered a response to our repeated requests for a return to the bargaining table and decent wages and benefits for its Italian workers. We'll just have to keep going at it!' (Emphasis in the original.)

The experiences of the author were similar: by late afternoon a large group had gathered outside the Business Centre. There was lots of conversation in Italian, English, French, and Spanish, partly sharing experiences of the day, partly discussing where pickets were most urgently needed and partly talking about how Second Life worked. But there was also a shared sense of excitement in taking part in what UNI called 'a first in labour history', and chatting about where people came from, what union they were in and how they had got involved. Co-location led to the closer interaction of co-presence, expressed in collective self-organization, mutual assistance and learning, the sharing of experience and informal sociability.

While coordinated international solidarity action is not new in labour history, what was new was the bringing together of a global collective in a shared cyberspace that allowed direct communication, social interaction and a collective presence at a location. The latter is, in Lefebvre's account, central to the creation of a social space that can overcome the dominance of the spatial practices of capital: 'The form of social space is encounter, assembly, simultaneity... [it] implies actual or potential assembly at a single point or around that point'. The form of the action in Second Life was able therefore to articulate a counter-force to IBM's commercial presence in Second Life.

The aftermath

In the period immediately following the Second Life event participants used the UNI blog to discuss possible tactics to follow it up in the real world. A total of 1849 avatars were counted as having taken part in the

Second Life action (Barillari, 2008a) and though this does not translate directly into numbers of real people, figures of 1000 on the email list of participants and 700 sending online petitions to IBM Italy seem broadly to correspond to the number registering for the action. Its international nature was also impressive, with participants emanating from 30 countries. Despite this, there was uncertainty whether this would translate into a real-life success in getting IBM to back down.

However on 24 October, within a month of the Second Life protest, the CEO of IBM Italy resigned. IBM denied this had anything to do with the strike but negotiations with the Works Council also resumed and the performance bonuses were reinstated. The aims of the Second Life action were therefore achieved, though, as with cybersolidarity actions in general, it is difficult to assess the relative importance of IT-mediated and other forms of action in determining the outcome of an industrial dispute (Robinson, 2006, 2008). Christine Revkin, organizer of the Second Life protest for UNI, commented on the blog: 'The threat of strike action in the "real world" by the Italian unions after the virtual protest has certainly also helped to break the deadlock. Yet the impact of this historical action in Second Life must not be underestimated'. It was perhaps also the novelty of the protest and its consequent press coverage that were particularly important in creating pressure on IBM.

Two other actions against IBM took place after the 27 September strike. The first on 27 March 2008 was a protest rather than a strike requested by IBM workers in France to draw attention to IBM's outsourcing of jobs to AT&T and RICOH 'so we maintained a low profile and we got less results than the first virtual strike'. The same type of organization was used as in the strike and 'it was very simple and easy'. Though there was less publicity in the mass media, the outsourcing was stopped in France following an intervention by a major customer. However, there was a fall in the number taking part in Second Life despite the action having been publicized through many of the same labour and Second Life channels as before. The second was a strike at IBM Turkey over recognition in August 2008 (Barillari, 2008a).

From event to place

Union Island

The success of 27 September acted as a catalyst to bring together UNI, RSU, the British TUC and the German public sector union Verdi and others on a common project to create a long-term union presence in Second Life. This was Union Island, a Second Life 'sim' with a landscape and buildings inaugurated on 1 May 2008. It contains exhibitions on labour history and current union campaigns; an area to learn how to use Second Life; another on why you should join a union; a museum dedicated to the IBM strike; and, last but not least, a bar complete with dartboard and pool table, where informal discussions can take place. There are also private rooms for formal meetings (see Figures 8.3 and 8.4).

Figure 8.3 The Union Island bar.

Figure 8.4 The arena on Union Island.

While different sponsors had differing priorities, many goals were shared (Revkin, 2008; Wood, 2008), that is:

- having a place where trade unionists from around the word could meet both formally and informally without travel costs;
- having a place where people could be introduced to trade unionism;
- having a base on the net for campaigning and actions like the IBM one;
- forging new partnerships with groups active in Second Life (NGOs, political groups) and 'digitally creative' people;
- learning more about virtual worlds and what people are doing in them;
- promoting the use of 'Web 2.0' tools by unions.

So far Union Island has attracted 'a few hundred people a month' (Wood, 2008) and hosted campaigns on May Day and World Day for Decent Work. There is a user group which provides input on and assistance with the further development of Union Island. At present, Union Island is usually uninhabited by avatars but there will soon be 'an everyday staffed reception' as 'Second Life islands that don't run regular public activities aren't really visited' (Revkin, 2008). Staff will both help users with Second Life and provide information on joining a union. It is hoped to attract users of Union Island through publicity and support within unions, as well as passers-by in Second Life, those seeking to learn more about the labour movement (a number of university politics classes have visited Union Island), and those who simply encounter Union Island through publicity material such as the Union Island blog (http://www.slunionisland.org/).

Union Island remains in its early stages and is seen by its originators as an experiment aimed to supplement other online efforts such as blogs and e-lists and more traditional union activities offline. The use of Second Life is 'a bit of blue sky thinking' (Wood, 2008), 'an extra tool to add to our "communications" ark and not something to replace our current ways of operating'. More generally, though, Web 2.0 tools do provide a new dimension where 'collective knowledge-based tools which highly improve our members' participation, involvement, and mobilization' (Revkin, 2008) can lead to the creation of 'an open digital community' with user-created content and activities and 'a horizontal organization without hierarchies', not a new union but a new evolution from within existing structures (Barillari, 2008b).

Contrasting modes of action

The modest start to Union Island contrasts with the sudden invasion of Second Life by hundreds of trade unionists on 27 September 2007. What are the causes of this gap between a one-off event and a long-term project?

Media coverage and the novelty of a 'first in labour history' doubtless played a part in attracting participants to the IBM action, as did the fact that many of those involved worked for the same company. However, there are also important distinctions in the modes of action and participation of the two openings for trade union activity. The IBM action involved a highly focused and instrumental use of Second Life as a means to the well-defined end of getting IBM to restore bonuses and bargaining rights in Italy. It could appeal not just to IBM employees but to a broader constituency of labour activists. It required a short burst of involvement in Second Life with detailed guidance provided by the organisers. It is unclear how many of the IBM pickets have ever returned to Second Life.

In contrast, Union Island provides a Second Life location and environment with the potential of becoming the space for a whole range of activities. It is far more open-ended, leaving users with potentially a lot of control over how the space is used, which requires both an awareness of the possibilities the technology offers and a higher level of commitment. In the preparatory stages, potential users were asked on the Union Island blog to suggest how they might take advantage of the site, though suggestions and instructions on how to use Second Life are also provided.

The organizers are aware of this gap and see one way to increase involvement as organizing one-off solidarity events such as the IBM strike to draw people into seeing the potential of Second Life and Union Island. Therefore Christine Revkin of UNI (2008) writes:

> 'People seem eager to participate in SL events, almost as if they were anxious for there to be a new IBM-like dispute they can join! That kind of enthusiasm is valuable...so, in a way, I'm looking forward to the next big union problem we'll come across!'

Another aspect of building up use of Union Island involves increasing a more general awareness among trade unionists of the value of Web 2.0 tools and providing training opportunities to learn about them. Here more traditional union channels are used to distribute material both on the tools generally and how to get started in Second Life.

Apart from 'in-world' solidarity and propaganda actions, the major value of Union Island must lie in its role as a direct channel of communication that allows co-presence and therefore the prospect of more directly social and many-to-many interactions than other media such as e-lists. As a direct channel of communication it can also be the foundation for new networks and collectivities. Participants in Union Island include Mongolian trade unionists who face travel difficulties and therefore have few direct contacts outside their countries. Wood (2008) also gives the example of 'getting a few organisers together in a virtual bar and finding two of them are facing the same union busting firm on different sides of the Atlantic, and can make vital link-ups in tactics for responding to it. Fascinating "little sparks" that point the way to something very exciting, but that will be hard to replicate systematically without serious resource, at least until the technology mainstreams, and users are able to steer it much more for themselves, letting a lot more of these sparks happen'.

From counter-space to counter-place?

How does the shift from event to long-term presence affect the theory of the production of space used to analyse the IBM action? In one respect, Union Island confirms Nunes' view that cyberspace is relational and enacted and emerges from forms of social practice. For months afterwards the ephemeral nature of the social space created in the strike could be seen in the deserted state of the IBM strike Second Life site on Commonwealth Island, littered with relics of the September action – a virtual physical space that had ceased to be a social space. Participants withdrew to their Real Life location; the collective subject of 27 September had dissipated. Nunes points to dispersal as the specific means by which network relationships end. Yet the potential for reconstitution of the network also existed. A willingness to take part might be re-created by the means used for their initial recruitment together with UNI's central email list of participants.

Nunes' insistence that cyberspace is 'always structured as an event' and Lefebvre's view of counter-spaces as 'assembly at a point' miss a dimension that can be found in David Harvey's work and which emerges from consideration of a project such as Union Island. That is the role of what Harvey (1996) calls 'permanences', such as places, that emerge from the flux of social practice as 'reifications of free-flowing processes' and have a structuring (enabling and constraining) effect upon them. 'Such permanences come to occupy a piece of a space in an exclusive way (for a time) and thereby define a place...they are contingent on the processes that create, sustain and dissolve them'.

Lefebvre's resistance to the creation of permanences on the grounds that they bring the authoritarian closure of possibility means, according to Harvey, that he cannot conceive of alternatives to domination, even in Utopian terms: 'For [Lefebvre] the production of space must always remain as an endlessly open possibility. The effect, unfortunately, is to leave the actual spaces of any alternatives frustratingly undefined' (Harvey, 2000: pp. 182–3). Instead, places are for Harvey (1996: pp. 316, 318) 'the focus of the imaginary' and possible sites for the construction of 'a form of community which is expressive of values outside of those typically found in a capitalist materialist and highly monetized culture'.

Looking at Second Life in this way enables us to see more clearly the relationship between Lefebvrean events such as the IBM action and the construction of a 'permanence' such as Union Island. Union Island becomes something closer to a 'counter-place' in Harvey's sense of a more enduring spatial structure through which flows of social activity counterposed to the dominant order can flow. It is far easier to construct such places in Second Life than outside it and to escape the domination of monetary transactions. Their creators are then faced with the task of making such places into lived social spaces.

From space to place and back again

The 27 September Second Life action meets the picture of space and its remaking by labour painted by Herod when he writes: 'the manipulation of space by workers and unions is a potent form of social power [which] flows through spatial structures just as it flows through social structures' (Herod, 1998b: p. 5). For the startled IBM executives and the pickets forcing the closure of the Business Centre there could be little doubt about the social power emerging from the exploitation of the spatial characteristics of Second Life by the trade unionists. Two alternative social spaces collided in contesting control of the mapped territory of IBM's islands in Second Life and the spatial processes associated with them: Were they a space for business activity or a site of protest?

This social power – along with the verbal and physical interactions among the participants – points to the real material nature of the action even though it took place in a virtual world. The sense of place referred to by Ondrejka and in Lefebvre's idea of points of assembly did come into existence at the sites of the protest, though probably none of the participants would have been able to say exactly where the action was taking place. As a lived experience, the mediation of an everyday trade union activity (picketing) by Second Life led to a strange dis-location and feeling of being in two worlds simultaneously.

Union Island marks an attempt to re-create this sense of place, 'our place' for trade unionists in Second Life, on a longer-term basis and open to a wider range of activities, from exploiting the capacity of Second Life for gathering distant individuals in a common space of co-presence to campaigning actions and possibly even formal negotiations with employers. Its success is dependent on its becoming somewhere where its potential as place and the range of activities enabled by Second Life are exploited through the creation of new social spaces marked by the activity of a constituency for whom using Second Life is another tool in their armoury as trade unionists. This in turn requires a consistent nurturing in the form of information, training, and opportunities to get involved.

In Robinson (2008), this author suggested that labour solidarity based on use of the Internet needed to be rooted in place-based industrial action such as a sympathy strike or a refusal to handle an organization's goods if it is to be a tool in winning disputes. The nature of virtual worlds both blurs and reinforces this statement – blurs it in that the status of Second Life as a place is ambiguous and reinforces it in that it is precisely the material and physical form taken by the action in Second Life that gave it its force. Whether it was the action in the virtual world or the threat of real-world, place-based action that led to the satisfactory outcome for the IBM workers is impossible to judge. Whatever its contribution to the final result, the materiality and the resultant social power emerging from the action in Second Life are evident. These associations remain, however, more fragile than those forged by daily real-life existence in the workplace – as is the case for Internet-based trade union actions of any type.

Emerging from this analysis is a double dialectic of the spatial and the virtual as seen in the world of Second Life: the dialectic of space as event and network and place as permanence; and what Aoyama and Sheppard (2003: p. 1152) describe as the 'dialectics of geographic and virtual space...meaning that neither is reducible to the other; dialectics, inter alia, of specificity and universality, of liberating flows and grounded forces, and of the contrasting logics of distance and proximity'. Both are mediated by a range of – often conflicting – human activities and goals and a complex and multi-layered technology that potentially allows them to be realized. Such technological mediation can in its turn lead to the emergence of new cultural practices 'reflecting and conditioning the emergence of new forms of environmental knowing'. (Dourish, 2006)

Implications for trade union action in a virtual world

Our analysis of the 27 September action and the creation of Union Island has a number of implications for union use of virtual worlds. Many of these lessons have already been drawn from the IBM action by its organisers, in part through the creation of Union Island.

First, the materiality of activities carried out in Second Life points to its possibilities as an arena of online trade unionism beyond its function of allowing better contact across distance. Second Life is not just a game or leisure activity. Insofar as companies such as IBM use virtual worlds as a vehicle and location for their real-life activities, it can also be an arena for trade unions that shares many of the characteristics of place-based actions such as picket lines. At present, it is unclear how far business use of virtual worlds will grow but the potential to pursue union aims in the virtual realm has been clearly demonstrated. Unions are already watching how far companies do begin to use virtual worlds and Unions 2.0 is looking at technological developments that can be used by unions to pursue their aims.

The IBM action brought together a number of elements, all of which are essential for successful trade union action involving Second Life or the Internet. They are: one or more constituencies that can be mobilised to become an active collective actor and possibly motivated to take part in subsequent activities; an infrastructure that allows users to exploit the possibilities of the technology and to take part in the activities; and a group of 'intermediaries' (Robinson, 2008) who set up actions, seek to involve potential participants, and create the infrastructure. Neither an active network nor the infrastructure comes about spontaneously, so in order to bring about an event such as the IBM action that can create a new social space in Second Life, a group needs to take on responsibility for the organization. The setting up of Union Island is in part an attempt to create a permanent infrastructure that can serve many different actions, thus cutting the cost of each campaign in terms of time and effort, and also to provide a focal point in Second Life for both those willing to get involved in the 'back room' work and also those just generally interested in finding out more about unions in Second Life.

The most difficult aspect of this is maintaining awareness and commitment so that there is a constituency that can be mobilized in response to a need for action or other union campaigning in Second Life. There are a number of groups that may be appealed to in terms of a pre-existing identity, not just trade unionists and labour activists but also young people who may be convinced more easily to join a Facebook group than a trade union. The initial novelty may fade and, while there will usually be a group for whom participation springs from political commitment or fascination with the technology, the sustaining of a group of potentially active supporters requires attention on a consistent basis.

Implications for research

Our analysis of trade union use of Second Life points to two directions in which further research can be undertaken. The strike raises questions about the transfer of real-world social relations into the virtual realm and how the use of Second Life both reproduces and transforms them. In turn, this requires analysis of the social and economic structures encouraged or imposed in Second Life by Linden Labs – for example, by presenting it as a realm for commerce and entrepreneurship, basing it around the sale and purchase of land and developing its own currency and markets – and how those structures are taken up or rejected. The political economy, governance, and social structure of Second Life need further critical investigation.

The second direction relates more directly to trade union use of Second Life and the Internet. While the role of the Internet in trade union action is now an established fact, there are few recent detailed case studies on the means by which ICTs and trade union action interact. As we have seen, the content of a technology and the way it is used can be central to attracting the participants necessary to making an action effective. The development of new technologies may create new opportunities both for unions and those with whom they have to deal so that awareness of this area must become more central to union practice and therefore to research in this general area. Research in this area needs to pay close attention to the contributions of the technological, the social and the industrial relations frameworks in the promotion of trade union activity through the Internet.

The nature of virtual worlds also poses new challenges for researchers. In observing what goes on in Second Life, it is necessary to be 'in-world' and there exists one or more added layers of mediation to negotiate to make sense of the meaning of what appears to be going on. One aspect of this is the identity and role the researcher should adopt in Second Life – the choice of avatar, clothes, and name might affect how the researcher is seen. In addition, in the case of this author, the role of the activist as researcher is already complex and many-sided in that she is both a committed participant and a recorder of what occurs (Shah-Shuja, 2008). Research stories that investigate these issues would be valuable as part of the broader area of Internet research.

Conclusions

The 27 September UNI action in support of IBM trade unionists and the creation of Union Island have enabled us to examine the mechanics of the production of space and the relationship between space and place in a virtual world. The mobilization of trade unionists and labour activists for 27 September led to a new social space being created and superimposed on the landscape of Second Life, contesting the physical and functional boundaries established in that landscape and shifting its spatial relations in pursuit of their social and economic goals. In both the strike and Union Island there is a distinctive coming together of three dimensions: the spatial, the virtual, and those aspects concerned with the specific nature of trade unionism and labour as a social actor.

The spatial aspect of the IBM action points beyond the standard conception of space towards seeing the production of space as a social process involving the employment of social power. Space as the product of this process both enables and constrains social practices such as picketing and business meetings. The action also shows how different forms of social order are embodied in space and the creation of new forms of social space that take on the character of counter-spaces. However, this analysis, though recognizing the need to 'materialize the context' (Nunes, 2006) and recognize the material element in the production of cyberspace, downplays the role of place as something relatively permanent that, even in Second Life, can not merely evoke meaning but also provide a spur to and location for activity. Union Island therefore attempts to provide a location at which to encourage trade unionists to exploit the possibilities of Second Life. It in turn requires a social infrastructure for its creation and maintenance.

The virtual world of Second Life is not just any space but one that imposes certain material, social, and geographic forms by virtue of its nature as a particular type of cyberspace. Its character as a software representation accessed through the net and manipulated by simulated humans creates spatial relationships which are distinct from those characteristic of the production of space or cyberspace in general. Users experience being simultaneously in two places – one virtual, one based on a physical location in relation to the computer – leading to an ambiguous sense of location. At the same time, new social groupings come into being, enabled by the virtual environment and permitting direct interaction of a type previously impossible. On 27 September this made possible the coming together of a widely dispersed set of actors, who appeared 'as if' they were at a single location and were able to interact with one another. This gave the protest a social power that it might not otherwise have had if it had been restricted to the sending of emails or to demonstrations at separate real-world locations.

What gives the IBM Second Life action and Union Island their distinctiveness was the action's connection to a particular group of actors: trade unionists and their supporters. They brought to Second Life particular sets of established social practices (strikes, picketing, and collective bargaining) and institutions (unions, works councils) alongside distinctive identities and dispositions such as the formation of a collective based around ideas of solidarity. The spatial dimension of the action confirms Herod's view that unions can derive social power from exploiting spatial structures and relationships. The remaking of space can also affect industrial relations outcomes and union strength, even if, as after 27 September, spatial relations revert to normal.

The extent to which labour can take advantage of the features of virtual worlds such as Second Life – whether by making actions such as 27 September an established form of cybersolidarity or by establishing them as a means of attaining broader union goals – remains an open question. The ultimate value of action in Second Life as a method of cybersolidarity depends on the long-term future of Second Life as a space for business activity, the ability of those subject to virtual world protest to protect themselves, whether via technical or legal means, from 'info war', and the development and pervasiveness of the technology. Union Island demonstrates the willingness of trade unions to invest in developing the infrastructure needed to make exploitation of Second Life by trade unionists easy and effective and to enable them to take advantage of the particular spatial and social relationships it offers. The key to this is increasingly the human factor – the education and involvement of trade unionists in a new, virtual world.

Acknowledgements

Thanks to Davide Barillari of RSU, Christine Revkin of UNI and John Wood of the TUC for their help in the writing of this chapter. An earlier version of the material on the IBM virtual strike ('Picket Lines in a Virtual World: Labour and the Production of (Cyber)Space') was presented at the ISTAS E-Society conference in Portugal, April 2008.

References

Aoyama, Y. and Sheppard, E. (2003). 'The dialectics of geographic and virtual space.' *Environment and Planning* A(35): 1151–6.

Barillari, D. (2008a) Interview with Davide Barillari, RSU and IBM Italy Works Council. September 2008.

Barillari, D. (2008b) Presentation to 'Unions 2.0' meeting, Milan, 11 July 2008.
Brunsting, S. and Postmes, T. (2002). 'Social movement participation in the online age: Predicting offline and online collective action.' *Small Group Research*, 33(5): 525–54.
Dourish, P. (2006) Re-Space-ing Place: Place and Space Ten Years on, in Proc. ACM Conf. Computer-Supported Cooperative Work CSCW 2006, Banff, Alberta, 299–308.
Harvey, D. (1996) *Justice, Nature and the Geography of Difference*, Blackwell: Oxford.
Harvey, D. (2000) *Spaces of Hope*, University of California Press: Los Angeles.
Harvey, D. (2006) *Spaces of Global Capitalism*. Verso, London.
Herod, A. (1998a) Of Blocs, Flows and Networks; The End of the Cold War, cyberspace and the geo-economics of organized labor at the fin de millenaire. In O. Tuathail, A. Herod and S.M. Roberts (eds) *An Unruly World? Globalization, Governance and Geography*, Routledge: London.
Herod, A. (1998b) The Spatiality of Labor Unionism: A Review Essay. In *Organizing the Landscape: Geographical Perspectives on Labor Unionism*, 1–36.
Herod, A. (2001) *Labor Geographies: Workers and the Landscapes of Capitalism*. New York: Guilford Press.
Herod, A. (2003) Geographies of Labor Internationalism. *Social Science History*, 27(4): 501–23.
Herod, A., Rainnie, A. and McGrath-Champ, S. (2007) Working space: why incorporating the spatial is central to theorizing work and employment practices. *Work, Employment and Society*, 24(2): 247–62.
Kendall, L. (1999) 'Recontextualizing "Cyberspace": Methodological Considerations for On-Line Research'. In S. Jones (ed.) *Doing Internet Research*. Thousand Oaks and London: Sage Publications, 57–74.
Lefebvre, H. (1991) *The Production of Space*. Oxford: Blackwell.
McDougall, P. (2007) IBM Issues Employee Conduct Rules for Second Life. *InformationWeek*, 27 (July).
Nunes, M. (2006) *Cyberspaces of Everyday Life*. University of Minnesota Press: Minneapolis.
Ondrejka, C. (2004) Aviators, Moguls, Fashionistas and Barons: Economics and Ownership in Second Life. http://ssrn.com/abstract=614663
Ondrejka, C. (2007) Collapsing Geography: *Second Life*, Innovation and the Future of National Power. *Innovations*, 2(3): 27–54. http://ssrn.com/abstract=1023493
Revkin, C. (2008) Interview with Christine Revkin, Union Network International. September 2008.
Robinson, B. (2006) Cybersolidarity: Internet-based Campaigning and Trade Union Internationalism. In *Social Inclusion: Societal and Organizational Implications for Information Systems: IFIP TC8 WG 8.2 International Working Conference*. Limerick, Ireland, 123–36.
Robinson, B. (2008) Solidarity Across Cyberspace: Internet Campaigning, Labour Activism and the Remaking of Trade Union Internationalism. *Work Organisation, Labour and Globalisation*, 2(1): 152–64.
Shah-Shuja, M. (2008) *Zones of Proletarian Development*. Openmute: London.
Walker, S. (2002) *To Picket Just Click It! Social netwar and industrial conflict in a global economy*. Leeds Metropolitan University School of Information Management, IMRIP 2002-1.
Wood, J. (2008) Interview with John Wood, TUC, London.
Zhao, S. and Elesh, D. (2008) Copresence As 'Being With', *Information, Communication & Society*, 11(4): 565–83.

9
Community as Commodity: Social Networking and Transnational Capitalism

David Kreps and Erika Pearson

Introduction

Social Networking Sites (SNSs) are one of the most publicly discussed innovations of the Internet and particularly of 'Web 2.0'. While community-building and social networking are certainly not new, the speed, scope and reach facilitated by these sites have heralded unprecedented innovation in the ways in which networked individuals approach their social networking. SNSs continue to grow, yet the balance between the technological features of such sites which support social networking and those which facilitate online advertising remains precarious, and frequently makes national and international news.

One factor that has received little attention in the literature on SNSs is the notion of 'cultural fit'. Searle and Ward (1990) introduced the concept of 'cultural fit' into the literature on intercultural relations. The premise is that it is not a personality per se that predicts the nature of an adjustment, but the 'fit' between a personality and a new cultural background. Human resources and recruitment experts have taken up this notion, but as yet it seems little applied in the context of membership of and engagement with online communities. But, more importantly, for the purposes of this chapter, this notion of cultural fit has been used in the marketing literature (Goad and Mooney, 2008) addressing the needs of entrepreneurs in a rapidly changing market, and used to emphasize the need for venture capital to be directed towards economically unexploited but pre-existing activities for maximum return on investment. The message here is that to ensure that cultural fit is achieved between new product and potential consumer, the new product should locate itself within the potential consumer's pre-existing activities and not attempt to shift the consumer into new and potentially ill-fitting activities.

While much has been written about the implications of social networks themselves, there has been little research on the nature and activities of those who develop and maintain the platforms upon which these networks rest. In particular, the venture capital which often seeds the growth of these sites is often treated as an anonymous and unremarkable part of the process.

This chapter seeks to interrogate these aspects of SNSs by going further than the concept of cultural fit into cultural concepts originally developed by Antonio Gramsci. Gramsci's cultural reworking of Marxist understandings of the nature of society, and particularly of capitalist societies, has given us the notion of hegemony, which we explore in some depth and apply in our reading of online communities. Facebook and Google's OpenSocial are used as specific case examples to exemplify these issues.

The phenomenon of massive virtual communities

Since the turn of the millennium – and especially since the bursting of the dot-com bubble – we have seen the World Wide Web grow from a static resource into an interactive space that is frequently referred to as Web 2.0 (boyd and Ellison, 2007; Madden and Fox, 2006). From the once purely text-based communities of the early Web, social networking and interaction has now developed to include visually rich environments (at least 180 or so at the time of writing), which are quickly developing a strong presence online (Plant, 2004).

From their introduction, SNSs such as MySpace, Facebook, Bebo, and Habbo have attracted tens of millions of users, many of whom have integrated these activities into their daily lives. These sites allow users to connect or reconnect with people both locally and globally, via email, instant messaging, sharing in business or social exchanges, and videoconferencing, and even to immerse themselves in virtual worlds that constitute both an escape from the real and a place within which to undertake real socialization (Turkle, 1995; Hardy, 2002).

Through SNSs, we are able to (rediscover and) talk to (old) friends from school or college, connect to existing or potential business contacts, or make new acquaintances regardless of the limits of physical geography. We are able to build relationships with people without being so rigidly bound by region, nationality, ethnicity, social role, family, or occupation as to the kinds of companionship we can forge and call our own. This allows us to meet people based on shared interests, political views, or other social activities, or on common language or shared racial or sexuality based identities. It is the formation of these communities of interest (Anderson, 1983/2006; Feenberg and Bakardjieva, 2004) which is arguably SNSs' biggest strength.

SNSs offer a range of different technological features which cater to a wide range of interests and practices. While these key technological features are fairly consistent, the cultures that emerge around SNSs are varied. Some – for example, Ecademy or LinkedIn are specifically professional; others such as MySpace, are centred on music and popular culture. Bebo, Habbo, ClubPenguin, and others are almost exclusively for children or teenagers, and others still, such as Facebook, attempt to bring many disparate social groups together in one multilayered virtual space.

While there has been a fair amount of scholarship – for example in the computer-mediated communication (CMC), and human computer interaction (HCI) fields – concerning SNSs, much of it has focused on the interactions and networking of such sites, and much of the criticism upon the meaning of friendship there: for example, does competitive 'friending' turn these so-called friends into mere cyber-acquaintances? Such 'friendliness' is no substitute for genuine friendship, according to Professor Ray Pahl, co-author of *Rethinking Friendship* (Spencer and Pahl, 2006), and only leaves us feeling dissatisfied. In his opinion, Facebook is a form of immaturity: 'It's not a real social network', he says,

> 'it mimics the playground insecurities of primary school kids piling up best friends to find their social niche. When people grow up and settle down, they realise that real friendship isn't about turning on the computer – it requires real effort and taking the rough with the smooth' (Independent, 2007).

Scholarship in the IS field has similarly focused on the 'friendship' issue, and on the nature of networked communication (boyd and Ellison, 2007). The main strands of enquiry have focused upon 'the generation of online ties and their integration into the individual's existing social network', on the one hand, and the 'role of new communication technologies as a new channel of communication', on the other (Mesch and Talmud, 2007). Other work in the computer science field has included an extraordinary hoovering up of data from 100,000 SNS profiles into a semantic map of personal tastes (Liu et al., 2006). Livingstone and Helsper's work offers a particularly interesting insight into how issues of 'anonymity, disclosure of intimate information and exchange of resources' (2007) affect communication.

Facebook was originally built for Harvard college students, in February 2004, by Harvard student Mark Zuckerberg and his 'friends'.[1] It grew during that year to include Stanford, Columbia, and Yale colleges. By May 2005 it had grown to support more than 800 college networks, was expanding into United States high-school networks, and then went international in October. In May 2006 it 'grew up', adding to its existing six million-plus userbase non-student networks based around the workplace – at first college staff, but soon businesses, corporations, and institutions. By the end of 2006 it had 12 million users. The summer of 2007, however, was the pivotal moment for Facebook as an SNS. In April there were 20 million users; in May they launched Facebook Platform, an application program interface (API), that allowed external developers to create and offer applications within Facebook, and by late summer 2008 the site boasted 100 million users. At this present rate of growth, Facebook will have around a quarter of a billion users by Summer 2009 (it is arguable, of course, whether all of these are 'active users'). From being based on an exclusive membership model (Harvard students) Facebook has opened up membership to anyone who can log in. These users can not only find and maintain connections with existing friends and colleagues (as the site intended for its original Harvard cohort), they can also use the site to form new, entirely virtual social network ties. New 'virtual' groupings are springing up daily – many simply for fun, to be discarded tomorrow (e.g. People Who Always Have To Spell Their Names For Other People); some with business in mind (e.g. the virtual twin of real-world trade association, Manchester Digital); political import (e.g. Support the Monks' protest in Burma); some with strange challenges (e.g. If 100,000 people join this group, I will legally change my name to Optimus Prime); and some with more personal gratification in mind. The networking and socialization supported by Facebook is in many respects a hybrid, replicating 'real-world' social interactions alongside facilitating the formation of new contacts based on interest rather than physical proximity. The complex webs of social ties this generates argues against claims regarding the 'immaturity' of social networking friendships.

Like many other SNSs, Facebook has grown from being a focused community built around the commonality of studenthood in the United States into an international community where you can find almost anyone who might ever join an SNS – and many for whom Facebook is their very first experience of online social networking. Users' personal profiles change daily with the news of the activities of all of their linked friends, who are forever sending each other messages using new applications which users must first install – and send to everyone they know – before they can receive and read the message. It is a virtual place of constant change, and perhaps this (at least appearance of) busy-ness is as much a part of its appeal as its ubiquity.

From MySpace to OurSpace: Google and OpenSocial

The continued growth of SNSs as they spread out from specialized groups and subcultures to encompass wider social networks has been matched by growing debate and discussion (particularly in the media) about the place and function of such SNSs within wider social practices. One common theme is the tensions between 'private' and 'public' behaviour on SNSs as users try to negotiate the contradictions between the intellectually known openness of these SNSs and the intimacy and emotional contact they feel as they actively build their own fragment of the wider social networks.

Another debate running parallel to this public–private tension is social–commercial conflicts exemplified by the introduction of Facebook's commercial system called 'Beacon' (which is discussed in more detail later in this chapter). Such disparities are not new, and have only become more accentuated as these social networks have evolved from the grassroots-style Bulletin Board Systems (BBSs) of the 1980s and 1990s, and other similar text-based forums, to the massive multimedia virtual environments of[1] today whose populations rival cities, and now even countries.[2] Social networks and virtual communities are no longer dominated by amateur enterprises. SNSs are a big and growing business concern, often requiring the efforts of sometimes hundreds of professionals and generating revenues that are attractive to investors.[3]

This formalizing and commercialization of SNSs occurs not only in the underlying code and infrastructure; it is also encroaching on the front-end of these sites, the spaces where users meet, socialize, set up profiles or avatars, and build what they may feel to be organic, natural, or unforced networks. The DataPortability project (http://dataportability.org) is one such formalization that will have an impact on multiple, currently discrete SNSs. Data portability involves cross-linking identity data – the profiles which form the core nodes of most SNSs – across multiple platforms (i.e. from MySpace to YouTube to del.icio.us). Data portability will link one large social network to another. While the aggregate number of users from this cross-platform interoperability is difficult to estimate given the number of both inactive and multiple identities, it is easy to argue that the end result will be truly massive extended virtual communities of overlapping networks. The social networking patterns will mimic the underlying infrastructure of the Internet itself.

One of the more immediate and intriguing outcomes of this push towards formal data portability in SNSs is the OpenSocial initiative being led by Google.[4] It works by connecting the 'containers' of the various SNSs (the codified structures which support the social interactions) and allowing information and applications to move freely from one container (say, Orkut) to another (MySpace). While this raises issues of identity management and questions as to who controls the information being disclosed by users at an individual level, in terms of social networks at a macro level, OpenSocial allows for information to be passed on or tracked back – information which includes details and patterns ripe for exploitation by companies and marketers. Unsurprisingly, this potential is not one of the features of OpenSocial hyped in the coverage: the focus instead is on how OpenSocial is the first true multiplatform initiative, and how a number of the largest and most influential SNSs are taking part.[5]

But not all: Facebook continues to hold out as more and more SNSs sign on to develop compatibility with OpenSocial. While the technical chatter regarding the cross-compatibility of applications and containers is interesting in its own right, what is more fascinating in terms of the discussion here is how both these approaches – OpenSocial's push towards openness of information exchange versus Facebook's extensive and popular but 'walled garden' approach to massive social networks – demonstrate the movement towards the commodification of virtual communities. To that end, these two approaches will be examined using ideas drawn from the work of Gramsci and Gill.

Gramsci, Gill, and the hegemony of the transnational historic bloc

This brings us to the critical core of this paper. Commodification, consumerism, and the power of rich elites constitute the field of enquiry of cultural and political theorists and philosophers. One philosopher whose writings have had a profound affect on our understanding of power in society is the early 20th-century Italian thinker, Antonio Gramsci, who 'recognised that social power is not a simple matter of domination on the one hand and subordination or resistance on the other' (Jones, 2006). Gramsci thus re-evaluated traditional Marxist understandings of modern capitalist societies by arguing that rather than being determined by underlying economic necessities, culture and politics formed a web of relations with the economy in which there is a continual shift of emphasis and influence. For this process he coined the term *hegemony*. 'Rather than imposing their will', Gramsci maintained, 'dominant' groups (or, more precisely, dominant alliances, coalitions or blocs) within democratic societies generally govern with a good degree of *consent* from the people they rule' – they achieve *hegemony* – 'and the maintenance of that consent is dependent upon an incessant repositioning of the relationship between rulers and ruled' (Jones, 2006: p. 3). Insidiously, a dominant bloc, in order to maintain its dominance, must be able to 'reach into the minds and lives of its subordinates, exercising its power as what appears to be a free expression of their own interests and desires' (Jones, 2006: p. 4).

This aspect of unwitting collusion on the part of the ruled with the strategies and tactics of their rulers is perhaps the best-known feature of Gramsci's concept of hegemony; that those strategies and tactics must constantly adapt to the shifting needs of the ruled is perhaps less appreciated. Dick Hebdige's work on subcultural groups perhaps expresses this dynamic best. A simple example of this approach is that of Punk. In the late 1970s the wearing of safety pins in one's ear and of torn fabrics loosely arranged as clothing was a statement of rebellion, of rejection of fashion – similar to Dada earlier in the century (Hebdige, 1979). By the early 1980s, however, this 'look' had become a fashion in itself. What was revolutionary had been absorbed, packaged, and sold back to the revolutionaries. Lifestyles becoming available in the shops in this way brings consumerism into sharp relief. Everything is allowed, so long as it can be absorbed into the dominant socioeconomic model (i.e. if it contributes to the market). Thus arises the pluralistic nature of the modern consumerist society.

This dominance of the market economy has been analysed with incisive clarity by Stephen Gill, Professor of Political Science at Canada's York University. Gill's work on the New World Order created after 1945 – of which he describes the world after 1991 as but the third phase – outlines the dominance of the market, of transnational capital, the G7 (and more recently G8 and G20) and the central role of US power in supporting and spearheading this dominance. The world after the Second World War, with its Marshall Plan, its NATO, and its emerging EEC, involved what Gill terms (using Gramscian language) an *international historical bloc* built on a *pax Americana* (Gill, 2003: p. 58). In the aftermath of that terrible worldwide conflict the American New Deal state became the model for the whole Western world, albeit somewhat modified by the changes required by wartime mobilization and the 'military–industrial complex' this had spawned. Roosevelt's New Deal of the

1930s – although it went further, at the time, and was later substantially cut back – nonetheless represented a significant shift in political and domestic policy in the United States, with its most lasting changes being an increased government control over the economy and money supply; intervention to control prices and agricultural production; the beginning of the federal welfare state, and the rise of trade union organizations. The Second World War tightened the relationship between government and economy through mandatory 'mobilization' of industrial units and workforce for the production of arms. This mobilization was not 'stood down' in 1945, as the Second World War became the Cold War, but evolved into what has since been termed the military–industrial complex – the combination of a nation's armed forces, its suppliers of weapons systems, supplies and services, and its civil government. This military–industrial complex, moreover, through European and transatlantic treaties, special relationships and political settlements under American leadership, soon established what Gill terms an international military–industrial complex, in which many countries' armed forces, weapons manufacturers, and government agencies are knitted together in co-dependent alliances. This international military–industrial complex, moreover, underpins an international and American-led economic model, an internationalized New Deal, termed by Gill an *international historical bloc*. (Gill, 2003: p. 58)

Despite Bush Senior's talk of a New World Order in 1991, Gill argues that the *hegemony* of American capitalism became a *supremacy* after the first Gulf War, with the collapse of the Soviet bloc and its absorption into the Western economy. Russia's recent attempts to re-establish its own sphere of influence have thrown this into sharp relief. This third phase, New World Order, was also a result of the gradual evolution through the 1970s and 1980s of a more integrated global political economy in which organized labour had become increasingly marginalized and capitalist elites with significant investment in many different nations had emerged. Such elites include those in 'key positions in transnational companies, banks, universities, think tanks, media companies, governments, and international organizations such as the IMF, World Bank and OECD', linked by the discourse of neo-liberal globalization (Gill, 2003: p. 169). Thus the 1st and 2nd phase *international historical bloc* became transformed into an 'American-centred and -led *transnational historical bloc*' (Gill, 2003: p. 59) at whose 'apex are elements in the leading states in the G7 and capital linked to advanced sectors in international investment, production and finance' (Gill, 2003: p. 59) – increasingly American firms – whose activities 'seek to make transnational capital a class 'for itself''' (Gill, 2003: p. 169).

Again, it is axiomatic in the analysis Gramsci provides that any 'ruling coalition will have to take on at least some of the values of those it attempts to lead, thereby reshaping its own ideals and imperatives' (Jones, 2006: p. 4). The exercise of power by a dominant bloc becomes a continuous and interpenetrative process in which society becomes saturated with the meticulous negotiations between the desires of the dominant and the needs of the subjugated. Power becomes 'something that is actively lived by the oppressed as a form of common sense' (Jones, 2006: p. 4). Power as understood through the concept of hegemony becomes exceedingly difficult to pin down, since it is always 'in the process of becoming' (Jones, 2006: p. 5).

Gramsci's work is today situated within the literature of cultural criticism alongside other writers such as Louis Althusser, Mikhail Bakhtin, and Michel Foucault, all of whom have their criticisms of Gramsci's approach, and present their own alternatives. This is not the place for a wider discussion of these issues, save to present the caveat, in using the notion of cultural hegemony, that there are fundamental assumptions about the nature of capitalist societies, divisions in society related to the concept of class, and a particular understanding of the nature and expression of power inherent in Gramsci's work that are not shared by other cultural theorists in the field. Foucault in particular refused to see power as something exercised by a dominant over a subservient class, insisting that power is derived from discourses – accepted ways of thinking, writing, and speaking – and practices that amount to power.

As for Gill's sometimes rather bleak analysis of the chances for a more democratic world, for advocates of transnational democracy his (and others') analysis is not a valid ground for abandoning the project but, on the contrary, for advocating it more vigorously. Nonetheless, moves towards transnational democracy in the 21st century (McGrew, 2002) will be mediated by information communication technologies (ICTs) and facilitated by those ICTs which foster and encourage links between people across national boundaries – such as the global social-networking tools being discussed in this chapter. Our concern is that the media through which such links are being made are prey to forces quite antithetical to transnational democracy.

Transnational capital and social networking

It is our opinion that SNS display precisely the Gramscian constellation of behaviours between a dominant bloc of venture capitalists – who have achieved hegemony in the New World Order – and the tens of millions of us who willingly surrender our personal data and the conduct of our friendships and (online) social ties to their marketplace.

Recalling our introductory comments on the notion of cultural fit, there is an understanding among marketing professionals, for example, that 'the reason that people are attracted to social networks in the first place is that reliance on user-generated content is seen as relatively *free of traditional corporate content and advertising*' (Goad and Mooney, 2008) (our emphasis). Any advert, in other words, must 'fit' the environment in which it is placed. Moreover 'if users perceive that a social network is becoming 'polluted' they will leave – and the evidence suggests that this can happen extremely quickly' (Goad and Mooney, 2008). Indeed, there have been a number of developments during the very recent past that have begun to highlight a much more sinister underbelly to the social networking phenomenon described above.

For example, the most successful SNS at present, Facebook, was guilty in the closing months of 2007 of appearing to become 'polluted' by advertising and privacy invasion, and was forced by overwhelming pressure from its users to back down. This commercial intrusion, called Beacon, worked by tracking users' Web shopping patterns on partner sites outside Facebook, and then sold adverting space within the social network based on user purchases. Beacon was introduced by Facebook in the autumn of 2007 and became the subject of instant harsh criticism from users. From their perspective, this was as if Facebook had started following them outside the walled garden of Facebook and into their personal, non-Facebooked affairs. This was seen by many as a gross invasion of privacy, the online equivalent of a stranger rifling through their bags. In short, Beacon broke the complicit conceptual gap between Facebook-as-SNS and Facebook-as-business. A group on the website calling itself 'Facebook: Stop Invading My Privacy' grew rapidly to more than 50,000 members, and several other organizations, including political activism site MoveOn.org, protested about the new system. At the end of November 2007 Facebook changed Beacon from an opt-out system to an opt-in one. Mark Zuckerberg, the young founder and CEO of Facebook, issued a press release that was published widely on national news websites, stating that Facebook users would be able to switch off Beacon completely.

With that Facebook users felt they had won a victory over the encroachment of the marketplace into their social space. The reality, of course, is that no such victory was achieved at all – only the appearance of one. As Zuckerberg himself recently noted, in answer to a question from a reporter at the launch of 'Facebook Ads', Facebook is an ad-supported business (Schonfeld, 2007). Even though Beacon was modified under pressure from users, advertising, run through the Facebook Ads system, is still a key component of Facebook's normal operations.

The Facebook Ads system has three basic components: Facebook Pages, Social Ads, and a reporting interface dubbed Insights. Just as users do, brands can create profile pages with applications and content, such as music sharing, discussion boards, and widgets specific to the advertiser's product or service. They can also define the actions users can take with their pages, for instance declaring oneself a fan of the brand[6] or RSVP-ing for an event. Facebook users can declare to all their Friends on the network that they are Fans of a particular brand. This declaration, published on the profile and the news feeds that all Friends see, therefore enables these Friends to visit the brand's own Facebook Page themselves. By publishing links to Brands alongside more social-oriented activities (such as new social ties), Insights masks commercial activity under the guise of social activity. Just as they click on the published link to find out more about a new social tie, Friends can click through to find out more information on the Brand – and, in doing so, are exposed to the opportunity to buy.

This shift in the framing of the economic activities of Facebook-as-business within Facebook-as-SNS does not, of course, mean that users have ousted such concerns from their 'social' space. These concerns have just been repositioned and re-oriented to better *fit* the imaginary construct of the SNS as a primarily *social* space and the implied balance between front-end social networking and back-end economic interests. From the perspective put forward in the previous section, Beacon is of interest precisely because it unbalanced the relationship between users and owners: the understated and understudied hegemonic relationship between these two sides of the SNS. In launching Beacon as originally intended – an opt-out, third-party, 'behind-the-scenes' collector of personal and commercial data – Facebook *assumed* that the consent of their users to such practices would automatically extend from existing subtle displays of commercial encroachment (such as AdWords) to this more obvious, explicit, even labelled display of authority over the data on which the SNS and its social networks rested. This was data which the SNS users assumed they, and not their hosts, owned and controlled.

Beacon, particularly in its original formulation, was a clumsy attempt to appropriate and repackage the SNS values of the extended social relationship based upon the community-of-interest (regardless of how deep or shallow such ties are, as is being debated in the IS literature) for economic and commercial purposes. The backlash against Beacon was not only against the exchange of personal data. It was also in reaction to the way Beacon and, by extension, Facebook's management, shattered the 'suspension of disbelief' that had developed between the front-end users and the back-end business. For users of SNSs such as Facebook, such sites must retain and foster the *appearance* of a divorce between the non-hierarchical, non-commercial socializations on the site and the businesses and commercial concerns that *run* the site. As was noted at the beginning of this section, when this separation fails, users desert the 'polluted' site.

However, this is all appearance. SNSs are no longer hobby activities but large commercial enterprises. And for them the users and communities on these sites are resources to be exploited. Facebook, as a protected and bounded SNS, provides an excellent example of these tensions between the social aspects of the network (the public face of the SNS) and the venture capitalism that goes on behind-the-scenes. If the question for users is 'Can I make friends through Facebook?', then the question for owners of and investors in such sites is, in the words of reporter Tom Hodgkinson (2008) in his coverage of this issue, 'Can you make money out of friendship?'. Few, if any, of the media reports on the phenomenon of social networking look at this aspect of Facebook-as-business, preferring to focus on the front-end social activities it supports. In contrast, Hodgkinson's report on the commercial foundations of Facebook is of particular interest, not only for its novelty, but also for what it suggests about Facebook and similar SNSs when considered from a Gramscian perspective. In particular, he highlights three interrelated aspects of Facebook operations which engage with the issues raised earlier in this chapter.

First, Facebook utilizes transnational networks such as the Internet, which are architecturally structured to transcend and subvert geography while at the same time emphasising locality and the institutional, political, or economic context in which the user is physically situated. Facebook's own 'About Facebook' page constructs a rhetoric of communities-of-interest within communities-of-place. From the perspective of socialization, this may seem little more than a gimmick or an artifact of Facebook's evolution. But considered from an economic perspective, communities-of-interest within communities-of-place can be called by another name: markets. As Hodgkinson notes, 'We are seeing the commodification of human relationships, the extraction of capitalistic value from friendships' (Hodgkinson, 2008). Whether investors or advertisers wish to capture all Facebook users in a place (e.g. Harvard), or of a type (e.g. movie-goers), or both (Harvard students who watch movies), this information is given freely and willingly by Facebook users. By adopting and repositioning itself as 'social facilitator' rather than, say, market researchers, Facebook develops a hegemonic relationship with its users. It is only when Facebook over-assumes on the relationship, as with Beacon, that users become fully aware of the situation and withdraw their consent. But when the illusion of divorce is maintained, the 'unwitting collusion' that Gramsci spoke of is perpetuated.

This tendency to give up information freely online without consulting privacy policies or other information management statements is an interesting phenomenon, one that anecdotal evidence suggests recurs across SNS sites (not just on Facebook). It is also a tendency upon which projects such as OpenSocial fundamentally depend. Again, the rhetoric of Facebook's public statements jars with the actions of behind-the-scenes innovations such as Beacon. On the 'About Facebook' page is the following statement on privacy:

> At Facebook, we believe that people should have control over how they share their information and who can see it. People can only see the profiles of confirmed Friends and the people in their networks. You can use our privacy settings at any time to control who can see what on Facebook. (2008)

This statement implies that privacy begins and ends with social network privacy – the front-end social exchange of information. On this important issue, this social focus continues as users follow link after link; and whereas the privacy statement on social exchange (what will be termed here 'front-end privacy' for simplicity's sake) is written in fairly plain, non-jargon language, the statement on the data Facebook-as-business collects ('back-end privacy') uses more opaque language, and shifts quickly from mentions of automatic information collection (though cookies and IP logging, though there is no mention of Beacon and the information it collects) back towards the social rhetoric of front-end privacy issues.

While there are important privacy and data security issues here, in terms of issues of hegemony, this (unwitting?) surrender of personal information only fuels the collusion between the rulers and ruled which puts the lie to the narratives of the SNS as a non-hierarchical space. By using this information to fund its 'ad-supported business', SNSs such as Facebook and those in the OpenSocial network are, in a sense, appropriating social networking innovations, ideas, and creativity and repackaging them for safe consumption within existing social hierarchies. Users may feel they are creating something new, vibrant, *theirs*, not 'polluted' by existing structures and institutions, but behind the scenes it is literally business as usual. Punk rockers may have felt the same way before they saw their styles and tropes for sale on the high street.

If it can be accepted that these users can be traded, repackaged, and sold as commodities, then what of their social ties? When considered from the perspective of the hegemonic dominance of the commercial interests over the social, the social networks take on new importance. For users, their ties allow them to build social networks (both intimate and distant, or strong and weak, to use Granovetter's (1973; 1983) term) – but, as noted above, these groups can also be articulated as a market. The 'commodification of friendship' can occur between two friends, or two hundred.

This commodification of friendship may be even more enticing in networks such as OpenSocial, which combine multiple platforms and multiple tie networks in such a way as to allow even broader access to the web of relationships which make up most users' online social networks. For users, OpenSocial links together the different 'containers' of online social networks to facilitate 'friendship' and social ties. Spencer and Pahl (2006), concerned with social dynamics, argued against the 'friendliness' of online Friends, but in economic terms the strength of the tie or the 'genuine-ness' of the friend makes no difference. What is of interest to them is the information exchanged between these ties, across these networks (and with little concern for privacy policies). As long as the illusion of distance between the social and the commercial is maintained and the network is not 'polluted,' then the behind-the-scenes operations of such SNSs can maintain hegemony (and may even, it could be argued, head towards some notion similar to supremacy).

What will be interesting to observe is whether, with the fall-out from Beacon, privacy and network information will be made accessible or protected on an individual basis or whether the lower common denominator approach will rule. That is, will information privacy levels be set differently for each individual in an exchange, or will an individual who has otherwise 'opted out' have their information made accessible through their interactions with another user whose data is being collected? When considering the network as a market, the individual as a commodity, it may not be outrageous to expect owners and site operators to spread their nets as wide as they can.

Beyond the walled garden: OpenSocial and cultural hegemony

Facebook is not isolated in considering the network as a marketable commodity – the backlash against Beacon just makes it the most visible example. For the purposes of comparison, it may be useful to return in more detail to the OpenSocial project, to explore how what appear to be radically different approaches to online social networking are in fact very similar in terms of capitalist orientation.

Facebook is often referred to using the metaphor of the walled garden, which highlights the fact that Facebook shies away from cross-platform compatibility. Despite the advertising approaches (including Beacon) opening up 'gates in the wall' to selected commercial sites, Facebook has tended towards remaining self-contained and apart from other SNSs. As was noted earlier, this is in stark contrast to the data portability project and OpenSocial. If Facebook is a walled garden, then OpenSocial is a river with many tributaries – many social networking sites and sources, each contributing and sharing information about their users among themselves. To stretch the metaphor a little further, this sharing of data allows marketers and others interested in the user data a way to acquire user information from multiple sources without having to recast their net at each social networking site. This possibility is of obvious interest to those who see SNS users and their networks of friendships as valuable commodities.

This potential for data collection is, as was briefly noted earlier, not a 'feature' that proponents of OpenSocial emphasize when promoting SNS data portability. As with Facebook, the SNS-as-business aspects of the service must be kept apart from the SNS-as-social space aspects if an SNS (whether a discrete site such as Facebook or MySpace or an amalgamation such as OpenSocial) is to be seen as 'unpolluted' by 'mainstream' capitalist or commercial interests. That these sites have two sides that need to be kept apart (in perception if not in actuality) tends to reinforce the concept of the dominant bloc and the 'unwitting collusion of the ruler and ruled'.

To maintain their position of authority in the rapidly growing online environments, the dominant bloc (socioeconomic powers, as represented by groups such as venture capitalists) needed to react to and even absorb some of the aspects of the once marginalized subcultures who developed the proto-virtual social networks which fed into more recent versions of SNS: Facebook, MySpace, etc. As social networking becomes more mainstream, moving from hobbyist/subcultural Bulletin Board Systems (BBSs) to multiplatform, multimedia SNSs that attract the attentions of some of the largest software and Internet corporations on the planet, Gramsci's notion of cultural hegemony becomes even more relevant. Cultural hegemony explains how even the most marginal of subcultures (who is unfamiliar with the stereotypical computer nerd, bathed in the light of a monitor as they sit alone in a dark basement?) can be absorbed into the dominant socioeconomic model if there is profit in it for the ruling elites. Like punk, sanitized and repackaged for the masses, social networking has been appropriated from the DIY, hacker, and geek subcultures, cleared of its need for coding ability or technological sophistication (measures by which, in part, these subcultures defined themselves), and resold.

From the perspective of the user, Facebook and OpenSocial seem to be two different ways of approaching online social networking. But behind the social activities of millions of users, these two approaches share the same model: how to turn a community into a commodity.

Implications for policy and research

This two-sided perspective of SNSs – as both social and commercial spaces – has important implications for future work. As more and more citizens incorporate online activities, such as building Facebook networks, into their everyday practices, and as the notion of the Information Economy gathers momentum, an understanding of this commodification of online social networks may feed into important debates on issues such as online privacy. Without a clearer understanding of the roles and strategies adopted by SNS-as-business, it would be difficult for legislators and policymakers to cultivate a balance between the often disparate interests of the users themselves (who see the site as 'their' social space) and owners (who see users as commodities to be moulded, courted, or sold outright).

Such an understanding is vital for policy as online activities become less and less distinct from offline ones. As such, it is feasible to predict that the actions of social networking sites and users will recur more frequently in issues of governance and social control. Examples of this have already arisen, such as admission of Facebook profiles as evidence in court cases (Richards, 2008) – which raises with it not only these questions of privacy, but also whether and to what extent the rights (and duties) of citizens extend into cyberspace. The transnational nature of global networking sites and the fledgling nature of international law collide here with potentially alarming implications for national policymaking.

A dialectic approach which contextualizes social relations of SNSs, such as friending, within the systems which support those activities (i.e. the business of SNS) is also vital to extending academic research in this area in ways which more fully account for the influence of systems on subsequent online behaviours. As was noted earlier in this chapter, the effect of decisions made by SNS-as-business can be seen rippling through

SNS-as-social network – users deserting sites 'polluted' by overt commercialization. A more detailed understanding of the relationship between these two aspects of SNSs would better account for the influences each has on the other.

In the context of the Russian-doll-like Informal, Formal, Technical (IFT) model of information systems (Halperin, 2006), and with respect to the burgeoning research field of online identity, the crystallization of the *informal* world of power relations in transnational capitalist societies offers another fruitful arena for further research. These power relations may be observed through the *formal* world of Web 2.0 conventions such as the personal profile and friending, and the coding languages used, and then on into the *technical* implementation of specific sites, and how personal data are recorded and then shared and sold.

What is made clear from this approach to SNSs is that it is no longer sufficient to analyse such sites purely in terms of friending and the social dynamics of end users. Such behaviours are important, but without engaging with the dialectic of social space and business, studies of these sites are incomplete.

Discussion and conclusion

Utopian rhetoric surrounding Web 2.0 social networking creates an image of a social space mediated by transnational communication tools that is democratic, anti-hierarchical, open, and unconcerned with excessive capitalist agendas. However, as this chapter has argued, this perspective ignores the hidden aspects of SNSs as corporate entities with obligations to venture capital investors and shareholders. This chapter puts forward the position that, rather than separate from the capitalist institutions and histories within which the Internet is embedded, the Internet, including SNSs, is in fact a continuation of these practices and ideologies.

Having made the move from hobby activity to corporate entity, SNSs have been appropriated to become part of a hegemonic transnational capitalist strategy for globalized and unregulated market dominance. As the Internet moves further away from its hobbyist origins and deeper into the mainstream of activities in capitalist societies (putting to one side for the moment the question of the international digital divide), what does a Gramscian analysis suggest might be in store for future permutations of online social networks?

Certainly, the question of 'pollution' will retain some of its importance for end users. However, like Punk before it, as online social networking is repackaged and further removed from its hacker-hobbyist origins, it might be plausible to suggest that the taint of commercial influence will not so automatically lead to users' deserting that service. As hegemonic groups further appropriate the codes and tropes of the users, the distinction between owners and users – rulers and ruled – will decrease. This in turn might result in users being more accepting of offline power dynamics being replicated in online spaces: online social networks will therefore shake off their ties to countercultural ideologies and instead begin to replicate and resemble existing offline power dynamics. In doing so, the distinction between online and offline engagement may subsequently recede. As the opportunity to make pocket money through SME becomes more and more open to small-to-medium enterprises and individuals (Goad and Mooney, 2008), in similar fashion to the 1980s sale of council housing (which transformed the working classes into property-owning middle classes in the United Kingdom), the distinction becomes sufficiently blurred for the rulers to rule not only with the consent but with the explicit support of the ruled. Through this process, offline economic relations are replicated online.

More broadly, although the phenomenon of the 'Dark Net' (Biddle et al., 2002) is likely to persist as a virtual underbelly correlating to its non-virtual cousin, the hacker-hobbyist has, like the punk, been stripped of political significance and has already become a cultural figure of good repute. It is truly not that long ago that spending large amounts of time in front of a computer screen was regarded as the behaviour of a young adolescent male devoid of social skills. Now, more and more of us will be attached to our screens much of the time, at work and at home. This activity is increasingly seen not only as socially acceptable and a 'cool' thing to do, but crucial to our economic well-being. Here, indeed, we see the Gramscian overtones in our willingness to sit tight at our keyboards and contribute to the new online economy as we flock in our millions to populate these new online social 'worlds'.

Finally, it seems clear now that 'cultural fit' is something which can be, and *is,* manipulated on a grand scale by economic elites. Maintaining hegemony requires continual shifting and repositioning of the strategies and tactics that maintain consent, and requires that new, oppositional or countercultural movements, and socially revolutionary subcultures, are not only absorbed by the mainstream but, if potentially truly profitable, *become* the mainstream, once they have been cleansed of their political dimensions and can be harnessed to replicate existing power dynamics. Therefore the hacker-hobbyist of not so long ago has become the cool online social networker participating in a new transnational economy. The venture capitalists at the top of this pile are certainly not making these things happen, but those which are able to stay at the top in this rapidly developing area are adept at manipulating the information revolution for their own ends. We, in turn, are happily dazzled by the Spectacle (DeBord, 1995) of SNS, and seem to be gladly logging on and buying into it.

Notes

1. Zuckerberg was originally involved in the Harvard-based 'ConnectU' site, and has since been accused of stealing from ConnectU when he built Facebook: cf http://news.bbc.co.uk/2/hi/business/6914843.stm.
2. For example, the self-reported population of SecondLife is approximately three times that of the national population of New Zealand. (source: US Census Bureau, International Database: NZ http://www.census.gov/ipc/www/idb/country/nzportal.html. And Second Life Blog http://secondlife.com/whatis/economy_stats.php.
3. For press coverage, cf. http://www.businessweek.com/technology/content/sep2007/tc20070924_995913.htm.
4. Google themselves make an interesting case study in the tensions and contradictions between being non-commercial with 'hacker' ideologies ('information wants to be free') co-existing with the economic imperatives of Google as a corporate entity.
5. For the list of current OpenSocial partners, see: http://code.google.com/apis/opensocial/partners.html.
6. In doing so, users may also start to feel some kind of 'ownership' or personal association with the brand, which is also a desired outcome for marketers.

References

'About Facebook.' (2008) http://facebook.com/about.php
Anderson, B. (1983/2006) *Imagined Communities* (rev. ed.). London: Verso.
Biddle, P., England, P., Peinado, M. and Willman, B. (2002) *The Darknet and the Future of Content Distribution*, Microsoft.
boyd, D. and Ellison, N.B. (2007) 'Social network sites: Definition, history, and scholarship' *Journal of Computer-Mediated Communication*, 13(1): article 11.
DeBord, G. (1995) *The Society of the Spectacle*, Cambridge, Mass: Zone Books.
Feenberg, A. and Bakardjieva, M. (2004) Virtual Community: No 'killer implication'. *New Media and Society*, 6(1): 37–43.
Gill, S. (2003) *Power and Resistance in the New World Order*, Basingstoke: Palgrave.
Goad, R. and Mooney, T. (2008) *The Impact of Social Networking in the UK* Experian Integrated Marketing.
Granovetter, M.S. (1973) The Strength of Weak Ties. *The American Journal of Sociology*, 78(6): 1360–80.
Granovetter, M.S. (1983) The Strength of Weak Ties: A network theory revisited. *Sociological Theory*, 1(1): 201–33.

Halperin, R. (2006) *Identity as an Emerging Field of Study* FIDIS Datenschutz und Datensicherheit 30:9 http://www.fidis.net/fileadmin/fidis/publications/2006/DuD09_2006_533.pdf

Hardy, M. (2002) Life Beyond The Screen: Embodiment and identity through the internet. *The Sociological Review*, 50(4): 570–85.

Hebdige, D. (1979) *Subculture: The Meaning of Style*, London: Routledge.

Hodkinson, T. (2008) 'With friends like these…' http://www.guardian.co.uk/technology/2008/jan/14/facebookIndependent News and Media 'Facebook Scares Me', 26 August 2007.

Independent (2007) 'Facebook Scares Me', 26-08-07 Independent News and Media. http://www.independent.co.uk/news/science/facebook-scares-me-one-man-explains-how-his-use-of-a-socialnetworking-website-spun-out-of-control-462738.html

Jones, S. (2006) *Antonio Gramsci*, London: Routledge.

Liu, H., Maes, P. and Davenport, G. (2006) *International Journal on Semantic Web and Information Systems*, 2(1): 42–71.

Livingstone, S. and Helsper, E.J. (2007) 'Taking risks when communicating on the Internet: the role of offline social-psychological factors in young people's vulnerability to online risks', *Information, Communication and Society*, 10(5): 619–44.

Madden, M. and Fox, S. (2006) Riding the Waves of 'Web 2.0,' *Pew Internet and American Life Project*. http://www.pewinternet.org/PPF/r/189/report_display.asp

McGrew, T. (2002) Transnational Democracy: Theories and Prospects. In A. Carter and G. Stokes (eds). *Democratic Theory Today*: Polity, Chapter 11. Polity Press, Cambridge.

Mesch, G.S. and Talmud, I. (2007) 'Editorial Comment: e-Relationships – the blurring and reconfiguration of offline and online social boundaries', *Information, Communication and Society*, 10(5): 585–9.

Plant, R. (2004) Online communities, *Technology in Society*, 26(1): 51–65.

Richards, J. (2008) *'Fake Facebook profile' victim awarded £22,000* The Times Online, 24 July 2008. http://technology.timesonline.co.uk/tol/news/tech_and_web/article4389538.ece (accessed on 18 September 2008).

Schonfeld, E. (2007) Liveblogging Facebook Advertising Announcement (Social Ads + Beacon + Insights). http://www.techcrunch.com/2007/11/06/liveblogging-facebook-advertisingannouncement/

Searle, W. and Ward, C. (1990) The prediction of psychological and sociocultural adjustment during cross-cultural transitions. *International Journal of Intercultural Relations*, 14: 449–64.

Spencer, L. and Pahl, R. (2006) *Rethinking Friendship: Hidden Solidarities Today*. Princeton, NJ: Princeton University Press.

Turkle, S. (1995) *Life on the Screen: Identity in the Age of the Internet*. Simon and Schuster, London.

10
Virtual Intimacy: Desire and Ideology in Virtual Social Networks

Rickard Grassman and Peter Case

Introduction

There are few social phenomena in contemporary Western society whose magnitude can match the viral spread of virtual social networks (VSNs). Every minute of the day hundreds of new Myspace, Flickr, and Facebook accounts are set up throughout the world and users ready themselves to interact with the many millions already in operation. What characterizes the current tendencies of our consumerist society are not so much the industrial goods in the marketplace, nor the excess beyond use-values engendered by branding but the *commodification of culture* as such. In the network economy intangible ideas and images are being bought and sold rather than any physical embodiment of what they represent. Indeed, the embodied commodity seems at best secondary if not downright superfluous (Rifkin, 2001). At the same time, we hear loud voices from the academy and beyond requesting a radical rethinking of identities, social formations, and businesses as they move from physical structures to virtual rhizomic networks (Boltanski and Chiapello, 2005; Flieger, 2005; Hayles, 1999).

The essence of a commodity is not to be found in its endless array of physical manifestations, which is why Marx's commodity fetishism became a mystical endeavour if ever there was one (cf. Marx, 1992). Instead the lure pertains to the very act of commodification itself that inscribes upon an object, service, or screen the desiring gaze of the Other. To flesh out what this means let us turn to one of the most infamous aphorisms of French psychoanalyst, Jacques Lacan, who polemically announced that 'Man's desire is the desire of the Other' (Lacan, 1998: p. 235). The most salient reading of this remark is that human desire is engendered by a belief in what it is that others desire. Essentially this is to say that the key predicate for commodification within an economy of demands is not to be found in any actual quality embodied in the commodity form, but that which is more in the object than the object itself – *the gaze of the Other*.

Scholars have already noted how subjects in the brave new world of late capitalism endow their identity and lifestyle with the mark of particular brands and products (Lash and Urry, 1994; Giddens, 1991; Parker, 2000). To be sure, this is still very much an ever-escalating propensity in its own right, due to the fact that it may still convincingly represent what subjects take to be the Other's desire. But even more radically we witness how subjects are beginning to embody appearance itself by enacting images of their lives to be framed by the brands of these online platforms such as, for example, Facebook and Myspace, and presented for the Other's gaze.

In this chapter we aim to analyse the human desire that has facilitated the widespread propensity to join, interact, and develop intimate bonds within the realm of VSNs. The word *intimacy* comes from the Latin *intimus*, the superlative of interior, which we couple with *virtual*, basically indicating that something is real in its effects rather than in its essence. Moreover, this inclination towards what we refer to as *virtual intimacy* resonates well with what Boltanski and Chiapello (2007) believe to be one of the most fundamental features of our network society, describing it as the natural preoccupation of human beings to revel in the desire to connect with others and in doing so avoid isolation. Apart from making sense at an intuitive level, this propensity also helps explain how the subject's desire mirrors that of the Other – a point that we develop below in the section entitled 'Who is the gazing Other?'

In addition to this fundamental point, however, we argue that the proclivity for virtual intimacy depends largely on two supplementary factors that mediate the lure of the Other's gaze. The *first* factor, developed in the section 'The Panopticon of intimacy', is the experience of virtuality as such that stages a notion of being at a safer distance from the most salient contingencies, inhibitions, and social conventions associated with real-life encounters. There is a certain sense of personal 'security' that arises from the peculiar narcissistic *control* that computer technology lends to virtual encounters, since many of the complexities of face-to-face interaction are suspended by the reductive communication medium (Turkle, 1984).

The *second* factor is the notion of exclusivity, primarily dealt with in the section called 'From intimacy to ideology', which, we argue, strengthens the bonds within the network by defining it against an antagonistic outside. This is, of course, a particular instantiation of the ubiquitous social psychological motif of inclusion/exclusion as evidenced, for example, in the homogenizing effects on society pertaining to incarcerating criminals and diagnosing abnormality (Foucault, 1995). The motif is also always already present in nationalistic inclinations, which are exacerbated by the formation of a scapegoat (Burke, 1969). Witness, for example, the immense unifying force of nationalism that 9/11 and the 'War on Terror' has produced in the United States (and elsewhere in the West) by conjuring up the paranoiac spectre of a pervasive yet amorphous 'enemy'. The centrality of the scapegoat to identity formation is a motivational pattern, also thoroughly explored in the literary works of George Orwell; in particular *Nineteen Eighty-Four* (Orwell, [1949] 1973) and *Animal Farm* (Orwell, [1945] 1973).

In essence, what is at stake here, and what we try to foreground throughout this chapter, but specifically in the section entitled 'From virtual intimacy to ideology', is the potential *ideological dimension* that we argue may be embryonic in a community that is, as it were, unified in conformity with the logic of exclusion. To this end we maintain that our investigation of virtual intimacy will render possible an exploration of the latency of power embedded in these networks.

In light of the Marxist dialectical ubiquity of class struggles, social capital has been perceived as an extension of economic capital by other means (Bourdieu, 1991). However, we argue that the current proliferation of VSNs may constitute a novel ability to accumulate and 'instrumentalize' social capital, both de-essentializing and deracinating its link to economical capital and hence further endowing it with sovereign political force.

We begin our analysis by providing a tentative working definition in order to position our object of study theoretically. *A virtual social network is a relational complex made up by subject positions that are mediated by an online platform whose purpose is to facilitate inter-subjective interaction.* A commonality to all these networks is that members are required to invite outsiders in order for it to expand (e.g. Facebook, A Small World, LinkedIn, etc.). To assist our theoretical analysis we draw on selected examples of networks to illustrate both the desire for virtual intimacy and the way in which this produces 'loyalties' that may be reified to serve political purposes.

Who is the gazing Other?

The way we conceive of VSNs operates at two different levels. The first is *ontological*, which refers to the very conditions of possibility for a virtual subjectification to take place. We have in mind such necessary conditions as the network interface, Internet access, the material resources and the time necessary to get engaged, and so forth (Castells, 1999; Warschauer, 2002; Zheng and Walsham, 2008). This is obviously a dimension in which socioeconomic factors still constitute a fundamental threshold, excluding most people in abject or relative poverty, and people in developing countries and beyond, simply because they do not possess the fundamental means to access VSNs.

Nonetheless, once we pass this threshold, we enter into a realm in which exclusion is still very much at work, but in a more insidious manner. What we encounter is a virtual space harbouring networks within networks and the unbounded potential for anyone to try to join an existing network or found a new one. This apparently liberal structure may well disarm any *prima facie* allegation of systematic discrimination on grounds of ethnicity, race, religion, gender, disability, socioeconomic class, age or sexual preference etc. that may be predicated on the structure itself *qua* the ontological level.

Conversely, what may be conceived as a radicalized democracy can easily turn into anarchy by virtue of it being as fragmented, hegemonized, or chaotic as is performatively generated by the confluence of virtual interactivity. Within this rhizomorphic realm of networks there is, of course, a plethora of different interests to be pursued regardless of whether they are financial, social, sexual, political, or of any other nature. No doubt the biggest financial interests are first and foremost manifested in what we call *macro-networks*, such as the overall platforms, most notably, for example, Facebook, Myspace, Linkedin, etc. and the prime generator of value is, of course, the sheer breadth of all the users they manage and the current and prospective income to be derived from marketing on such a wide scale.

No doubt, one may equally find financial interests being represented and pursued within the more anonymous constellations of users that make up *micro-networks*, especially in such networks that encompass a financially powerful set of members. As opposed to *macro-networks*, in which the only commonality among users is that they share an overall structure, a certain interface and frame of functionality that is distinct, *micro-networks* are the performative constellations that emerge and are shaped by every discrete act of interaction. As a consequence financial interests and power may be one determining characteristic behind some of these micro-networks.

However, this chapter is not primarily concerned with interests that are reducible to simple finance. This is indeed what we have tried to capture in the title *Virtual intimacy*, by which we refer to the emotive dimension of subjects desiring affective bonding within VSNs. Still, as we will see later on, it would be impetuous to let oneself be blinded by the benevolence of such desire for reciprocated affection on the assumption that this inclination cannot be used instrumentally.

But let us suspend the instrumental dimension for now and proceed from the ontological to what we conceptualize as the *ontical*, to borrow a term from Martin Heidegger (1962). This is to say that we are no longer dealing with the fundamental structure of different macro-networks as an overarching 'plane of immanence' (Deleuze and Guattari, 2004). In contrast, at the ontical level we are engaging with the world of networks from the confines of a subject position, which means that any alliance to a network depends not on the liberal politics of the macro-network but on so-called micro-networks. In other words there is no Rawlsian *'original position'* within VSNs (Rawls, 2005), where subjects can choose in a detached and rational way the conditions of their participation. Instead inclusion requires a leap into an already operating power constellation – *a micro-network*. By 'micro-networks', in this context, we are thinking of organizational framings, or ongoing power struggles, that are quite analogous to what Blanchot (1969) describes as *the encounter*, Foucault (1995) accounts for in terms of *micro-politics*, and Deleuze and Guattari (2004) view as a *structure of relations*.

In other words, in order for any network membership to occur, recognition and consent are required from at least one external subject position – *the Other*. However, in the light of Lacanian theory, 'the other' is a complex subjective notion and we are therefore required to lay bare some further nuances if we are to make use of this theory. Lacan distinguishes between *the other* (as in any other person) and *the Other*, with a capital O, which is sometimes referred to as 'the big Other'. This Other is much more generic than the simple presence of another subject and literally constitutes the otherness against which the subject can experience a sense of self (Lacan, 1991). Moreover, the Other must 'first of all be considered a locus', and that is, according to Lacan, 'the locus in which speech is constituted' (Lacan, 1993: p. 274). It is not a positive symbolic fact but a performative quasi-transcendental structure of signifiers, what Lacan refers to as the *symbolic order*, in which the subject is always already inscribed (Salecl, 1998). The Other is engendered by language and yet at the same time it constitutes the symbolic support by means of which the subject comes to know itself. What we witness here is a radical shift; the commonsense assumption that *we use language to speak* gives ground to an inverted perspective of *language speaking through us*.

This entails that the Other is reducible neither to something internal and psychological nor to something completely external and exclusively embedded in language or in the institutions of our social reality. It is nevertheless an experience of a meaningful alterity which, even if particularized to each subject (Evans, 2005), confers on the subject a notion of symbolic objectivity from which the subject's own symbolic mandate may be derived.

What is perhaps most significant about the Other, still resonating well with the multifaceted Lacanian maxim above, is that it teaches the subject *how and what to desire*. By endowing the subject with a specific position, or role, with which the subject identifies, the symbolic support is discerned from what is perceived to be the external context, with a certain excess, a notion of intentionality or 'objective' perception – *the gaze of the Other*. To illustrate this distinction further, let us recall the train of thought indicating that in order for any network to emerge there has to be at least one reciprocal act from *the other* in the sense of another subject. This is indeed true but then again the other subject is most certainly consenting from the locus of the big Other and thenceforth the intimacy as experienced by the subject from the established virtual bond is not necessarily as dependent on the other subject as on the big Other of the symbolic order.

Now, to demonstrate further what this means let us turn to some prevalent tendencies that are easily observable in the everyday interaction of VSNs. As a rather distinct element of the research underlying the present chapter, one of the authors opened up a Facebook account to get a better inside glimpse of how VSN dynamics play out. The first curious experience was somewhat uncanny in the sense that, to a certain extent, the author was always already a member. Other users had already searched for his name and connected with his profile, which had been registered and saved by Facebook. As a result, a certain symbolic space was reserved for his profile long before he himself decided to join. It truly gives another dimension to the old Groucho Marx joke, 'I would never belong to a club that would have me as a member', a sentiment that we might paraphrase in this context as – I would never belong to a club in which I was always already a member.

From this little *virtual ethnographic* (Hine, 2000) excursion into the realm of VSNs, it is easy to discern a quite salient tendency characterizing the nature of some of the interactions that take place on the network. In fact, many of the messages posted on the so-called profiles – which are the online identities that interact and concomitantly constitute each micro-network – diverge quite significantly from ordinary speech. These accounts appear more as monologues than anything else. There was a certain 'diary-like' feel to them embracing everything from elaborate narrations of holiday trips to quite trivial accounts of shopping for groceries. What these accounts emphasize is that a virtual bond may not necessarily need to be maintained by the reciprocal interactive participation taking place between two or more distinct profiles.

Kierkegaard once said that in every love relationship there is always a third party and that is love itself: 'First there is the lover; then the one or those that are objects; but thirdly, there is present love itself' (Kierkegaard, 1962: p. 280). Now, as we will see, some of the accounts we find on VSNs illustrate this point perfectly and the third party, in Lacanian terms, is indeed nothing short of the ubiquitous gaze of the Other. Put differently, the big Other is the symbolic support that appears in many cases to be confirming or even reinforcing the notion of being in love and this we find to be a quite significant and visible feature in VSNs.

One of the profiles, for instance (let's call him Daniel), had a mainframe picture of himself with his girlfriend passionately kissing in the sunset at the edge of a breathtaking ocean view. As if a picture could not speak a thousand words or Daniel, just to make sure, fed the Other a thousand more, his chat book was overloaded with a dizzying array of affectionate descriptions. Some highlights would be 'Daniel is waiting for his true love...his life elixir' and so forth, sensations of 'butterflies in the stomach', and elaborate descriptions of the immense happiness he feels.

Now we are in no way questioning that one may feel all of these things in love relationships; however, the way these things are being narrated, indeed 'narrativized', and staged for *the gaze of the Other*, leads us to suspect that this is not the whole story. It is almost as if he is trying desperately to convince himself of his own love by insisting, as he does, on symbolically inscribing it in the register we refer to as 'the big Other'.

At the more extreme end of this spectrum of virtual intimacy, or indeed narcissism to the extent of severe self-delusions, we might consider, for a moment, 'the virtual life of Neil Entwistle' (Raban, 2008). Entwistle, an Englishman, was recently convicted of the double homicide of his American wife and baby in New Hampshire. Before committing these brutal acts he created a website containing many photos depicting a 'blissful marriage' and the 'perfectly happy middle-class family'. There was no indication in these virtual images of the double life he was leading. It turned out that he was living with increasingly unmanageable levels of debt due to his attempts to maintain a façade of affluence against a backdrop of failed e-business entrepreneurism (of the 'make-a-million-quick' and Internet porn varieties). Moreover, as police analysis of his email correspondence revealed, he was frustrated by the lack of sexual gratification in his marriage and prompted, therefore, to fantasize about extramarital affairs and flirt online with prospective sexual partners.

Another curious example of how this presence of the Other may influence love relationships is currently a rather widespread wedding practice in China.[1] Not too far from Beijing there are some newly constructed European towns, one of which is designed to be a facsimile of the 'typical' British town and hence including all the stereotypical icons necessary to signify 'British Culture'. (Although, it should be pointed out, this particular cultural simulacrum leans more towards Cambridge than Blackpool.) These towns are, more or less, unpopulated by permanent residents and, rather like Disney's Epcot Centre, have the sterile feel of a film set. For example, the 'typical' British red GPO telephone box appears quite authentic even though it contains no functioning telephone; and while all the residential accommodation has been sold, purchasers merely keep it as unoccupied investments as the Chinese do not like secondhand flats. However, albeit a postmodern twist to the good old modernist 'form follows function' doctrine, it seems as if, quite inversely – function follows form, considering how these towns have come to serve another purpose – the 'set' for wedding photos. Chinese couples travel in their droves to these towns, not to get married – a bureaucratic formality normally effected weeks after – but to have their pictures taken. Who needs a real-life ceremony when the Other thinks you have had one, in a romantic, faraway town such as Cambridge?

Our point in evoking these examples is that whether we consider a single person reporting on grocery shopping or someone waiting for his life-elixir or Chinese wedding photos, the important thing is not necessarily who or even *whether* anyone looks at the texts or images produced, but that the *imagined* gaze of the big Other never falters. Hence, once this bond has been established, and as long as it is not subjected to any active forms of exclusion, the virtual bond can operate quite smoothly, being, as it were, largely a relationship between the subject and the big Other. This bond, to that extent, therefore authorizes a high degree of narcissism on the part of subjects, who feel empowered to describe intimate details of their lives regardless of whether there is an *actual* public to read and/or respond to the narratives that are produced. It is enough to *imagine* the gaze of the Other in order to confirm subjects in all manner of narcissistic indulgence.

The Panopticon of intimacy

What these practices bring to mind is, we suggest, an information-age equivalent of Jeremy Bentham's infamous nineteenth-century architectural design of the Panopticon prison facility, in which every cell was to be visibly structured in a circular shape around the Panopticon tower (Bentham, 1995). In Bentham's scheme, lighting conditions would make sure that each and every cell could be observed at all times from the tower but no one from the inside of any cell could ever see the guards of the Panopticon tower. Consequently the inmates could never assess whether they were actually being watched at any particular moment. What this illustrates – and what Foucault (1995) has, now famously, developed at great length – is the moment when the inmates, as a natural reaction to never knowing when they are being observed, actually internalize the gaze. Consequently, it doesn't matter who is being watched, or even whether a guard is even present in the tower; once the gaze is internalized, inmates start governing themselves as if they are under constant surveillance.

In a similar vein, a directly isomorphic structure of relations is present within VSNs. The VSN member takes on the role of the inmate whose subjectivity is influenced by the internalized gaze of both a prospective other (definite article) or the Other (in-definite article). However, instead of dealing with the desire for resistance, integrity and relative freedom which may be expected from prisoners who would most certainly shy away from the gaze, we are actually dealing with the opposite desire of the love-sick multitude of subjects desperately seeking recognition, intimacy, and attachment.

What is increasingly evident as a feature of 'the search for love' in our contemporary society of grand romantic narratives is not simply finding that 'special someone' as much as *finding love itself*. Rather than having to deal with the intrusiveness of a real person that may lead to all kinds of emotional friction and conflict, one can, with the help of a network's fleetingness, reinvent a more germane concept of love. Perhaps this is what Zygmunt Bauman had in mind when, in the preface to one of his latest books, *Liquid Love*, he asserts that 'while relations cease to be trustworthy', people are inclined to 'swap partnerships for networks' (2008: p. xiii). The prospect of love with the imagined (or virtual) Other becomes the *sine qua non* of self-love. All the autoerotic dreams of the narcissist can proliferate and be sublimated through the technological opportunities afforded by VSNs.

What networks offer is a middle ground between 'the drive for freedom and the craving for belonging' (Bauman, 2008: p. 34); that promises an anodyne surfing 'between the reefs of loneliness and commitment, the scourge of exclusion and the iron grip of bonds too tight' (2008: p. 34). Perhaps this can explain some of the tendencies we are witnessing within VSNs. The real-life partner that one might conventionally share everything with – be it personal philosophies, political opinions, travel experiences, childrearing experiences, or everyday trivialities – can now be supplanted by the very concept of 'love' and/or the support of an imagined O/other. The real partner is substituted by the virtual gaze of imaginary 'someones' or by that multitude which is 'no one in particular'.

In *The structural transformation of the public sphere* Jűrgen Habermas demonstrates how modern media, mainly the press and television, pacify the public by providing a vehicle for vicarious engagement in 'discourse' and hence subverting the need to gather in public spheres or engage in debates (Habermas, 2008). People are stripped of their autonomy and political consciousness and, instead, are transformed into docile bodies to be moved and mediated by the interests of those who control the various mass media. It might be thought, however, that the rise of VSNs challenges this critique to the extent that levels of prospective interactivity are significantly enhanced for people utilizing these new forms of medium in their homes.

As we argue in the following section, it may well be the case that the *potential* for political action has extensively increased with the emergence of this new form of medium. Nonetheless, it should be acknowledged that Habermas' critique is not without relevance to the phenomenon of virtual intimacy within VSNs. Although some of the barriers that potentially inhibit people finding a voice, facilitating public debate or mobilizing collective political energy have been dismantled by the onset of VSNs, there is, we contend, still a certain element of pacification occurring within VSNs. Our suggestion is, paradoxically, that action itself is rendered passive by VSNs. It would be premature, therefore, to counter Habermas's critique by asserting that the level of interactivity within modern media – VSNs in particular – has revived the public sphere of communicative action.

Instead we fear that this new mode of interactivity is first of all not a neutral means of interaction. The *form* such interaction takes influences the very substance of what is expressed. Keeping people in their homes and rooted in front of their computer monitors, regardless of whether they may engage in public debate or private social interaction, severely desensitizes the subject to the other and to the realism in the actions they perform. In other words, what is at stake in this new form of social interaction through VSNs is not only a subtle undermining of the feelings of compassion that become salient when people are continually interacting through real-life face-to-face encounters, but also a fictionalization of reality as such. What seems to be happening is something Robert Pfaller (1992) has referred to as *interpassivity*, which is a gradual transformation of the subject into being reactive and passive even in the guise of activity itself.

Slavoj Žižek (1999) has developed this concept further by noting the phenomenon of interpassivity in practices as disparate as sitcoms with laughter included in the soundtrack and Tibetan Buddhists' use of prayer wheels. In the case of sitcoms, subjects do not have to laugh or make discriminatory judgements about the humour on offer insofar as the television does the laughing in their stead. To put it bluntly, the big Other does the laughing for us, so we can just sit back, relax, and enjoy the symbolic support of the Other letting us know that we are having fun. Tibetan monks praying by ritualistically spinning a wheel, according to Žižek (2007), render their inner beliefs redundant insofar as the ritual does the 'believing' for them. Using parallel reasoning, it is easy to see how VSNs provide subjects with a sense of 'interactive satisfaction' by supplanting actual engagement and social interaction with people in a conventional way with 'profiles' that ostensibly interact on their behalf. What is your excuse for not mingling and socializing when it can be done virtually, from your own couch, in splendid solitude?

From virtual intimacy to ideology

So far, our analysis has largely revolved around what we take to be the meaning of *virtual intimacy*. This, we suggest, is the semantic and performative force that serves a crucial role in prompting the desire necessary for instigating, sustaining, and proliferating the phenomenon of virtual social networking. Furthermore, *ideology* is, of course, a highly complex and controversial concept which has been used in a variety of ways to denote and connote very different things. Scholars attribute the dawn of ideologies with the diffusion of enlightenment ideals that occurred towards the end of the 18th century (Gouldner, 1976). The onset of this new 'age of reason' saw challenges to some of the previously taken for granted sources of authority, such as religion and sovereign rule, that had until that period sustained social order. The Age of Reason witnessed the rise of new 'rational' belief systems that offered an alternative basis of authority. An ideology is not only concerned with making sense of the world in a novel way but, simultaneously, it seeks to transform the subject's relation to it.

According to Gouldner, it 'does so in a way that is liberating in relation to some other, older conception of the world' (1976: p. 47). Moreover, what is being changed is nothing short of subjects' identities, which needs this alteration in order to be re-attuned to the world in a manner that resonates better with the new ideology. This process is not necessarily conscious, which is why Marx famously exclaimed, '*Sie wissen das nicht aber sie tun es*' – 'they don't know it but they are doing it' (Marx, 1957: p. 79). This quote is often associated with Marxism proper, implying, as it does, that the capitalist forces of production are what condition people (notably the proletariat) to act in certain ways, and which, according to Marx, mask the fact that people are not serving their own interests but that of capitalism itself (Marx, 1992). However, the quote as such, regardless of who voiced it, does not necessarily have to bear the mark of Marxism but could equally serve as a minimal description of how an ideology functions. In the light of this, an ideology is, irrespective of its content, a mindset that, on the one hand, *primes* action and, on the other, *blinds* the acting subjects to the interests that are being facilitated by that action. Indeed, what this conception of ideology signals is some form of 'constitutive naivety', a misrecognition, 'a divergence between so-called social reality and our distorted representation' of it (Žižek, 1999: p. 28); in other words, what Marx himself refers to as 'a state of false consciousness' (Marx, 1992: p. 74).

The question is, however, to what extent this classical concept of ideology may still be pertinent to our post-industrial society of information and networks. According to Peter Sloterdijk (2005), we live in an age of cynical reason in which subjects are very much aware of the discrepancy between the ideological mask and social reality but, nonetheless, insist on the mask. Consequently, Sloterdijk (2005) proposes an alternative way in which ideology in contemporary society operates in the form of cynicism. This he describes in terms of an enlightened state of false consciousness in which people are quite aware of what their actions entail, but, rather than strengthening peoples' ethics, it generates a moral numbness or cynical distance between awareness and action (Sloterdijk, 2005). In Žižek's words, interpreting the position of Sloterdijk, we find a radical modification of Marx's quote in which people 'know very well what they are doing, but still, they are doing it' (Žižek, 1999: p. 33). This we believe, nevertheless requires some further embellishment in order to capture the contemporary workings of ideology, especially in the context of VSNs.

This is to say, most people are quite aware of what they are doing when they are interacting in these VSNs. However, rather than serving as a pretext, or a mask, for disregarding some deeper level of moral conscience, we argue, and in particular concerning VSNs, this cynical distance is inherent in the very mode of interaction. What we mean is this: whether we are dealing with narcissistic indulgence vis-à-vis the Other, power of exclusion, or interpassivity, it is not so much the veiling of our inner ethical convictions as much as the continual shaping of social reality as such. In other words, unlike both Marx and Sloterdijk, we do not believe in any deeper-seated truth, essence, or structure that is consciously immanent or unconsciously lurking beneath our engagement in the world. Rather, it is our engagement in the world, albeit through virtual interactivity, which shapes our conscious and unconscious experience of it. In short, the mask is what constitutes social reality.

As a result, in order to investigate the ideological potential embedded in VSNs, we are not looking for some mystical message that is operating underneath the surface of virtual interactions. Instead, we believe VSNs to be the surface phenomenon *par excellence* and it is precisely this apparent lack of substance which makes ideological influence, we argue, potentially even smoother and more unperturbing than in face-to-face social relations.

The unity of any political class, gathering, or movement is necessarily a symbolic one (Laclau and Mouffe, 1985), and nowhere is the predominance of the signifier, sign or symbol over what is actually being signified clearer than in the realm of VSNs. The superior performativity of a virtual identity, in respect of being a pure appearance, is therefore much more likely to overcome some of the inherent antagonisms associated with real-life intimacy or indeed the founding of collective identities and networks.

What is bound to transpire, in one form or another, through micropolitical processes in these VSNs is a new form of *hegemony*. Laclau and Mouffe (1985) predict that hegemony 'will emerge precisely in a context dominated by the experience of fragmentation and by the indeterminacy of the articulations between different struggles and subject positions' (1985: p. 13). What happens is that this state of indeterminacy, the lack of 'substantial' identity formations, renders possible the emergence of certain signifiers, which become inextricably intertwined with an emotive and imaginary excess. The only quality required in such a signifier is a certain level of performativity, paradoxically a certain lack in signification, in order for it to abridge, or symbolically veil, the heterogeneity of a multitude into a coherent collective identity (Laclau, 2005).

Once this 'identity' is inscribed in the symbolic it creates hegemony, a preference for the Other, because certain signifiers are taken to symbolize what makes a collective identity (and its members) distinct from others. Consequently subjects may derive narcissistic pleasure from identifying with these defining characteristics. Moreover, this form of narcissism, through the collective, is not necessarily confined to affirmative patterns of identification, but may indeed create an even more forceful hegemony by dis-identification with an antagonistic outside. These tendencies are easy to discern in most groupings harbouring racist, nationalist, and elitist beliefs and, so, too, we argue, in many of these VSNs. This is why the power of exclusion may introduce the taint of ideology within the virtually intimate relationships they facilitate.

Lacan (1993: p. 268) refers to this hegemonizing signifier as *point de capiton*, a quilting point, which produces certain fixity in the otherwise indeterminate sliding of signifiers, by elevating this one signifier and endowing it with libidinal force. This hegemonic signifier, also known as the *master-signifier*, albeit embodied in a leader, in a certain idea, or perhaps even in an enemy, achieves this privileged position only insofar as the symbolic also gives rise to imaginary associations in which subjects may recognize themselves. In other words, the master-signifier is dependent on being equipped with this emotive charge, the 'libidinal investment', which Lacan (1978: p. 326) locates in the imaginary order and describes as narcissistic. A libidinal investment occurs when a subject, with the help of fantasy, endows a certain signifier with a 'passionate attachment', to borrow a term from Judith Butler (2004), which from that time forward is perceived to bear the mark of the subject and therefore satisfy narcissistic desires (Lacan, 1978). Moreover, by virtue of providing symbolic support for subjects to see themselves in a distinct collective, the master-signifier goes further elevating these symbols into an imaginary unity so that the enchantment of narcissism may be realized by enacting this image *en masse* for the gaze of the Other.

Furthermore, by structuring symbolic coherence, the master-signifier establishes the defining characteristic of a certain symbolic identity, which inevitably needs to be counterposed to an outside. As mentioned above, this outside may also strengthen the bonds within a network or community if it is interpreted as antagonistic, that is, members either fear it directly or fear being associated with it. It is precisely in this split between the desire for recognition *qua* virtual intimacy and its inherent dependency on exclusion which foregrounds the ideological dimension of any network.

It is easy to observe how this phenomenon operates in VSNs and how certain homogenizing trends are inclined to crystallize over time. The clearest examples are when networks are dominated by certain subject positions that, so to speak, set the tone for the rest of the network. One illustration of this is a rather restricted and secretive network known as the 'Elite List' founded by a celebrity 'profile' in Stockholm called Alexander Bard, also co-author of the book *Netocracy* (Bard and Söderqvist, 2002).

The 'Elite List' consists of no more than 100 affiliates, ranging from members of the Swedish parliament to select artists, scientists, journalists, and other media profiles. Because of the rather limited number of profiles, whenever new members are selected others are excluded, which no doubt produces a sense of 'loyalty' to the perceived preference of the gaze – which, in this case, is none other than Alexander Bard himself.

Now, considering the different profiles that are under the sway of this 'loyalty', the hegemony of this particular network is bound to have extensive influence beyond the realm of its members, seeping into what is covered by media, not to mention what is discussed in parliament. Furthermore, we contend, there is not necessarily any homogeneous socioeconomic class, political conviction, or particular financial interest that underlies this emergent 'loyalty' which one may witness in such a network. However, this is not to say that political dimensions may not emerge and retroactively fuse with the 'loyalty' produced by the desire for virtual intimacy. In fact, this is where, we contend, the instrumental aspect of VSNs re-emerges through the performativity of the master-signifier, that is the way it shifts into new domains of meaning.

Let us recall the way Roland Barthes (1972) drew the link from the sensorial to the ideological, with something as intimate as taste becoming inextricably embedded with symbolic values, and thus, for example, the enjoyment a Frenchman derives from eating a steak may be unconsciously reified to strengthen patriotic values. While remaining within the realm of sense experience but yet entering a more nuanced and less ideological strand of the symbolic spectrum, Marcel Proust (1982) takes us on a journey depicting the intrinsic relationship between sense and symbolism in *Remembrances of things past*. We are reminded of his description of how a 'Petite Madeleine' cookie involuntarily invokes this immense richness of childhood memories.

In contrast, what we are dealing with in VSNs is enjoyment in meaning, *'jouis-sense'* or 'enjoy-meant' (Žižek, 1999: p. 44), which, unlike the examples of Barthes and Proust, are always already within the realm of symbolism. In other words, the enjoyment that pertains to virtual intimacy resides in the way the subject through fantasy recognizes its own image in the symbolic, invoking self-love (Lacan, 2006). The ideological turn *par excellence* therefore occurs when the master-signifier, established through a narcissistic desire for recognition, acquires evermore symbolic and political connotations.

In the case of the 'Elite List' it is, for instance, only recently that Alexander Bard himself has expressly come out as a political figure. Although falling short of suggesting that this will compel every member of the 'Elite

List' to pledge the same political allegiance, we nonetheless believe that the hegemonic position he has achieved in this network and his recent political move are not easily separable. Instead we believe that Alexander Bard and this political turn is a perfect example of a master-signifier that performatively accumulates political connotations. Therefore, as far as the other members are concerned, there is a certain element of reification in which their desire for virtual intimacy becomes inextricably intertwined with their subjection to ideology.

Conclusion

Let us now draw the main conclusions from our analysis. In the present chapter we have moved from pointing out how *the commodification of culture* has been accelerated by the arrival and proliferation of VSNs, through to investigating how this new medium may nevertheless provide novel capabilities for political action beyond the most prevalent influences of financial power and market forces. In this attempt we have identified three main factors – *the gaze of the Other, virtuality* and *the power of exclusion* – that we argue to be crucial dimensions of the desire for *virtual intimacy*. Furthermore, we suggest that this desire for virtual intimacy is the principle motive behind the formation of micro-processes, micro-politics (Foucault, 1995) and *micro-networks* inherent to the phenomenon of VSNs.

To recapitulate, the *first* of the three factors informing virtual intimacy derives from our interpretation of the Lacanian dictum, 'Man's desire is the desire of the Other' (Lacan, 1988: p. 251). According to this principle, subjects are rendered prone to desire that which is symbolically inscribed as an object of desire and thus interpreted as desirable to the other. This has led us to problematize the other, which in Lacanian theory does not have to signify the *actual* presence of other subjects, as much as the symbolic inscription of Otherness may suffice. This imagined gaze, we contend, is a quintessential feature of VSN-mediated interaction.

The *second* factor is that of *virtuality*. This emboldens the subject by introducing the idea of being at a safer distance from the contingencies of face-to-face encounters. However, this inclination may indeed be seen as a double-edged sword: on the one hand instigating action but on the other domesticating the very experience of action, which, paradoxically, renders it passive (interpassivity). What is at stake here, we argue, is not only that this mode of virtual interaction undermines compassion by desensitizing the subject to the other, but also introduces a gradual fictionalization of social reality as experienced by the subject.

The *third* factor, we argue, is *the power of exclusion*. This resides in the inherent dependency that any form of *intimacy* has upon an exterior from which this intimate space may be distinguished. Indeed, there are countless instances in which bonds are strengthened within this intimate sphere by emphasizing these distinguishing characteristics. Portraying the 'outside' as coloured by elements of aversion, threat or enmity also reinforces a sense of unity within a collective identity. This is perhaps most notably present in the identity-work sought through macro-political rhetoric associated with, for instance, the current 'War on Terror', but it is indeed also present at a more micro-processual level, as in the case of racist, nationalist, or elitist groups.

Finally our analysis has led us to investigate the way in which *virtual intimacy*, as a consequence of these three factors, may be *hegemonized* and thus reified to converge with the political. This, we argue, may take place at a symbolic level in which a signifier attracts a 'libidinal investment' and thus becomes an imaginary construct from which subjects can derive narcissistic pleasure, recognizing themselves in the signifier. This is what helps to promote hegemony within VSNs. Through what we have described in terms of 'passionate attachments' (Butler, 2004), a signifier may become elevated to the level of the Lacanian *'point de capiton'*, a *master-signifier*, a point of confluence between imaginary and symbolic signification, which structures an emotive hierarchy within the symbolic order.

The ideological turn, we conclude, therefore occurs when the master-signifier transforms from being a mere principle of affectionate bonding into an instrument of ideology. Far from being harmless or politically neutral domains, VSNs may be understood as prospective vehicles of a new and insidious form of social control. However, in so stating, we are not really referring to the muscular use of political ideology of the sort witnessed in national regimes of the Right or Left throughout the 20th century. The processes we have aimed to illustrate in this chapter are far subtler, more reticular and rhizomic in form.

We hope, in this chapter, to have provided some theoretical insight into the emerging micro-political and intersubjective dynamics of VSNs. Now, in terms of more precise implications for further research and practice, we are reluctant to offer any specific or concrete suggestions on how these findings may be used, considering what we see as the ideological peril of 'colouring the big Other' with predesigned aims and strivings. Instead, what we have tried to offer is not reducible to a conventional means–end petition towards social change, but rather a 'sensitizing framework' to assist further reflection on, and observation, and expansion of what we perceive to be some of the most prevalent tendencies of our time.

Note

1. This was well captured in a Channel 5 documentary entitled *Paul Merton in China* (directed by Barbie MacLaurin and shown on British TV in October 2008).

References

Bard, A. and Söderqvist, J. (2002) *Netocracy*, London: Pearson Education.
Barthes, R. (1972) *Mythologies* (A. Lavers, trans.), New York: Hill and Wang.
Bentham, J. (1995) *The Panopticon Writings* M. Bozovic (ed.), London: Verso, 29–95.
Blanchot, M. (1969) *L'entretien Infini*, (The Infinite Conversation), Paris: Gallimard.
Boltanski, L. and Chiapello, E. (2007) *The New Spirit of Capitalism*, New York: Verso.
Bourdieu, P. (1991) *Language and Symbolic Power*, Boston: Harvard University Press.
Burke, K. (1969) *A Grammar of Motives*, London: University of California Press.
Butler, J. (2004) *Bodies and Power Revisited*, Chicago: Univeristy of Illinois Press.
Castells, M. (1999) 'Information Technology, Globalisation and Social Development', *UNRISD Discussion Paper*, No. 114.
Deleuze, G. (2001) *Pure Immanence: Essays on a Life*, New York: Zone Books, 102.
Deleuze, G. and Guattari, F. (2004) *A Thousand Plateaus: Capitalism and Schizophrenia*, New York: Continuum.
Evans, D. (2005) *An Introductory Dictionary of Lacanian Psychoanalysis*, London: Routledge.
Flieger, J.A. (2005) *Is Oedipus Online?*, Boston: MIT Press.
Foucault, M. (1995) *Discipline and Punish: The Birth of a Prison*, London: Second Vintage Books.
Giddens, A. (1991) *Modernity and Self-Identity: Self and Society in the Late Modern Age*, Cambridge: Polity.
Gouldner, A. (1976) *The Dialectic of Ideology and Technology*, London: MacMillan Press.
Habermas, J. (2008) *The Structural Transformation of the Public Sphere*, Cambridge: Polity.
Hayles, N.K. (1999) *How we became Post-human: Virtual bodies in Cybernetics*, Chicago: University of Chicago Press.
Heidegger, M. (1962) *Being and Time*, New York: Harper and Row.
Kierkegard, S. (1962) *Works of Love* (H. and E. Hong, trans.), London: Collins.
Lacan, J. (1978) *The Ego in Freud's Theory and in The technique of Psychoanalysis, Book II, 1954–1955*. In J-A. Miller (ed.), S. Tomaselli (trans.). Cambridge: Cambridge University Press.
Lacan, J. (1991) *Freud's Papers on Technique, Book I, 1953–1954*, J-A. Miller (ed.), J. Forrester (trans.). London: W.W. Norton and Co.
Lacan, J. (1993) *The Psychoses, Book III, 1955–1956*. In J-A. Miller (ed.), R. Grigg (trans.), London: Routledge.

Lacan, J. (1998) *The Four Fundamental Concepts of Psycho-analysis, Book XI*. In J-A. Miller (ed.), A. Sheridan (trans.). London: W.W. Norton and Co.
Lacan, J. (2006) *Ecrits*, London: W. W. Norton and Co.
Laclau, E. (2005) *On Populist Reason*, London, Verso.
Laclau, E. and Mouffe, C. (1985) *Hegemony and Socialist Strategy*, London: Verso.
Lash, S. and Urry, J. (1994) *Economies of Signs and Space*, London: Sage.
Marx, K. (1957) *Das Kapital - Kritik der politischen Ökonomie*, Moscow: Marx-Engels-Lenin Institut.
Marx, K. (1992) *Capital: Volume 1: A Critique of Political Economy*, Penguin Classics.
Orwell, G. ([1945] 1973) *Animal Farm: A Fairy Story*, Harmondsworth: Penguin.
Orwell, G. ([1949] 1973) *Nineteen Eighty-Four*, Harmondsworth: Penguin.
Parker, M. (2000) *Organizational Culture and Identity*, London: Sage.
Pfaller, R. (1992) *Die Illusion der Anderen*, (The Illusion of Others), Frankfurt: Suhrkamp.
Proust, M. (1982) *Remembrances of Things Past: Swann's Way*, London: Vintage.
Raban, J. (2008) 'The Virtual Life of Neil Entwistle', *London Review of Books*: 14 August 2008.
Rawls, J. (2005) *A Theory of Justice*, Cambridge, Mass.: Harvard University Press.
Rifkin, J. (2001) *The Age of Access*, New York: Tarcher.
Salecl, R. (1998) *(Per)versions of Love and Hate*, London: Verso.
Sloterdijk, P. (2005) *Critique of Cynical Reason*, Minneapolis: University of Minnesota Press.
Turkle, S. (1984) *The Second Self: Computers and the Human Spirit*, London: Granada.
Warschauer, M. (2001) 'Reconceptualising the Digital Divide', *First Monday*, 7(7).
Zheng, Y. and Walsham, G. (2008) 'Inequality of what? Social Exclusion of the E-society as Capability Deprivation', *Information Technology and People*, 21(3).
Žižek, S. (1999) *The Sublime Object of Ideology*, London: Verso.
Žižek, S. (2007) *How to Read Lacan*, New York, W.W. Norton and Co.
Zygmunt, B. (2008) *Liquid Love*, Cambridge: Polity.

Index

Addiction 78, 93
Age 78, 79, 91–92, 114
Anonymity 6, 54, 59, 63–64
Avatars 11, 27, 36, 43, 98–100, 104
  Creation options 100
  Customization 105–106, 110
  Design 100, 106
  Diversity 104
    Outfits 108
  Sexism 107, 111

Blogging 3
Boundaries 4, 20

Capitalism 12, 155, 163, 171
Castells 14
Charities 42
Chat rooms 52
Clans 80, 88
Co-location 138
Co-presence 138
Collectivity 12, 138
Commercialization 12, 13, 159
Commodification 12, 13, 160, 168, 175
Community of Learners 37, 38, 41, 48
Community of Practice 25
Computer-mediated
    Communication 3, 52
  Asynchronous 52
Computerized Cognitive Behavioural
    Therapy 61
Conflict 13, 29
Constructivist 47
Consumerism 160
Contextual Design 115–116
Cookies 116
Cooperation
  Group 46
Creative destruction 19
Cultural Fit 155, 172
Cybersolidarity 137, 143
Cyberspace 6

Data protection 13
Digital immigrants 22, 26
Digital natives 22, 26, 32
Disability 56
  Sex and disability 58
Disclosure 63
Disinhibition 59
Distance 65

e-learning 21
Education
  Adult 27
  Management 28
  system 25
Email 3, 5, 55
Equality 45–46

Face to face communication 3
Facebook 8, 10, 12, 14, 22, 158–170
Friendship 157, 168

Gender 11, 100
Genres 80
Google Generation 23–24
Government 36
Guild 88

Health
  Google 61
  Information 52
  Mental 54
  Sexual 53, 57–59
Hegemony 161, 167, 169, 187
Human Computer Interaction (HCI)
    115, 129, 157

IBM 134, 138–148
Identification 6
Identity 6, 7, 15, 187
Ideology 185
Information processing 23–24
Information richness 3
Innovation 18

Index 195

Instant messaging 55
Internet 18–20, 33
Intimacy 176
Involvement 46

Knowledge 25
Knowledge management 44

Language 30
Learning 10, 11, 20, 22, 32
   Active 28, 44
   Critical 45
   Social 24
   Styles 26, 32, 54

Massive 7, 8
Media choice 3
Message boards 54–55
Misattribution 5
Mobile phones 18
MMOGs 8, 11
MMORPGs 76, *see also* online games
MUDs 3, 77
Multidisciplinary 41, 44
Multimediated 7, 8
Multiplayer 7, 8
Multitasking 22, 24
MySpace 12, 37, 157

NGOs 42
Ning 10, 30–31

Online advertising 155
Online Communication 54
Online Communities 6, 60, 129
Online Gamers
   Age 78, 79, 91–92
   Composition 78, 98
   Education 81
   Gender 78, 89, 100–102
   Stereotypes 90, 101, 108
   Styles 103
   Types 77
Online Games 75, 76, 84, 98
   Action games 86
   Design 99, 115
   MMO 98
   MMORPGs 37, 48
Online Gaming 75, 80, 84

Motivations 77–78, 102
Risks 77
Social aspects 87
Usage 76, 78, 85, 86, 103
Online Support 54
   Dilemmas 60
   Membership 66
   Methods 62
   Type of 67

Panopticon 182
Participatory Design 117
Patients 11, 52
   Interactions 53
   Preferences 52, 61, 68–70
Pedagogical research 45
Pedagogy 10, 11, 18, 27–33, 36
Presence 7, 36
Privacy 6, 13, 119
Propaganda 147

Second Life 7, 9, 10, 12, 27, 36–48, 56, 106, 134–135, 151–152
Security 6
Seniors 114, 121–123
Simulations 47
Situated Cognition 45
Social Capital 114, 129, 177
Social construction 3, 135
Social inclusion 93
Social networking sites 1, 14, 155
   Commercialization 159, 170
Social networks 9, 156
Social Presence 43, 47, 64
Solidarity 7, 137
Space 136, 141, 149

Teaching 10, 20
   Methods 26
Technology
   availability 3
   Disruptive 19
   Value of 18
Terrorist 27–28
Trust 14, 62

Unions 143–145, 150
University 36
User interactions 3

Values 12, 115, 117
  Categorization 115, 124–129
  Identification 116
  In Design 116
Value Sensitive Design 115
Virtual
  campus 38, 44
  collaborations 5
  community 46
  interactions 3
  intimacy 175, 178, 185, 191
  laboratory 44
  learning 21
  life 76
  strike 12, 134
  teams 3

Virtual Communities 6, 60, 159
Virtual social networks 1, 6, 8, 9, 177
  Emerging themes 12
  Heterogeneity 14
Virtuality 1, 190
  Growth 2
  Levels of 2, 9
  Scope of 9

Web 2.0 1, 8, 20, 23, 25, 37, 155
Wikipedia 21
World of Warcraft (or WoW) 8, 11, 37, 75, 84, 88, 99–109

YouTube 20, 37